Praise for *MATTER*

"*Matter* is a must-read intellectual roadmap for all those courageous leaders looking to make an actual difference. It's not just about making change happen, it's about making change that actually matters."

—*Jeremy Gutsche, CEO, Trend Hunter, and* New York Times *bestselling author*

"This book inspires us all to build companies that matter; where customers' best interests fuel innovation. It teaches us how to embrace a disruptive edge as a defining competitive advantage—and make our company the obvious choice by focusing all our attention and actions on people. This book should be compulsory reading inside companies that want to lead."

—*Ken Fenoglio, president, AT&T University*

"If you want to be a Leader that Matters this is the only book that matters. Surprising. Provocative. The obvious choice for leaders everywhere."

—*Mel Robbins, award-winning CNN commentator, TEDx Sensation, and bestselling author*

"*Matter* walks the razor edge between strategy and execution. It's obviously written by real-world business leaders, and not just talking heads. In a hyper-competitive world, *Matter* will give you the road map to finding your edge of disruption and offer specific tactics for exploiting the opportunities you find there, and ensure you become the obvious choice in the process."

—*Josh Linkner, four-time tech entrepreneur and* New York Times *bestselling author*

"This book provides an invaluable road map to differentiating yourself from the competition and becoming the obvious choice. As the authors rightly explain, in today's world unless you matter, you don't have a right to exist and remain in business. Now more than ever in our fast-moving environment it's necessary to fight against commoditization and add value, this book provides not just case studies of how companies are achieving this but practical guidance on how to achieve the same in any business."

—*Charles Stanley, president, Forevermark at De Beers*

"*Matter* recognizes that we are living in volatile times and gives you the tools to succeed. *Matter* helped me to realize the importance of being curious and having courage, of relentlessly asking questions, and challenging assumptions."

—*Donna Lynne, DrPH, group president, Kaiser Foundation Health Plan, Inc. and Kaiser Foundation Hospitals*

"A truly impactful book that challenges you to re-think the lens by which you view your business, your customers, competitors, and how you thrive in this new economy full of disruptive opportunities."

—*Bruce Johnson, president and CEO, GHX*

"*Matter* left me energized with a new perspective on how to create value for our customers, investors, employees, and communities. The book provides an approach that is relevant to any leader, regardless of their position, industry, or scale of operation. These insights and tools are as applicable to business as they are in life. After all, don't we all really want to *matter*?"

—*Zachary T. Neumeyer, chairman, Sage Hospitality Resources*

"Peter Sheahan and Julie Williamson possess that rare and dazzling intellect required to define a new space, and bring true thought leadership to the changing world of business. Their new book *Matter* shows us how to stand up, stand out, and make a world-changing difference to people that matter most—our customers, our communities, and our employees."

—*Sally Hogshead, CEO and founder, Fascinate Inc.*

"*Matter* provides a road map for anyone seeking to become the obvious choice and win in a hyper-competitive world. More importantly, it provides a pathway to do work that matters— to your client, to your community, and to you. The case studies are rich and insightful, and the strategies are simple, but not simplistic. It's robust and evidenced based, without ever being academic or theoretical. We all want to do work that's significant. We all want to feel significant. Ultimately, the power of this book is that it will inspire you to become a company that matters, and to do the work that really matters."

—*Dr. Peter Fuda, principal, The Alignment Partnership*

MATTER

MATTER

Move Beyond the Competition, Create More Value, and Become the Obvious Choice

PETER SHEAHAN and JULIE WILLIAMSON, PhD

BenBella Books, Inc.
Dallas, TX

BenBella Books, Inc.
10300 N. Central Expressway
Suite #530
Dallas, TX 75231
www.benbellabooks.com
Send feedback to feedback@benbellabooks.com

Printed in the United States of America
10 9 8 7 6 5 4 3 2 1

Library of Congress Cataloging-in-Publication Data
Names: Sheahan, Peter. | Williamson, Julie.
Title: Matter : move beyond the competition, create more value, and become the obvious choice / Peter Sheahan, Julie Williamson.
Description: Dallas, Texas : BenBella Books, 2016. | Includes bibliographical references and index.
Identifiers: LCCN 2015029946| ISBN 9781941631768 (hardback) | ISBN 9781941631775 (electronic)
Subjects: LCSH: Value. | Expertise. | Excellence. | Competition. | BISAC: BUSINESS & ECONOMICS / Development / Business Development. | BUSINESS & ECONOMICS / Decision-Making & Problem Solving. | BUSINESS & ECONOMICS / Leadership. | BUSINESS & ECONOMICS / Customer Relations.
Classification: LCC HB201 .S549 2016 | DDC 658.4/01—dc23 LC record available at http://lccn.loc.gov/2015029946

Editing by Debbie Harmsen
Copyediting by James Fraleigh
Proofreading by Laura Cherkas and Kristin Vorce Duran
Indexing by Debra Bowman, Indexing Services
Jacket design by Sarah Dombrowsky

Text design by Publishers' Design and Production Services, Inc.
Text composition by PerfecType, Nashville, TN
Cover design by Faceout Studio, Kara Davison
Printed by Lake Book Manufacturing

Distributed by Perseus Distribution www.perseusdistribution.com

To place orders through Perseus Distribution:
Tel: (800) 343-4499
Fax: (800) 351-5073
E-mail: orderentry@perseusbooks.com

Significant discounts for bulk sales are available. Please contact Aida Herrera at aida@benbellabooks.com.

This book is dedicated to the courageous souls who do work that matters, and who do the work to matter!

CONTENTS

INTRODUCTION

"The purpose of life . . . It is to be useful, to be honorable.
It is to be compassionate. It is to matter, to have it make
some difference that you have lived."

—Leo Rosten

DOES YOUR COMPANY REALLY MATTER? Has it moved beyond the commoditized and substitutable solutions readily available in the market, and created more value for its customers, communities, investors, and employees? *It could!*

Is your team focused on doing the work that really matters? Are team members solving the most difficult challenges your internal and external customers face, and going above and beyond to create more value for your organization? *They could!*

What about you? Does your work matter? Are you just working hard, or are you focusing on the hard work that moves the needle in the areas your team most needs, generating more value for them and for your organization than if you just stuck to the basics? *You could!*

Just ask Doug Woods, Jeff Moore, and Angela Ahrendts. In their own ways, in their own industries, each has taken on work that matters. The world is different because of the challenges their companies have solved for their customers, their partners, and their employees.

Doug Woods and his team at DPR Construction matter because they build great things. Their relentless pursuit of powerful and effective ways to collaborate in the construction process has changed their clients and partners forever. The construction industry is evolving because of their leadership.

Jeff Moore and his team at transportation management company Lakeside matter because they had the chutzpah and the vision to be something no other trucking company had imagined. They decided to move beyond the competition, challenging embedded practices that historically had plagued the logistics industry, and in doing so became a trusted partner to their clients—capable of reducing costs, freeing up resources, and lowering carbon emissions in the process.[1]

Angela Ahrendts and her team at Burberry matter to the legacy of the 160-year-old brand they helped to resurrect by leaning into the digital disruption that threatened the viability of not just the Burberry brand, but retail as we know it. She and her team committed to reinventing the brand, the shopping experience, and the customer base in an ambitious and bold way. The result? Customers are back, investors are back, the brand is set up for the next 160 years—and retail has a new shining beacon for thriving in an omni-channel, digital world.

The work you, your team, and your company choose to do on a daily basis matters. It matters to the people you serve because of the problems you solve, and it matters for your own sense of pride, progress, and achievement. People want to buy from companies that matter. People want to work for companies that matter. People want our communities to be filled with organizations and people that matter.

This book is about building companies that *matter*—companies that create more value, that move beyond the competition, and as a result become the obvious choice in their markets. It's also about teams that matter, and doing work that matters to you. The observations and lessons we have provided here work at any level for people who want to matter more through the work they do.

You will meet big companies, small companies, B2B companies, and B2C companies. You will even meet a spy agency along the way. And you will meet some exceptional individuals. We will dissect the journeys the individuals inside these organizations took as they sought to escape the morale-crushing cycle of commoditization to become the obvious choice for their customers, their most talented employees, and the investors and communities they serve.

This has been our obsession here at Karrikins Group (formerly ChangeLabs). We have spent more than fifteen years studying what it takes to matter, and working alongside companies striving to matter—to create more value, move beyond the competition, and as a result become the obvious choice. We have observed companies that succeeded, and also some that failed. We have learned from all of them, and we felt it was important to share those lessons. This book is the result of our realization that we needed to codify what it took to become the obvious choice. We wanted to map the journey of those who succeeded and offer it to you, here in these pages.

So we embarked on a research study, designed to uncover and document the practices of successful companies that have become the obvious choice—those that matter most in their industry. More than thirty companies, representing more than fifteen countries, hundreds of interviews, thousands of transcribed pages, years of analyses, and tens of thousands of words written to try to describe what we learned have led us to one strikingly simple, consistent, and powerful insight: To become the obvious choice, to be a company that matters, you need to consistently create outcomes that are valued more than those of your competitors and that are not easily replicated. As the definition of value evolves in the marketplace over time, you also must sustain your ability to perpetually create new and valued outcomes that are beyond what your competition is capable of doing. Period.

Sounds simple, right? But perpetually creating new and valued outcomes is clearly an accomplishment that only a select group of companies are able to achieve. How are some companies able to be the obvious choice in their markets year after year? We realized the "what," "where," and "how" questions about providing value were riddles worth solving. We pushed our analysis to answer these three questions, believing this would be the most useful to us and to your journey:

1. What does it take to create more value?
2. Where do you find the opportunities to create more value?
3. How do you build the capability to deliver more value, year after year?

These three questions formed the basis of our continued research. The answers form the premise of this book.

WHAT DOES IT TAKE TO CREATE MORE VALUE?

Jeff Moore set out to transform the way Lakeside did business, moving from a highly commoditized, super-low-margin operation to the obvious choice for innovative consumer goods companies in Canada. He knew the only way to get there was to solve more complex problems and to create more valued outcomes than his competitors. Doing that meant solving the most important problems his clients have—high freight costs—in a way others in the market couldn't easily replicate.

That is what we mean by value: If you don't want to be commoditized and you want to become the obvious choice, you need to create solutions to the complex problems that are most important for your customer, those that few others are capable of solving. In theory, that's pretty straightforward. In practice, definitely not.

In Jeff's case, the only real way to do that was through using single-source logistics management models, challenging entrenched industry practice, and creating efficiency and optimization opportunities along the way. This is complex work. It takes vision, intellect, effective processes and systems, and commitment to do it at scale. If you have those things, the complexity is a good thing; it is where the opportunity to differentiate comes from. Defining and solving complex problems that have economically significant outcomes attached is very hard work. It is not easily replicated, but the scarcity of scalable solutions is why it is valued.

> That is what we mean by value: If you don't want to be commoditized and you want to become the obvious choice, you need to create solutions to the complex problems that are most important for your customer, those that few others are capable of solving.

Jeff's willingness to commit to navigating this complexity is what has made his company, Lakeside, the obvious choice for his customers. You're going to hear a lot more about how they did that in Chapter 4. For now, we shift our attention to understanding how to identify the most complex and important problems—those where we can find the opportunity to create more value for your customers' lives (as well as for your employees, your communities, and others in your industry).

WHERE DO YOU FIND THE OPPORTUNITIES TO CREATE MORE VALUE?

When Angela Ahrendts took the reins as CEO of Burberry, the brand was in decline. The trench coat was no longer cool, their brand was associated with an older, less influential demographic, and their traditional strategy was being undermined by powerful online channels capable of selling the same products they sold in store, for some 25 percent less. In short, they were being disrupted.

Like most retailers, Burberry had been determined to hide from the disruption, hold on to legacy business models, and hope that the threat would pass. Not Angela. Under her leadership, Burberry would move toward the disruption and stand right at its edge, where the old brick-and-mortar world met the new digital world. Her vision was to build an omni-channel brand

and business model capable of serving customers where they were, not where Burberry had historically wanted them to be.[2]

We would suggest that she walked right up to what we call the *edge of disruption*, and looked out toward a future where retail for Burberry was reimagined. What single-source freight models were to Lakeside, an omni-channel consumer experience was to Burberry.

We have found in our work and our research that the opportunities to create the most value are found at the edge of disruption—at the intersection of old and new, where the profits, reach, and reputation of your past enable you to test the models of the future. This is where the most complex problems, with the fewest solutions, are found. Burberry didn't abandon the traditional store model and go exclusively digital. Instead, it embraced an omni-channel model at the edge of disruption. It harnessed the emerging digital disruption, merged it with its existing business model, and moved confidently into the future armed with the solutions and business models required to thrive in the new world.

The edge of disruption for your organization is that point from which you can see both past and present changes in technology, regulation, customer demand, cost structures, employees, investors, and other variables converging into a larger wave of disruption that threatens the relevance of your existing value proposition and business model. As you project these changes into the future, you can see the erosion that turns your products or services into a commodity business, where you can only compete on price, volume, and a reduced cost structure, all the while burning your people out by asking them to do more with less.

Instead of erosion, you can also see a different future at the edge of disruption—where multiple new challenges for your customers emerge in the complexity that the disruption brings, and therefore where opportunities exist for you to create more value. It is at this intersection of old and new that the chance to differentiate yourself is found. In this book, we will help you define where your edge of disruption is and show you what to do when you get there to become the obvious choice.

So you now know *where* you want to go—to the edge of disruption, where you can synthesize existing and emerging business models and create more value. And you want to do more than just go there—you want to solve the problems that you find there and exploit the opportunities that arise. You want to use the vantage point of the edge to challenge assumptions and beliefs effectively. You want to create new and differentiated ways of doing business—with products and services that meaningfully change how business gets done.

To do that means figuring out *how* to get to the edge and stay there, continuously learning and moving as the edge moves. The sneaky little truth about the edge of disruption is this: It doesn't stay in the same place for too long. You have to learn to perpetually move with it. When you can do that, you will remain the obvious choice for your customers, employees, investors, and communities, year after year—you will be a company that matters to all of the people you serve.

HOW DO YOU BUILD THE CAPABILITY TO DELIVER MORE VALUE, YEAR AFTER YEAR?

When Doug Woods, Peter Nosler, and Ron Davidowski (the D, P, and R of DPR) founded their company in 1990, they knew they wanted it to matter in the construction industry. They wanted to be a force for positive change on multiple fronts.

- First, DPR wanted to change the way clients engaged with their general contractors (GCs). Traditionally, clients and GCs have had notoriously poor relationships, plagued by missed expectations, litigation, and substandard outcomes. DPR wanted to engage with clients in a way that improved the quality of their clients' experience while also improving on-time and on-budget project delivery.
- Second, DPR wanted to change the way it engaged both its staff and its contractors. In the "Vivid Description" outlined in its core ideology, DPR sets an ambitious goal that "over

the next 30 years our people practices will be recognized as being as progressive and influential as Hewlett Packard's were over the last 50 years."[3]

- Finally, DPR wanted to change the communities it served, by building great things with great business partners.

Consider that DPR has grown from a startup in the 1990s to a $3 billion success story, and has become the obvious choice for companies like Facebook and Genentech looking to partner with a GC to "build great things." At the same time, it has been included on multiple "Best Companies to Work For" lists (including for Millennials),[4] and has given millions of dollars to charity through its DPR Foundation. We think it is fair to say that DPR matters—to its clients, its employees and contractors, and its communities.

How does it manage to do this, not once, but year over year? By consistently identifying the best opportunities to solve more complex problems and then doing the hard work required to solve them. In DPR's case, the leadership team members readily acknowledge that they aren't perfect, but they lean into the complexity of the most technical construction projects and they dedicate themselves to leading the industry in its understanding of innovative new approaches, redefining best practice as they go, with a commitment to delivering more valued outcomes to their clients.

DPR's leadership team does something that we consistently saw in the companies we studied. To be a company that matters, you need to judge yourself by your impact, not by your intentions. Companies that matter don't just talk about opportunities to create more value; they do the hard work required to actually convert those opportunities to demonstrate value. When complex problems emerge at the edge of disruption—where the future meets the past—these companies don't shy away from the challenge, trying to protect a legacy business model. They are willing to take risks to develop and refine a new way forward. And they don't do it just for themselves.

Companies that matter talk incessantly about legacy and doing the right thing. They are committed to creating value for their clients and for their industry and communities as well. They see it as their role to ensure that everyone—even their competitors—and the community are better today than they were yesterday. Companies that leave their customers, employees, and communities better off by delivering the most valued solutions have an *elevated impact*.

DPR has an elevated impact because its leaders chose to work differently with their clients, their contractors, and their communities. The founders wanted to challenge how its business worked at the most basic level—the contracting relationship between the buyer of a building and its builder. They had been in the industry long enough to see all the problems with the existing litigious model, and decided to change the game by elevating their impact and redefining the contracting process.

> To be a company that matters, you need to judge yourself by your impact, not by your intentions.

That couldn't happen in isolation. DPR had to have great relationships with people of influence within the right client organizations who had the vision and ability to build great buildings. It had to vest its financial interests with the success of the project, putting more skin in the game and helping to pioneer new ways to partner. And it had to connect well beyond the client, to bring bankers, employees, subcontractors, and even universities along on the journey. When DPR's founders stood back and looked at the impact they were trying to have, they saw that they needed to influence the entire industry and market, so they built the broad relationships required to do just that.

They needed to have *elevated relationships*—relationships that gave them influence with people who had the ability to make decisions, partnerships to provide the deep knowledge of the nuances and cultural realities inside their client organizations, and connections to people and ideas required to create solutions

to one of the most complex problems in their industry: the contracting relationship itself.

Companies that matter elevate relationships with their customers and throughout their industry. They are the go-to companies when an industry voice is needed, and they have the ability
to pull together market-wide conversations to focus on innovation and collaboration. At the same time, companies that matter
can support intimate and nuanced discussions with their clients
about the client's strategies, challenges, and future. In other
words, through their relationships, they influence, partner, and
connect better than anyone else in the industry. Their relationships are part of what enables them to have an elevated impact.

DPR's edge of disruption these days is its adoption of
Integrated Project Delivery and risk-sharing models that are
redrawing the lines between client, designer, and general contractor. DPR knows where its edge of disruption is because,
like other companies that matter, it chooses intentionally and
methodically to define it, learn about it, and then share what it
has learned. DPR creates a point of view on emerging disruptions and sees the value that can be delivered to its clients and
partners, who in turn seek DPR's point of view whenever possible. DPR's team has been able to build a reputation powerful
enough to give them access to the most senior decision makers
and influencers in its industry. The company's *elevated perspective*
creates the access and credibility required to support its *elevated
relationships*, which combine to show DPR's leadership the path
to having an *elevated impact*. And therein lies the map for your
journey to become the obvious choice:

- Establish your elevated perspective by defining your edge
  of disruption and learning and sharing as much as you can
  about it.
- Use your elevated perspective to build credibility and gain
  the access you need to develop *elevated relationships*.
- Go deep with your customers and connect the dots
  between disruption and opportunity, and you will have the

understanding and influence required to have an *elevated impact*.

- Lean into the complexity required to solve higher-value problems, and answer the call to act in a way worthy of your leadership position.
- Do these things and you will be able to create more value for your customers, move beyond your competition, and as a result, become the *obvious choice* in your market, year after year. You will matter more.

Whether your clients are internal or external, large or small, local or global, you and your team can all move to do work that matters and build a company that matters. We are not saying it is easy, but it can be done. Join us and explore how you can develop the capabilities required to have an elevated perspective, elevated relationships, and elevated impact, and become the obvious choice. You will be inspired by the examples of others, and rejuvenated by the possibilities that emerge for you, your role, and your business as we progress. Read on!

The Matter Model

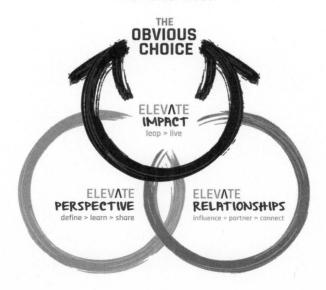

SECTION ONE

ELEVATED PERSPECTIVE

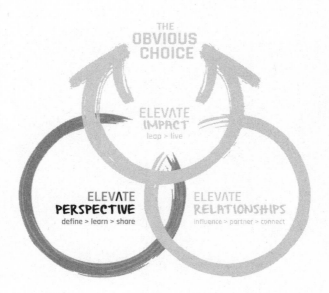

MAGINE YOU JUST ORDERED A PIZZA. Domino's Tracker will walk you step by step through the making and delivery of your pizza. Bought an Apple computer? You can track its progress through the production and delivery stages with the click of a button, and thanks to its seamless integration with logistics firms like UPS, you can watch its progress on a truck to your house. Speaking of apples, you can even find out exactly where a real apple in your local grocery store came from, which farmer grew it, and how it arrived at the store—all with the simple click of your camera phone and a tracking code on the apple. Each of these everyday products can be traced with ease through the supply chain, even by a consumer—it is so simple we usually don't even stop to think about it (except when we are wondering where the heck our new computer is, or why the delivery driver is taking so long).

Now imagine you are having $35,000 knee replacement surgery (or maybe you actually just did and are catching up on some reading). You are going to have a device implanted into your body that is destined to be there for a very long time, costs tens of thousands of dollars, and will have far-reaching effects on your health and well-being. Given how much it costs and where it is going, you would assume that you would wake up from surgery knowing exactly which artificial knee, which screws, and what other types of objects were put inside you. You'd likely be wrong. From the lot number to the exact device serial number, medical devices, or "implantables" as they are known in healthcare, are actually incredibly hard to track. The complexity of the supply chain, together with the intricacies of the operating room and the myriad players involved, make it a high-pressure, fluid process, where pieces and parts are quickly traded in and out to accommodate your precise needs and the physician's preferences for how to address your particular situation, neither of which will be fully known until surgery has started. As a result, the only system of record for identifying what was and was not used, and who will be billed for what, is often the operating room garbage bag.

You think we're joking about the garbage bag. We're not. Until a few years ago, and even today in many of the world's hospitals, the method for tracking inventory used during surgery is to collect discarded packaging from the trash for identifying markers that can provide a list of products used during the hectic operating room experience. This is coupled with the records taken by the operating room nurse and the manufacturer's representative, if he or she was in the room during the procedure. That's what is used to create a purchase order, and to identify what may have been implanted in your body.

It doesn't take a genius to realize that this is a problem. First, it is an extremely manual process with a high margin of error. In one study conducted by VUEMED and presented at the IDN Summit and Reverse Expo in 2013, billing inaccuracies were found in 100 percent of procedure records evaluated. Even more interesting, 80 percent of the records erred by overbilling patients, and 90 percent erred by underbilling.[1] So it wasn't unusual for the same person to be overcharged and undercharged on the same invoice! The net annual cost of waste, loss, and expiration in the US medical system alone is estimated in the billions of dollars, in part from processes like the garbage bag approach to inventory management, which seems ironically apropos.

Second, inaccurate and manually collected data can make it difficult to track down the patient if there is a recall or a problem identified with the part. We can do it with cars (think about those recall notices you get in the mail periodically), but not the often lifesaving devices inside your body.

Now consider this waste, and the potential threats to patient safety, in the context of the broader aims of the system. No matter where you sit in healthcare, you are focused on what's known as the Triple Aim. The Institute for Healthcare Improvement, which coined the term in 2008, defines the Triple Aim of healthcare as simultaneously improving the patient's experience of care, improving the health of populations, and reducing the per capita cost of healthcare.[2] Clearly, the way implantables were being managed was in conflict with all three of these goals. It is a complex problem that matters a great deal to suppliers, providers, and patients across the entire system. The company that could solve it would create massive value and be established as a company that truly matters. But this problem was even tougher, because no one company could actually solve it. It would require an industry-wide effort led by a company with an elevated perspective: the ability to challenge assumptions, to be optimistic about the possibility of solutions, and to explore the unanswered questions to find answers that would work. What really mattered was being able to define and facilitate the *full solution*, even if you weren't in a position to deliver on that full solution.

Governments, insurers, manufacturers, providers, and even patients wanted to understand why it was so hard to track implantables. What was each of the players doing at their step in the process that was causing the challenge, and why weren't they fixing those steps? What industry assumptions and beliefs were preventing solutions from being created? What types of interdependencies were at play and would need to be addressed to create a viable solution? One company with an elevated perspective had the insight to ask these questions, envision a solution, and get the right participation from others to answer them. That company was Global Healthcare Exchange (GHX). Founded by a coalition of healthcare suppliers, this Colorado-based company has established itself in the unique position of connecting suppliers and providers in the healthcare supply chain, committing both parties to the accurate exchange of data, in real time, to advance the Triple Aim of healthcare.

From its early focus on provisioning clean and accurate data exchange, GHX has taken on many edges of disruption since it was founded. GHX has been involved in some of the toughest problems in the industry: e-commerce in the company's early days; then contract synchronization, price accuracy, data sharing, and interoperability; and, more recently, new opportunities in vendor management and cross-industry solutions for challenges like accurately tracking implantables. Its CEO, Bruce Johnson, feels that GHX has learned through experience to deliver on the basics really well, earning the right to take on the bigger challenges that matter even more to the industry by proving its ability to deliver value to "both sides"—suppliers and providers. In doing so, the company has built robust knowledge and insight no one else has, giving its leaders an elevated perspective on the healthcare supply chain.[3] They are using that perspective to get the access to the people and relationships they need to create high-value, impactful solutions that involve many different players in the industry—the solutions no one company can craft alone. The result? For implantables, the industry has collectively defined a solution and has taken the first steps to clawing back some of those lost billions in waste, loss, and expiration, among other improvements. And that's just a small (and recent) part of GHX's business and the value it has delivered over the years.

We see GHX as a clear example of a company that invests in and delivers on an elevated perspective that uniquely positions it in the industry. Ever since GHX was created, its leaders have continually sought new edges of disruption for themselves and their industry. For example, in 2010, the executive team set out an incredibly ambitious goal, what Bruce and his team called "5 in 5." In five years, they wanted to drive $5 billion out of the cost of healthcare. How? By tackling some of the biggest cost challenges and inconsistencies in the supply chain. With this singular goal in mind, the company set out to create systemic change that would deliver these savings, and in the process would also improve patient outcomes and experiences. You will learn a great deal more about this fascinating company and how it uses its unique position and perspective to continually define new edges of disruption in the chapters to come (spoiler alert: GHX not only delivered on 5 in 5; it exceeded its goal). For now, though, let's turn to you, and think about how you might define your edge of disruption—the first step in developing an elevated perspective.

Take a minute and think about critical questions your buyers might need answered about a new market they are entering, legislation that is changing your industry, or a product they are developing. Like many in the healthcare industry, maybe they need to solve three apparently conflicting problems: lowering cost, improving outcomes, and making customers happy. Perhaps they are evaluating a new technology, or trying to figure out next year's business risks. Your buyers are looking for someone with an elevated perspective to help them think through those types of questions. Where do they go for answers? Who do they ask? Would they come to you? Are you or your company known for an elevated perspective, or as a trusted partner who can bring a different vantage point and can ask good questions that they aren't thinking to ask for themselves? Are you someone who knows what's happening at the edges of disruption that are most meaningful to them?

If your customer asked you a question like, "Why is it so hard to . . ." and the honest response is either "I don't really know much about that" or a more superfluous set of generic ideas and observations that don't really create progress toward a scalable solution, how likely are they to continue the conversation? Not very. But what if your response is "You know, we've been studying that exact question for a while now, and here's what we think about it," or "Funny you should ask, we are currently co-creating a solution to that very problem with some of our customers. Would you like us to come and talk to you and your team about what we are discovering?" These answers would very likely lead them to bring you in to talk to their boss. Or even their boss's boss. You would comfortably move right up the chain to the organization's decision makers, because you had a definitive point of view, grounded in reality, that you were willing to share.

We believe there are things that matter to buyers, and there are things that matter more. An elevated perspective that comes from the edge of disruption matters more. Your ability to have insight at that edge, and to share it in a compelling and applicable way, will matter in the most influential rooms of your most important clients. Clients can leverage that perspective to help differentiate their organization and solve their most complex problems. This is what is truly meant by the phrase *thought leader*.

Your ability to offer an elevated perspective from the edge of disruption is critical to gaining access to the right people, and to influencing them in a way that opens an opportunity for you to create more value than your competition does. GHX uses its elevated perspective to persuade partners in the industry to participate in joint problem-solving for challenges that matter most to their investors and customers, and that have the biggest impact on the industry's Triple Aim goals. Your goal throughout this section should be to define for yourself the right edge of disruption and build an elevated perspective around it. It is a critical first step on your journey to becoming the obvious choice. This is especially true when clients can better identify opportunities for themselves to be a part of something much larger, as is often the case with the work GHX does. We need to work together now to define what it is for you.

> An elevated perspective that comes from the edge of disruption matters more. Your ability to have insight at that edge, and to share it in a compelling and applicable way, will matter in the most influential rooms of your most important clients.

After we are done *defining* your edge of disruption—the place where you can add the most value to solving the most important problems your clients face—we will shift our attention to how you can go about *learning* as much as you can about it, and then critically *sharing* the point of view you develop there from a strong platform. By the end of this book, you should have an elevated perspective in an area that matters to your most important clients, and you'll have the reputation and access you need to develop the next capability, *elevated relationships*, which in turn will allow you to have an *elevated impact*. When you have all three, you will consistently matter more than your competitors and will be creating the capability and culture to stay that way. And that is what will result in you being the obvious choice, year after year, for your industry, your employees, and your community. Let's get started.

CHAPTER 1

DEFINE: Discover Your Edge of Disruption

AS WE DISCUSSED IN THE INTRODUCTION to this section, if the most value is created where complexity reigns, healthcare certainly has a lot of value creation opportunities. We could start with looking at how the insurance industry works (both patient coverage and practitioner malpractice), move over to the ways physicians and nurses are educated, skip along to hospital care and the outcomes hospitals deliver, maybe spend some time in rural community access, tally the overall cost of delivering care (plus there's the fact that the United States typically spends more on healthcare as a percentage of GDP than almost any other nation), and perhaps throw in changing patient expectations (admit it, you've diagnosed yourself via Google search—we all have), and we wouldn't even scratch the surface of the massive changes that are happening. There are lots of places to go to find interesting and meaningful edges of disruption in healthcare.

No one knows this better than GHX, which you met in the section opener. GHX was founded during the heady days of the internet boom. Healthcare buyers were being bombarded with what Bruce Johnson, current GHX CEO and member of the founding executive team, calls "PowerPoint Promises" that sounded something like this: "Sexy startup from the Silicon Valley promises data nirvana. Every transaction and piece of inventory in your system will be instantly trackable and traceable via electronic data interchange, and there will be no more waste in the system." Bruce and the founding team at GHX knew better. That vision described in the PowerPoint Promise was beyond the edge of disruption in 2000 and was deep in what we call "unproductive disruption," the space where the technology, processes, and infrastructure and other environmental factors are not yet in place to make the vision a reality. At the other extreme, more conservative approaches by single manufacturers attempting to use their proprietary websites as a competitive advantage were too close to the status quo, offering no meaningful progress for the industry. Doing nothing risked leaving a market opening for a third party to enter and dictate how the industry would interact with its customers—also not a good option.

That was the edge of disruption upon which GHX was founded—somewhere between the hyperbole of the internet startup mania and the industry status quo. To avoid duplicating e-commerce investments and third-party disintermediation, which would worsen already spiraling healthcare-system costs, five competitive manufacturers created a digital data exchange that would benefit the industry.

GHX has successfully become the obvious choice for much of its industry. It grew from a first-year target of $20 million in transactions annually flowing through its exchange to more than $60 billion annually today, with its systems handling more than 168 million transactions per year. Ironically, some people who in 2000 were, at best, avoiding being involved with GHX now like to fondly remember their early support for it, revising history a bit in the process! As an example of the shift that has occurred since the company's launch, Bruce noted that one of the early companies on the exchange back in 2001 took the minimum possible steps to be on it, sharing only very hesitantly and incrementally out of a fear of losing control of its data and contracts. Today it is one of the most active and vibrant members of the exchange, using its supply chain offering as a differentiator. It was tough at times, but GHX brought customers along to the edge of disruption with them. In doing so, GHX provided those customers with their own path to becoming the obvious choice for their customers.

With more than 417,000 unique trading partner pairs connected to the exchange, 22,000 healthcare facilities, and 85 percent of medical/surgical products represented by integrated GHX suppliers, the company is thriving. With metrics like that, GHX clearly has a track record in delivering from the healthcare industry's edge of disruption, providing more value, and as a result becoming the obvious choice for the suppliers and providers they serve. Even more, it delivers to both sides of the market—suppliers and providers. As Bruce Johnson told us in our interview with him, the ability of GHX to provide solutions that work across the supply chain gives the company an elevated perspective about what will advance the industry as a whole, rather than simply helping one side to win over the other.

> "Defining your edge of disruption should be driven by the question, What are the problems we are uniquely positioned to solve with a scalable solution?"

As GHX has learned what matters most to its customers and worked to deliver it, its elevated impact has pushed the industry into new potential edges of disruption, in the process opening up new opportunity for GHX to create more value. As we mentioned in the introduction, GHX has now tackled several edges of disruption. As Bruce explained to us, "Defining your edge of disruption should be driven by the question, What are the problems we are uniquely positioned to solve with a scalable solution?" As GHX grew, so, too, did its unique ability to solve problems that spanned multiple industry players—an ability supported by its engagement with both suppliers and providers.

It is worth pausing to consider the word "unique," and it's one to think about as you pursue your own edge of disruption. Keep in mind that one qualifier for "unique" may simply be that you are willing to take on a challenge where others are not. That shouldn't be your only qualifier, but it can be a powerful one. "Scalable" is another word that jumps out. Can you envision a solution where you can get to enough scale to have a reasonable impact? Remember that scale is relative—if you are in consumer products, it might mean millions of buyers in an off year, whereas if you are in the business of customizing jets like the 787 Dreamliner, it might mean dozens of buyers in a good year. Regardless of your market's actual size, "scalable" means you can address enough of it with your solution for it to matter.

Coming back to GHX, the company gained momentum in the market during its first decade, working through startup mode to stabilize itself and grow. In the process, it built up its ability to discover new edges of disruption that leveraged its unique capabilities, including its aptitude for standing in the center of a complex and often contentious environment, between competitors, providers, suppliers, distributors, and others. The team learned to see its inherent neutrality not as a limiter but as a distinguisher in terms of problems it is uniquely able to solve. As it solved for and scaled the first edge of disruption it was charted to deliver, the ability to have e-commerce between suppliers and providers, they quickly moved on to more ambitious edges. And as we mentioned earlier, GHX more recently has taken on leading the industry in defining the solution for documenting implantables used in patient care. We'll be getting deeper into that, together with advances it has made in tracking pharmaceuticals, in Chapter 2, "Learn." Given how often the company has done it, defining new edges of disruption is almost a core competency of GHX!

In any edge of disruption it defines, GHX looks for the challenge that matters most to the suppliers and providers that use the exchange, and to the broader population—including you as a potential patient. You might be wondering how all of this work on electronic data interchange could be relevant to you.

Isn't it really just about suppliers getting paid faster and providers getting more accurate billing? What does it have to do with patient outcomes or your experience at the doctor?

Consider this. Imagine you are at the doctor's office, and you have a latex allergy. With interoperable systems sharing accurate data about product descriptions, it is possible for your electronic medical record to be matched to the inventory being used for your doctor's visit. This could help ensure that the nurse setting up the tray is flagged to pull the right latex-free gloves from inventory and confirm that they are being used during all aspects of your treatment. Without accurate supply data, your risk of coming in contact with latex is exponentially higher. Clearly, the work that GHX and others in the supply chain do influences not just the flow of money but also the quality of care patients receive. Because of GHX's ability to scale solutions to inventory problems, the edges of disruption it tackles deliver against all of the Triple Aim goals, not just cost containment.

Developing an elevated perspective about the right edge of disruption is critical to success. In a space where trust between industry participants was a major barrier, GHX had to learn to navigate among its competitors, customers, and customers' customers. Through the trust it has earned, the results delivered, and the value created, GHX has been able to anchor itself as a neutral arbitrator of industry solutions that require broad participation and support to deliver. This position enables GHX to drive solutions across the industry for even more complex challenges—the ones that matter more—like the ability to track and trace implantables. That's a perfect edge of disruption for GHX to address, because the company has unique access to data, people, and the market to challenge industry assumptions, think optimistically about how to solve problems, and ask the yet unanswered questions about crafting a full solution.

You might be thinking that healthcare is so rich in opportunity that it is easy to find a "good" edge of disruption there and run with it—who wouldn't want to solve for something like tracking implantables? But let's think about that differently. Step back and consider some of the different edges of disruption available in healthcare. Consider for a moment that it is unlikely that GHX or its clients would benefit from GHX developing, for instance, a nuanced and in-depth perspective on the cost of medical education that synthesized all of the current issues in a credentialed and meaningful way. *Could* GHX do that? Probably. There are a lot of smart people working there who could direct attention to it. Would GHX working on this issue drive *significant* outcomes in terms of positive change in solving the problem, or in advancing the GHX core strategy, or that of its customers? Unlikely. Is GHX uniquely placed to have a meaningful and sustainable position on the issues surrounding the cost of medical education? No. Would a perspective on medical education help GHX get into the right conversation with its clients about how to positively impact the Triple Aim goals? Probably not. While there are plenty of disruptions happening in the medical education space, it is not the *best* edge of disruption for GHX to explore—it might be someone else's, but it likely isn't for GHX. Being selective about your edge of disruption is critical—remember Bruce's criteria of unique and scalable for GHX. As you look for the right edge of disruption, being able to say "no" is critical, and is a skill we will revisit in several of our case studies.

> Defining your edge of disruption is about looking toward the future, determining where your capabilities and credibility uniquely position you to take advantage of the wide array of changes you see there, and developing a unique perspective about the disruption these changes will bring. You then use that perspective to drive meaningful insight for the people you need to influence the most.

Likewise for you, there are many problems in the world to solve, and many exciting new opportunities and spaces to explore, but you need to be selective in defining *your* edge of disruption. Defining *your* edge of disruption is about looking toward the future, determining where your capabilities and credibility uniquely position you to take advantage of the wide array of changes you see there, and developing a unique perspective about the disruption these changes will bring. You then use that perspective to drive meaningful insight for the people you need to influence the most.

Let's think about where you might find your own edge of disruption. To be clear, we are not suggesting that with an elevated perspective, you need to be an expert on all areas of your business and that of your customers. We are, however, suggesting that you need to figure out the edge of disruption that is most likely to matter to your customers—where you can add the most value, and about which you have the most to say—and go there. Everyone has a different edge of disruption, depending on interest, industry, competition, customer base, strategic goals, and market position, so figuring out yours is critical.

As you work on defining your edge, you will need to take a hard look at what's going on around you. It might feel unsettling, or even scary, but it is a critical step to becoming the obvious choice. Places to look for your edge of disruption include the contracting process (especially if you are in a business-to-business model; we're going to share an example of how that can yield amazing outcomes), customer experience, product positioning, technology, customer relationship, service models, internal data and information, areas where legislation is looming, changes in adjacent industries, and other parts of the value chain. We believe that wherever you go to find your edge of disruption, it should ultimately generate *market-facing* value. It must have an impact on your customers, and if appropriate, your customers' customers. For GHX, its leaders look for edges of disruption where they can advance all three Triple Aim goals and uniquely deliver scalable solutions to their customers in ways that matter. So yes, healthcare has plenty of complexities to explore, but they aren't all good opportunities for every player in the industry. And even industries that seem more mundane and less complicated have pushed out onto edges of disruption to challenge norms and create new products, markets, and ways of working.

As you start to think about defining your own edge of disruption, let's consider an example that everyone has experienced—grocery shopping. In 1916, grocery shoppers typically made a list, brought it to the store, and handed it to a clerk, who would then fill the entire order, bag it, and give the shopper a total price. That's just how it was done. If you asked a grocer in 1916 about how his business worked, he would have talked about the importance of clerks knowing everything about all the inventory and managing the customer experience. If you had asked customers what they needed or wanted in their shopping experience, they likely would have said faster clerks and lower prices.

In the face of deeply held beliefs about how to shop for groceries, a guy named Clarence Saunders was optimistic enough about the industry to launch his own unique brand, and curious enough to challenge many of the deeply held assumptions about how people shopped for groceries. He set his sights on the customer's shopping experience as his edge of disruption when he opened the first Piggly Wiggly in 1916. It was the first grocery store to use checkout lanes and to price each individual product so that shoppers could browse and select for themselves—using a radical new object Saunders invented called a *shopping cart*. He was the first to create this self-service format, overcoming deeply held industry *and* customer beliefs about what the ideal grocery-shopping experience looked and felt like. Saunders didn't just ask customers what they wanted—the likelihood of them coming up with checkout lanes was incredibly remote. And he didn't try to do what his competition was doing, only better or cheaper or with nicer people. Instead, he looked at what was happening in retail and in the way shoppers were starting to behave, synthesized it with what he knew about the economics of his business, had the courage to challenge the assumptions almost everyone was making about shopping for groceries, and single-handedly reinvented the experience.[1]

> Saunders didn't just ask customers what they wanted. And he didn't try to do what his competition was doing . . . he looked at what was happening . . . synthesized it with what he knew about the economics of his business, had the courage to challenge the assumptions almost everyone was making about shopping for groceries, and single-handedly reinvented the experience.

Fast-forward almost 100 years and Saunders's self-service format, so radical when he first launched it, is still the norm for the industry. He was truly on the edge of disruption in 1916, and he created an enduring model as a result. In an interesting twist, today grocers are starting to experiment with "concierge service," where shoppers order online and drive up for curbside pickup, and a clerk loads their bags into the car (sound familiar?). Why take this on? Because grocers are seeing the disruptions that are happening around them and they are defining their new edge of disruption in the shopping experience.

As the grocery industry shifts to accommodate these changing shopping behaviors, one company, Homeplus (owned by Tesco), decided to take a radically new approach. It defined for itself a new edge of disruption to explore—one invested in technology, shifting cultural norms, activity in adjacent sectors, and the reinvigoration of a historic business model while solving for how to create a new shopping experience. While the competition installed self-scanner technology for customers to use in the traditional checkout environment, Homeplus ventured out into the real world of its customers. Let's take a look at what has become a case study for defining your edge of disruption in the real world.[2]

In 2015, Homeplus was succeeding as the second-largest Korean grocery retailer, with more than 400 stores serving 6 million customers weekly.[3] Flash back to 2011, though, and the company was concerned about losing sales to online retailers (e-tailers). Homeplus did have a conventional website for ordering products, but it felt vulnerable to dedicated e-tailers. South Korea was by most measures the world's most web-savvy country, with 84 percent of its more than 40 million residents using the internet. Residents especially loved using their smartphones to order all sorts of retail goods on the spot. But in 2011, grocery had eluded the e-tailing boom, and shopping for groceries online represented only 2 to 3 percent of Homeplus's market.

On the face of it, there was no need to push e-tailing forward. Indeed, it would seem to be in Homeplus's interest not to—it had plenty to focus on in its traditional business operations to

compete with the other traditional grocery stores. The more pessimistic or defensive-minded thinkers in the industry might have
been inclined to simply continue to work in the current model,
driving out cost and other internal operations in traditional environments—the place where they were comfortable working.

But Homeplus executives were reportedly curious about an
unanswered question in the market. They had noticed some
developments in other adjacent markets that pointed toward
e-tailing being important in Homeplus's own market. The staggering adoption and use of apps on smartphones was a cultural
phenomenon in South Korea. In parallel, in the United States,
online sales of staple products like diapers and razors were
exploding, with online subscription models claiming upwards
of 30 percent of the market. This new fringe behavior was gaining critical mass, and Homeplus saw a chance to answer the
question of how consumers would respond to a fresh take on
internet grocery shopping.

Homeplus chose to be optimistic about the future of grocery shopping in this new world by framing e-tailing as an
opportunity, and to be curious about how to accelerate it even
further. This was a stark contrast to most retailers' desire to halt
the progression of online grocery shopping for as long as possible. Standing back from the daily realities of their business,
Homeplus executives challenged deeply held industry assumptions by asking a very important question. Instead of considering ways to dissuade shoppers from going online for groceries,
they asked, "How can we remove barriers to ordering groceries
online and take the lead in online grocery sales?" We suggest
that solving this question became Homeplus's edge of disruption in 2011, and it was the perfect place to bring together its
understanding of the market, its enthusiasm for technology, and
its interest in the shopping experience.

The company's executives pulled together a team of partners
that included their ad agency in Seoul, which came forward with
an idea for making orders much easier for time-pressed consumers. The team hypothesized that consumers were reluctant to
take the time to get out their computers, log on to a grocery site,

and scroll through static lists of products to find what they liked to buy. It was all too much bother; worse, it didn't make sense in either the traditional model or the emerging model. To make headway with consumers online, Homeplus had to engineer a new kind of online shopping.

The team looked to cultural norms and technology trends in particular for insight. South Koreans relied heavily on public transportation to get around their highly urbanized country. As they waited for the subway, they liked to pull out their phones— maybe to do something important, or maybe to surf, check social media, or play games—it didn't matter. For Homeplus, this was a potentially disruptive way to engage.

The company invested in a dedicated app and outfitted train stations with images of grocery products. This allowed commuters to use their smartphones, stroll along the train station with its walls plastered with images of products just as they would a grocery store aisle, and capture the products they recognized and loved on their phones. With the help of their ad agency, Homeplus was able to mimic the visuals of a grocery store's aisles, with items displaying QR codes shoppers could scan with their phones.[4] As items were selected, the app added them to the consumer's shopping basket. Assuming payment details were filled out in advance on the app, a single click would allow the customer to make a purchase. During the campaign, online sales rose 130 percent.[5] Clarence Saunders would be proud!

Imagine for yourself the kinds of questions you need to ask, the assumptions you need to challenge, if you want to completely reconstitute your customer interactions. These market-facing, customer-impacting moments are rich and generative places to look for your edge of disruption. You may want to ask your customers, but remember that they likely will struggle to envision something different as well, so don't stop there. Ask your employees, talk to people outside your industry, and understand the cultural changes that are affecting your business. Take a good look at your assumptions and test yourself. Are you pushing out of the echo chamber of your own business far enough, or are you stuck on the model as it is known today? It is tough to do on your own—collaboration is great for brainstorming as you define your edge of disruption. Bring in outside voices; industry watchers, customers, board members, employees, vendors, technology experts, consultants, and others will help you to really focus on where you can create the greatest value for your organization and your customers.

If you feel like defining your edge of disruption is a little overwhelming, you are right where you should be. If it feels like it may change the fundamentals of your business forever, you are on it. Don't worry—once you get there, you will have the ability to stay there, while continuing to look forward and to push your customers, your industry, and your markets in new directions. But first, you need to learn about the three things required to get there.

When we looked at companies that have succeeded on the edge of disruption, that are delivering the highest value possible to customers, we observed that they brought three things to the journey. Every person and every company you meet in this book has these three things in common, and you need to find them for yourself if you wish to become the obvious choice in your market. The three things you must have are *the courage to challenge your assumptions*, the ability to *take an optimistic stance* about the future of your industry and your place in it, and a desire to *explore the unanswered questions*, to know more about the world around you. Let's consider each of these in turn.

HAVE THE COURAGE TO CHALLENGE ASSUMPTIONS

First and foremost, when you set out to define your edge of disruption, you absolutely, unequivocally must have the courage to challenge your assumptions and deeply held beliefs about your industry, including how you make money and provide value. You must step out of the container of your immediate environment and be willing to stretch your imagination and your understanding of possibilities.

Let's take a minute to flash back to 1916, and imagine what might have been on Clarence Saunders's list of assumptions. We're willing to bet "The highest level of service is to serve someone yourself" was on there, along with "Customers like to make a list of what they want," because it was assumed that browsing around a store was no way to spend precious time!

What about GHX? According to Bruce, in those early days plenty of industry players assumed no one would ever really be willing to share their data. They suggested that manufacturers would bias the exchange for their own benefit, or that providers would not be willing to participate, fearing a loss of influence over their suppliers. Everyone seemed worried about losing control of their data, which was a big assumption, given that many of them actually didn't have much control over their data when it was managed in-house at the time. Some leaders in the founding companies even admitted later to not believing GHX would succeed. Thankfully GHX did succeed, and it did in part because it was willing to challenge these assumptions head-on.

> Take a good look at your assumptions and test yourself. Are you pushing out of the echo chamber of your own business far enough, or are you stuck on the model as it is known today?

It would have been no different for Homeplus. You can hear critics saying, "People prefer to buy fruits and vegetables in person, carefully selecting their own." Another assumption might have been, "Growth in apps for phones isn't relevant to buying groceries." Whenever you are getting close to the edge of disruption, the assumptions become louder and harder to ignore.

Do it for yourself right now. Pull out a piece of paper and write down the five most irrevocable truths that you believe about how you do business. Truths that, when you are honest with yourself, may in fact be blinding you to opportunities that are right in front of you. Opportunities that the insular world of your industry and your organization are hiding in plain sight. Embedded in the results will be pointers to your edge of disruption—the ideas that are too precious to challenge are the very ones you must examine. Hang on to that piece of paper while you read this book; use it as a bookmark if you have a paper copy. You may feel the need to come back to it time and again.

We know it is hard to challenge your assumptions, but you must do it because those sacred beliefs and unconscious biases blind you to the opportunity that is hidden in plain sight all around you. You can challenge your assumptions about how you do business and what makes you special—what you believe about yourself and about your competition. You can also orient around the customer perspective and examine assumptions about what they expect from you. It may be necessary to tap into outsiders to gain access to thoughts on industry convergence, legislation, or cultural trends that are hard to see from an internal view. Take a broad inventory of the assumptions you have in each of these areas, and test them by talking to others, doing research, and getting diverse input to help you to see them differently. Test yourself. If you aren't feeling a little uncomfortable, if you don't see anything on your list that makes you think, "That's just not possible to change," you may not be pushing far enough.

TAKE AN OPTIMISTIC STANCE

Going along with the courage to challenge assumptions, defining your edge of disruption requires you to take an optimistic stance about the future of your industry and your place in it. People sometimes shy away from sounding overly optimistic, because they worry about sounding naïve. But without optimism that your industry and your business can thrive, there's almost no point in doing the work of heading to the edge of disruption.

Pessimism is the foundation of price wars. Because you can't see any other way to do business and charge a premium for your services, you focus on driving down cost and winning on price.

Time and again we've encountered people who feel deeply pessimistic about the future of their industry or their place in the market. This is a crushing situation to be in, because it diverts all of your energy into protecting where you are and prevents the best people from spending time thinking about what "could be."

We believe there are not really pessimistic and optimistic people; rather, there are pessimistic and optimistic questions. Finding your edge of disruption, and then thriving from what you learn there, is about asking more optimistic questions. Optimistic questions are *growth questions* for the future. Questions like "How can we use this to our advantage?" "What opportunities are hidden in this disruption?" and "How could we get ahead of this change and profit from an early-mover advantage?" Pessimistic questions are the *survival questions* about today's models. Questions like "How do we stop customers from moving to this new, more user-friendly technology-based experience?" or "How can we use our market strength to kill the spread of this new innovation?" We understand the need to be practical; sometimes you have to meet and outdo your competition where your buyers are today, not where they will be in a few years. But if you are optimistic about the possibility that the future can be even better than today, you will keep pushing out of the box you are in, even if it is a box that is currently serving you reasonably well.

Homeplus asked an optimistic question that focused on the future possibilities: "How do we help shoppers to buy our products differently?" A pessimistic question that kept them concentrating on the status quo would have been: "How can we keep shoppers coming into our stores and buying more from us in the model we know best?" Developing Piggly Wiggly's new format was an optimistic position to take as well. It asked "what if" questions about shopping—"What if the cost of service could be lowered?" "What if customer satisfaction could be improved?" "What if these things happened through a different experience altogether?"—rather than asking, "How do I attract more customers to the same experience that my competition offers?" The answer to that inevitably would have led to a "lower prices" conclusion, leaving Saunders to slug out a commodity pricing strategy along with all the other grocers.

The GHX founding companies did the same. Instead of asking a more scarcity-driven question like "How do we protect our data and ourselves in the process?" the founding companies asked, "How can we avoid duplication and create a data exchange that doesn't just reduce the cost to serve but also allows the industry to deliver even more value?" That same optimism is alive and well at GHX today as it forges ahead to solve the industry challenges present in implantables and pharmaceuticals, and as it works to create value in other markets, like those in European countries. There is a belief at GHX that they can make a difference, and that makes all the difference in how they define their edges of disruption.

> Over and over, we saw optimism, coupled with the willingness to challenge assumptions, as crucial characteristics for success.

During our research, embedded in the case studies, and in our work, we've consistently found that optimism was a foundational element of success for people who decided to re-create their businesses. By adopting a more optimistic stance, leaders asked better questions—questions that pushed them to identify the opportunities, not just the threats, at the edge of disruption. Over and over, we saw optimism, coupled with the willingness to challenge assumptions, as crucial characteristics for success.

The power of optimistic thinking holds true for companies of all shapes and sizes, and in all industries. Let's shift gears and look at an example of a company that is smaller in size, but not in impact: a mid-sized plumbing distribution company from the southwestern United States.

Standard Plumbing Supply is no multibillion-dollar giant like Homeplus. It is a family-run, increasingly vertically integrated plumbing supply business based in Utah, and it faced a competitor that strikes fear in the hearts of many established market leaders: Amazon. That's right, Amazon wasn't just unsettling consumer-facing retail giants like Barnes & Noble and Best Buy, but also business-to-business players such as electrical and plumbing distributors. Lowe's and Home Depot were tough enough competition, but now this plumbing distributor was squaring off against this disruptive online wizard and its world-class user experience.

In 2014, with Amazon encroaching, a group of plumbing suppliers invited Karrikins Group (then ChangeLabs) to address its annual convention and offer guidance on how to respond. In conducting a preconference briefing, Karrikins Group brought multiple business owners into the same room to explore their perceived challenges and opportunities. Richard Reese, CEO of Standard Plumbing, dialed in, and for much of the discussion, was content to listen. When the question "What opportunity does Amazon actually present to the distributor and its current role in the value chain?" was posed, the other plumbing suppliers responded with versions, some unprintable, of "Amazon is the devil."

Richard's response was very different. He noted that while Amazon was indeed a disruptive force, in that disruption lay tremendous opportunity to grow their businesses, both in store and online. We were shocked to hear this. It may have been the first time we heard someone speak so positively about a competitor and the change they were bringing, let alone one as aggressive as Amazon. If we had known the history of this family business, we might not have been so surprised.

Disruption was not new for Standard Plumbing. In fact, the company was founded as a disruptive force. In 1952, following a graduate degree from the New York University School of Retailing and a stint at Macy's, Dale Reese returned to his home state of Utah and did for plumbing supply what Piggly Wiggly had done for grocery retail—he made it self-service. Many years later, Standard Plumbing, now under the leadership of one of Reese's sons, Richard, faced a choice: ignore the emerging forces of online commerce that were starting to bubble up on the fringe of the industry, or lean into them, move to their edge of disruption, and embrace this mostly uncertain online channel opportunity.

The company chose to move toward the edge, with confidence and optimism, and set up an online department. Although a pallet in the back of the warehouse is hardly a "department," it was a symbolic move that the future was coming, and Standard Plumbing would be a part of it. Where did Standard Plumbing choose to sell most of its supplies? That's right: Amazon!

Like most entrepreneurial businesses leaning into the online world in those days, Standard Plumbing did not realize that by doing so it was essentially making transaction and product information (called a "stock keeping unit" or SKU) across almost every product category on earth available to Amazon. Amazon would track SKUs and categories, and when one reached a sizeable enough volume, Amazon would begin competing with those suppliers who had been listing on its site. The B2B industrial product space is twice the size of the entire retail market in the United States,[6] so it's no wonder Amazon decided to target a pretty large share of it.

Now one might be forgiven for crying foul, but Standard Plumbing's leadership team saw no value in complaining. They merely dealt with the facts and made future-focused decisions instead of exerting effort holding on to a world that would eventually crumble. Reese had been learning at the edge of disruption the whole time, and had come to know two things. First, in an online market, it was all about search. If you could rank higher than the competition, you won. And no one could beat Amazon in search. Amazon dominated organic rankings on sites like Google, and could also control rankings on its own site. Second, Reese also knew that to truly win with plumbers across North America, Standard Plumbing would need to stock and make available a much broader range than just the highest-volume SKUs, and this would include the heavy and bulky items that Amazon traditionally resisted carrying.

Here was Standard Plumbing's opportunity—its edge. Richard Reese asked the more optimistic question: Could Standard Plumbing become partners with Amazon, rather than the two being competitors?

The answer turned out to be a resounding yes. There were two relatively important and high-value challenges Standard Plumbing could solve for Amazon. First, Standard Plumbing could assume the inventory-carrying risk and storage cost for larger bulky items that have lower volume. And second, it could act as a direct distributor for these same expensive-to-ship items in the states where it has physical locations.

In our conversation with Richard, he noted that 85 percent of Standard Plumbing's sizeable online business is currently with Amazon, on its behalf.[7] Focused mostly on carrying inventory risk and associated costs, Standard Plumbing now makes available for Amazon customers some 63,000 SKUs, which are sent across not just Standard Plumbing's eight states, but the entire United States and Canada. This small Utah-based family business has become the obvious choice not just for its traditional market, but also for the biggest disruptor in its market, because it solved a relatively important problem for Amazon—the need to penetrate this important and growing market in a way that worked for Amazon and for its customers, which meant being able to manage inventory and delivery effectively at a local level.

Reese is not just optimistic about the disruptive opportunity that Amazon provides; he also speaks very positively about its approach to business. He admits that "when doing business with Amazon, there is the Amazon way and there is the Amazon way. Choose." And yet he adds that an abundance mind-set (an expression of optimism) pushes the company to do business with its competition as well. To Amazon, Reese explains, a "box is a box, and as long as they are part of the transaction, they are more than happy to share the margin."

The explosion of Standard Plumbing's online business has enabled the company to aggressively grow its brick-and-mortar wholesale supply business as well. With the increased volume came greater buying power, and therefore better prices and enough capital to expand its offering in the physical world, too. It was win-win. When Richard Reese took over from his father they had thirteen stores. In 2015 they had more than eighty, in eight states, and now do business across a North American footprint. "My father could never have imagined this world," said Richard. But he could raise a son with the same optimistic and entrepreneurial attitude he had way back in 1952.

This entrepreneurial attitude was evident not just in Richard's optimistic response to the threat of Amazon, but also in his response to the largest housing downturn since the Great Depression. As you can imagine, the plumbing business was battered by the bursting of the housing bubble in July 2008. It was a time when many manufacturers and distributors just like Standard Plumbing were struggling to survive. And it was during this time that Standard Plumbing was the most optimistic.

Change is how an environment continues to unlock new and vibrant forms of value, so you will have to keep moving.

The company was in no way enjoying the social consequences of such a severe downturn, but at the same time it looked for the proverbial silver lining.

As more and more manufacturers came up for sale, Richard began a process of vertically integrating his business, using his powerful distribution position—both online with Amazon and offline through its growing store footprint—to increase Standard Plumbing's sales by acquiring other distributors and bringing them into the Standard Plumbing processes. He bought real estate for pennies on the dollar as well, placing wholesale stores in increasingly convenient locations across a growing interstate footprint. We could not help but laugh during the research when Richard earnestly suggested that growth was tougher in 2015 than it had been in 2010 through 2013. He semi-jokingly suggested that the best years for growth were when companies were being sold below true value and real estate was being auctioned at fire-sale prices. He was optimistic in even the toughest times! It is no wonder he has grown the business his father started into the obvious choice not just for the local tradespeople, but for the disruptor (Amazon) as well.

Optimism underpins everything that follows. If you find it hard to be optimistic about your business, take a minute and think about what worries you. Is it that your current business model won't survive? Is it a new competitor driving margins down? Perhaps it is the burden of legislation slowing your ability to service your customers. The truth is, these things most likely will continue to happen. The trick to reclaiming your optimism is to realize that disruption is actually normal—people are always finding new ways to solve problems. No single offer or business model will ever stand the true test of time. Change is how an environment continues to unlock new and vibrant forms of value, so you will have to keep moving, keep looking for where you can have the highest possible impact. And to do that, you have to be optimistic about your ability to move with the changes; you have to be willing to understand them while looking outward. It takes curiosity to find the edge of disruption and stay on it.

EXPLORE THE UNANSWERED QUESTIONS

Being willing to challenge assumptions and being optimistic are the first two consistent characteristics we have observed in companies that have successfully found their edge of disruption. They all shared a third characteristic that is worth discussing. It became clear as we talked with these companies that you must have an insatiable desire to explore the unanswered questions that face your industry, your company, your team, and your customers, wherever you find them. This is fueled by a desire to know about what's going on around you, wondering what others are doing and what *might be* possible. That keeps you watching for the next opportunity, pushing to understand what's happening broadly and how you can create more value for your clients, and doing the work that matters most by solving complex problems with innovative solutions.

Unanswered questions that are worth exploring are the "what if," the "where else," the "how might we" questions. When was the last time you asked a curious question about your business?

Do you know the basics of your industry at the moment: the stock price of your own company and those of others in your industry, the health of your suppliers, the technology changes happening for your customers, what's going on with your competition, how new employees learn the ropes? These are serious questions—we are regularly surprised by how removed people can be from their own business and how their industry operates at a foundational level. When you lose touch with those kinds of basics, it is hard to contextualize larger, more important problems that need solving. Too often these types of questions are left up to a specific function like marketing or research and development, while the rest of us stay focused on the task at hand. This is not okay in companies that matter. Inside those companies, almost everyone is curious about their company, industry, and market—they are continually exploring. It is ingrained into the culture to be "ever forward," as DPR calls it.

If people in your company aren't investing in exploring those unanswered questions about how your business gets done, you will entirely miss the edges of disruption that can propel you forward. If *you* personally aren't exploring, the people around you likely won't be, either, so it is up to you to model the way. It is critical, no matter where you are in the company, that you take the time to be curious about your business and your customers, and that you allow others to explore, too.

If the people at GHX had not asked the big question of "What if we did business differently?" they wouldn't be tracking to take billions of dollars out of healthcare for the foreseeable future. If Richard Reese had not been open to asking how the internet could be useful to his traditional wholesale supply business, he would never have become the obvious choice for Amazon. If Clarence Saunders had not been curious enough to not only explore other ways groceries could be bought, but even go as far as to design a contraption to enable those other ways, shopping would be a very different experience today. And if Homeplus had not asked how it could take the converging disruptions of the internet, shopping behaviors, and cultural norms, it would never have discovered how to create whole new shopping models for the next generation of grocery buyers.

If you have the decision-making authority to make investments, invest in the curious questions, rather than proving what you already know to be true. Anyone can prove that their assumptions are correct. History generally provides plenty of data for them. But in our opinion, paying to have history researched and restated is often a waste of time and money (although we see it happen all the time). Instead, put your resources toward exploring the unknown, the ideas that challenge those very assumptions you may want to prove.

When you are ready to invest to satisfy your curiosity, take a page from Homeplus and put your money where it matters. Homeplus could have commissioned a study on how to drive more people into the grocery store after work and then launched a splashy subway campaign promoting the value of hitting the store on the way home. Instead, it chose to explore something new and different, unlike anything people had seen before, and the value it got out of pushing to a new edge of disruption has been ongoing for years now, far beyond the original investment in the pilot.

Interestingly enough, for Homeplus, despite staggering adoption numbers at first, the subway experiment was not a complete success, at least not initially. It turned out that there were some serious flaws in the initial model, and customers quickly fell off after the first experience with the new shopping approach. Homeplus still had to spend some time learning about what was happening on its edge of disruption, so it could anchor its position as the leader in the online grocery shopping experience. We'll dive into that in more detail in the next chapter when we unpack the challenges of learning about your edge of disruption. Even Piggly Wiggly continued to tweak and develop the shopping model that rocked the world in 1916 (earning multiple patents along the way). That's why defining your edge of disruption is step one on the journey; learning about your edge is the next.

Bring It to Life . . .

1. Develop a "disruption chart," listing or visually plotting the most likely disruptors your industry will face in one year, three years, and five years. Think in terms of macro-trends (social, political, economic, community, and cultural), internal developments (workforce, products, geography, structure, and leadership), and outside developments (competition, customers, regulation, technology, and supply chain).

2. Using your disruption chart, select the top five disruptors and develop three possible scenarios of how your industry will evolve over the coming years.
   a. Host a diverse team of creative thinkers to engage in debate over the scenarios you have developed. The goal of the discussion should be to challenge assumptions and produce specific outcomes that the group believes are viable.
   b. As you debate, compile a list of the assumptions that are the strongest in pushing you to accept or reject potential scenarios and opportunities that exist within them.
   c. Do a quick "alternative assumption" on each of these that is both optimistic and future oriented.

3. Using your new assumptions, refine the scenarios.

4. Based on these new possibilities, and coming from a place of optimism, what is the one edge of disruption that you believe offers the best opportunity to evolve your existing capabilities in a way that creates more value for your team, your organization, your company, and your customers?

5. Take that edge of disruption and identify three unanswered questions you could explore in a more intentional way.

6. Identify the people and process you could engage to explore these unanswered questions.

7. START exploring!

CHAPTER 2

LEARN: Establish Your Point of View

WHEN HOMEPLUS DEFINED the customer shopping experience as its edge of disruption, it invested in a six-week pilot that had remarkable success. The pilot was designed to interact with shoppers in a new way, and once an order was placed through the app, within three hours, Homeplus would have the order at the customer's door, guaranteed. Brilliant, right? The pilot sparked a massive public reaction, and Homeplus saw a spike in sales, but consumers overwhelmingly indicated that a three-hour delivery time was too long, and the spike quickly died down after the "first impression" bubble burst.

Before you become distracted by an internal soliloquy about the state of modern society and our impatience, it's important to understand that it was not that three hours was not an extraordinary logistical achievement, but rather that it was too long a window of time to not know when the Homeplus delivery guy would be at your home. It is understandable that the Homeplus team assumed customers would be wowed by the three-hour delivery window, and that they overlooked the effect of the length of that window on customers' lives. This is why Homeplus's willingness to take an intelligent and controlled risk—and actually test the concept in the market—was such a strong way to learn at its edge of disruption.

TAKE INTELLIGENT RISKS IN THE REAL WORLD

Homeplus had found a new edge of disruption—e-tailing. But it had to *learn* more about it to elevate its perspective and fully solve the challenge. Some investigating turned up interesting results. The company took a deep look at the market demographics for its targeted consumers. Residents of Seoul already work some of the longest hours on earth.[1] When they aren't working, they generally prefer to spend time in their neighborhood rather than at home. Given those cultural norms, three hours was too long a window; it did not offer enough flexibility to accommodate the typical lifestyle of the customers. So, after the initial six-week trial, Homeplus began tweaking the approach, looking at different delivery options and pickup stations, gradually growing its presence in the e-tailing space based on what it had learned. The original idea was ultimately a market failure in some ways, but what it taught Homeplus was invaluable. The knowledge helped Homeplus to develop a strong point of view on the future of the customer experience in buying groceries and the role Homeplus could play in that space. Thus the Homeplus leadership team invested in a relatively controlled, intelligent risk in exchange for valuable insight, without betting the farm. It shows the value of courage, optimism, and curiosity in defining a company's edge of disruption, and the need to push further into learning about the edge for a fairly traditional industry.

If a grocer can do it in the face of massive legacy real estate and capital investments, so can you. Think about your team, your region, your function, or your company—wherever you have line of sight. What controlled risks could you take to learn how you could matter more to your internal or external customers?

You might be thinking that grocery is one thing, but your business is *far* more complex than selling fruit to people (and trust us, so is the grocery business). The truth is, everyone has these challenges, but exceptional companies find ways to deal with them. As we shared in the introduction to this section, from its inception GHX has been faced with a Gordian knot—so many intertwined and dependent challenges that it can feel unsolvable. But GHX stepped into the complexity of the US healthcare system, and into other geographies as well. In doing so, it has created the space for customers, competitors, suppliers, and others in the industry to come together and collaborate on solutions. By bringing these diverse market views together, GHX has been able to continually redefine its edge of disruption and solve some of the most complex problems in the cost of healthcare. GHX has done this by being willing to take intelligent risks that are grounded in a core belief in the value of co-creating with its customers and its market.

CO-CREATE WITH YOUR CUSTOMERS AND YOUR MARKET

Henry Ford reportedly once said that "coming together is a beginning; keeping together is progress; working together is success." If you buy into that, co-creating with your customers and your market to learn about your edge of disruption and establish your point of view is the ultimate measure of success. In our experience, no one does this better than GHX. As its success confirms, engaging your customers and your market in co-creating—both in defining *and* solving for your edge of disruption—creates tremendous respect for your ability to bring people together around interesting challenges. And you often fast-track the sales process later on, because people are primed to buy solutions they helped to build. Working together to solve systemic problems creates more value for everyone—you, your customers, their customers, your competitors, and the industry as a whole. Starting this early by co-creating possible solutions with outsiders gives you the ability to create solutions that matter more than any that the participants can accomplish individually, and being the company that creates the space for co-creation gives you the strongest position for maximizing your value contribution.

Think back to what we've shared about GHX. It occupies a unique place in healthcare as a company that was created by five competitors and originally chartered to fill a very specific need. By its very founding, GHX was placed in the middle of its market, and it had to negotiate, partner, cajole, convince, and, yes, even push others in the industry to join in what was at the time a bit of an experiment in e-commerce. Over the years, this position has helped GHX to find a confident position as a convener of ideas, a place where its customers and the rest of the market can come together to co-create solutions to some of the most difficult challenges in healthcare today.

But it wasn't always a given that GHX would have the ability to effectively co-create with its customers and its market. It had some significant obstacles to overcome, including building trust among competitors and between suppliers and buyers, protecting its neutrality in the process, and convincing the industry that GHX had the capability and the influence to effectively create a collaborative space. You may encounter some of these obstacles as well. It can be scary to go out to customers or others and actually *not* have answers to the big problems, but what GHX has learned is that by asking the right questions, you demonstrate your strength and the value of your involvement, and you wind up with better solutions. Knowing what questions to ask and what solutions to invite your customers and your market into solving will enhance your reputation as an organization that matters more, because you will be creating more value for the industry, for your customers, and for yourself.

Knowing what questions to ask and what solutions to invite your customers and your market into solving will enhance your reputation as an organization that matters more, because you will be creating more value for the industry, for your customers, and for yourself.

Earlier in this section we mentioned the challenges related to tracking implantables. There were plenty of questions to ask, and even more solutions to explore for this problem. As we talked with GHX's Karen Conway, executive director, industry relations, and Margot Drees, VP of global strategy, about the evolution of the industry discussions, they highlighted three important outcomes from the process of co-creation.[2] First, GHX gained traction for the development of its own part of the solution. Second, by driving industry alignment, GHX had better visibility into the larger problem and how it could help add more value. Third, and related to product development, was a significant lesson from the process of co-creating with the market. It might seem counterintuitive, but this lesson is all about going broad and ambitious for a moment, and then narrowing your focus to a solvable piece to deliver that makes progress against the bigger challenge. Let's take a closer look.

In 2010 GHX started internally discussing the opportunity related to tracking medical devices, and in 2011 it invited its partners in the industry to begin the hard work of defining and learning about this new edge of disruption. In bringing all the right people together and fully appreciating the breadth of the problem, GHX was able to drive the creation of an exciting and creative demonstration of what "could be" for implantables. After two years of active and engaged debate, argument, consideration, and creation, and dedicated facilitation from GHX, the coalition working on the problem committed to building a demo for what they believed was possible—from an optimistic and curious position that challenged many assumptions being made in the industry about implantables.

They brought this demo to the GHX Supply Chain Summit in 2013 in the form of a site at the event set up to resemble an operating room, where they demonstrated how use of implantables in the scenario could be tracked and recorded for appropriate and timely billing, as well as to support patient notification. It was a big moment that really highlighted the success of the co-creation in defining the desired end state in a way that no single organization could have accomplished—all enabled by the discussions GHX prompted by going out to the market and saying, "Let's solve for this."

After the summit, stakeholders were eager to move forward on provisioning the whole solution. The insights generated from the co-creative process were enough to pique serious interest from influencers and buyers across the sector. This is just the type of access an elevated perspective creates, something we will dedicate an entire chapter to in the "Elevated Relationships" section. GHX was positioned to offer an even more powerful perspective on what could and could not be achieved in this space. But there was also a sobering realization: The "ideal" solution developed and showcased at the summit would be difficult to replicate in delivery because it required extensive technology, process, and behavior change from every single person end to end, including physicians and other highly specialized, highly trained people involved in the surgical processes. Coordinating all of this change at the same time simply would not be possible.

Armed with this refined perspective, GHX took a step back and reevaluated what would be the best edge of disruption to tackle first, now that the full problem set was defined. In the spirit of progress, in 2014 GHX decided to focus narrowly on AOM, Advanced Order Management, as a first step in solving for tracking implantables. Because the whole industry fully understood both the problem and the larger solution, solving for a piece of it became meaningful and important. Without that shared understanding, generated through the co-creation process, solving just a piece of the problem would have been out of context and potentially meaningless in advancing the industry toward the desired end state.

The result? Today AOM is improving accuracy and reducing invoice problems, and providing greater visibility than ever to implantables spend and use. It does this by automating many of the steps involved in managing implantables, from requisition to electronic purchase order creation. In the process, visibility of which implantables are being purchased and consumed becomes available. AOM tackles the first set of problems in the medical device supply chain that will move the industry toward the desired end state that everyone has co-created through the collaborative process. If GHX had not co-created with its market, it very likely could have developed a product that only solved for a tiny and potentially obsolete part of the problem. Because its leaders took the time to step back and invite others in, the solution fits today's realities and tomorrow's vision of an industry-wide, seamless integration of implantables management into the healthcare system, improving both costs and patient experience and safety.

Refining and learning about your understanding of your right edge of disruption is one of the underlying objectives of co-creating. You don't want to go around giving out PowerPoint Promises. That kind of reputation will never give you the access you need to influence the marketplace. As you define your edge of disruption, remember that refining your ideas and narrowing your focus are a part of the process. Once the larger problem has been clearly articulated, achievable step solutions are legitimate ways to add more value.

As you define your edge of disruption, remember that refining your ideas and narrowing your focus are a part of the process. Once the larger problem has been clearly articulated, achievable step solutions are legitimate ways to add more value.

GHX has co-created with its market in other areas as well. In 2008, it began a similar journey to facilitate traceability of pharmaceuticals, an area with problems similar to implantables. It is very difficult to track down the ultimate recipient of a prescription, making timely recalls and patient notification incredibly hard if not impossible. More importantly, the pharmaceutical industry has issues with drugs being counterfeited, adulterated, and diverted from their proper destinations. These challenges can be addressed with a comprehensive approach to tracking and tracing pharmaceuticals, but again, no one organization could possibly own and deliver that end-to-end solution. As a result, almost twenty organizations in the industry participated in early discussions about the problem, including suppliers, providers, regulators, industry associations, and of course, GHX as the host.

Phase 1 for pharmaceuticals was a collaborative effort to develop requirements for the industry to define an Interoperable Track and Trace System that would provide a simple and accessible solution for users across the healthcare system. Phase 2 included building a prototype of a working interoperable system, designed to use prototyping to uncover additional requirements and further learning about how to handle security issues in a potential solution. The insights from Phase 2 were further used to engage with and inform regulators and policy makers, who play a very active role in healthcare. Using this iterative process, the working team was able to produce an exciting result for everyone.

The effort culminated in 2013 with the delivery of an end-to-end solution in a "live" scenario that included AbbVie, Inc., McKesson, and the Veterans Health Administration to jointly deliver an award-winning proof of concept that demonstrated full traceability on an interoperable system.[3] In addition to those companies participating in the demonstration, Johnson & Johnson Health Care Systems, AmerisourceBergen, and others contributed to the development of the system. It was truly a collaborative effort from across the industry, and it provided a breakthrough moment in making what seemed impossible a reality. Out of that work, the industry is on its way to implementing real change in how pharmaceuticals are tracked, and everyone who participated in the effort has an opportunity to matter more as the solutions are designed and implemented across the industry.

Looking at these two examples, it would appear that the edge of disruption for GHX in this space isn't just implantables or pharmaceuticals—it's Track and Trace across the entire healthcare supply chain, or any other systemic problem that requires cross-industry collaboration! What GHX has learned about how to successfully define, develop, and execute co-created solutions in healthcare is unparalleled. The benefits to GHX of learning about the challenges it wants to solve through co-creation with its market cannot be overstated. The access these co-created activities provide is clear, especially as GHX nurtures elevated relationships (more on that in the next section).

For now, note that the co-creation approach gives GHX deep insight and knowledge to guide product development. It was also able to confirm that it was working at a meaningful edge of disruption, one that mattered more to its customers and other influencers in healthcare. Last, GHX has had an influential seat at the table for some of the most important conversations in their industry, and many clients would likely suggest that, going forward, it would be crazy to talk about something like Track and Trace without GHX in the room.

Consider that in September 2014, the US Food and Drug Administration (which regulates medical devices) published a final rule that includes the requirement for a unique device identifier to support tracking of medical devices, as well as a larger mandate related to product data. Luckily, thanks in part to GHX and its efforts to co-create a solution, the industry has already gotten a head start on solving this new challenge. Who do you think the manufacturers reach out to as they adapt to this new regulation, which is devastatingly complex to comply with in the real world? GHX may not own the end-to-end work, but having an end-to-end solution envisioned makes any individual piece more impactful and stickier—it matters more. The added value of co-creating when you are learning about your edge of disruption is that it amplifies rather than diminishes the value of the work you decide to do.

As a convener in the industry, GHX doesn't shy away from tackling big and thorny problems, or from spending time— sometimes years—bringing the market along and crafting viable solutions that will resonate with customers. GHX's success shows that you can't be afraid of big problems, or of solutions that take time to evolve. In a complex industry with many challenges, there may not be many "quick and easy" solutions for the problems that matter the most, but unless someone has the courage to step out and bring their customers and the market together, those problems won't get solved effectively.

The same is true in complex organizations. Perhaps you are trying to improve from within. Engaging people outside your team—your internal customers and your larger organization—to co-create a solution can be effective, but don't expect results overnight. You may have to authentically be in it for the long haul to create something that matters. Homeplus was able to test a new go-to-market approach with a few weeks of a strong marketing campaign supported by a reasonably isolated technology infrastructure, and it generated results that matter. We aren't saying it always takes years; however, don't be afraid of the solutions that do require more effort and time.

As you work to learn about your edge of disruption, you may find you have more questions than answers. You may not even have the problem fully defined. GHX is exceptionally good at co-creating a problem definition and solutions with its customers and its market, and we recommend you consider this approach as you work to learn about your edge. Another approach is to make sure you "know what you know." This takes a commitment to catalog and leverage your organizational knowledge and expertise to continually push forward on the edge of disruption, which helps you to learn as much as you can about the value you can create. And we haven't found many companies that know what they know better than DPR.

KNOW WHAT YOU KNOW

If you were to meet Doug Woods at a shopping center, you would think he was a knockabout kind of guy. Someone who attends every one of his son's football games, cooks good ribs, and appears to be in the manual trades. You certainly wouldn't think that he, and the company he cofounded, might have built the very shopping center you were in, and more likely built the highly complex data center that the retail brands in the shopping center use to give you that special loyalty discount you crave so much. Oh, and you probably wouldn't think that his company also may have built the high-tech science laboratory that sits next to the very field on which he likes to watch his son play football.

Doug Woods is a shockingly humble guy, which we are convinced is part of the reason that DPR (as we noted in the Introduction, he is the D in DPR) has a sustained discipline of seeking feedback, learning from its experiences, and pushing "ever forward" to matter more to its customers tomorrow than it does today.

Through our conversations with DPR, we discovered that you can often learn a tremendous amount about your edge of disruption when you look right in front of you: at your people, your suppliers, your contractors, and your customers. They all have experiences that help you to better understand your edge of disruption. It takes courage and humility to ask about those experiences, learn from them, and synthesize them to find and stay at your own edge.

The construction industry is known for its rough-and-tumble, almost cutthroat contracting processes. In the thick of deeply rooted industry assumptions about contractors, the bidding process, and how work gets done, DPR has managed to challenge everything.

DPR is a $3 billion technical construction company that was founded in 1990. For five years in a row starting in 2010, DPR ranked on *Fortune*'s 100 Best Companies to Work For, landing in the top ten in 2014. The *Huffington Post* included DPR in its list of "10 Companies College Students Should Want to Work For," alongside companies like Google and Zappos.[4] Even more astonishing, as of 2015, DPR received more than 80 percent of its business from referrals. DPR was so clearly the obvious choice for certain clients that 25 percent of them (and in some years as many as one-third) engaged DPR to deliver multimillion-dollar projects without undergoing competitive bidding. That's definitely not the norm in DPR's industry.

To truly appreciate DPR's accomplishment, you need to understand a little more about the construction industry's bidding process. Like many industries that run on competitive bidding, construction has over the years become a game where some contractors bid low to win the work and anticipate making up money in change orders later on—a game that is avidly supported by some customers who pit contractors against each other to drive down price, without regard for the actual cost of the program. The bidding process has become a deeply held assumption in the industry, making DPR's "no-bid" awards in a highly commoditized industry unusual and impressive. Pushing back on clients' procurement-oriented process, the company built strong, enduring, strategic partnerships to benefit clients and deliver better project outcomes.

This was one of DPR's most valuable moves to its edge of disruption. It set out to fundamentally redefine the way GCs and clients partnered to build great things. DPR was on a one-way mission to break the traditionally adversarial nature of the industry in which the three cofounders had spent their lives, and it wanted to create a company that did it better than anyone else. For DPR, this edge consisted of three key elements. First, it specifically *focuses on technical construction* in partnership with customers. DPR set out from its very inception to live at the edge of building construction and strived to seek and accept only work that was technical and complex in nature. Second, it is determined to be *"ever forward."* If a new and better way to do something emerges on the fringe of the industry, DPR embraces it. It believes in continual self-initiated change, improvement, learning, and advancement of standards for their own sake. For example, DPR is constantly taking new technology such as building information modeling from the edge of disruption and creating better outcomes for its clients in the process. And finally, DPR very purposefully *encourages different models for contracting.* The traditional bidding and contracting process itself was at times in conflict with building partnerships, and was a causal factor in the adversarial nature of the business. DPR refused to comply with the status quo and, with every opportunity over the years, continued to guide its clients, and increasingly the industry, in a more collaborative direction.

How did DPR pull that off? It's not because DPR is the only general contractor in its space (it's not) or because DPR has some proprietary way to build (it doesn't). And it isn't because Doug Woods, DPR cofounder, is a nice guy who is completely committed to his company (although he is). It's because DPR has spent time and energy making sure it is very clear about the type of clients it wants to work with (more on this in Chapter 4), and is always looking out to the future for ways to matter more. We're going to talk more about its approach to customers in Section Two, "Elevated Relationships." For now, though, let's consider how DPR knows what it knows, and how it uses that to challenge its assumptions about how work gets done.

DPR purposefully and methodically captures knowledge inside and outside the organization for subsequent use. It includes everyone in its collection process, even its customers and subcontractors. Its ongoing push to learn keeps the company continually on the edge of disruption in its industry when it comes to customer satisfaction, and it supports DPR's unique approach to project delivery and its overall business. How? Because it always works to understand what works and what doesn't, and that stops it from making assumptions about how work gets done. At the same time, its processes are visible to its customers, giving buyers the confidence to know that DPR is using the most relevant processes and techniques to build great buildings.

Think about it for a minute. You can't learn from your expertise if you don't know what it is or where it exists inside your organization. DPR is *obsessed* with cataloging and registering everything it knows. An obvious way DPR catalogs knowledge is simply by doing more than most companies do to solicit client impressions and perceptions. When we visited

> You can't learn from your expertise if you don't know what it is or where it exists inside your organization.

DPR's office in Redwood City, California, to interview senior leaders, everyone we met seemed to be either coming out of a feedback session or heading into one. One executive was conducting a customer satisfaction survey with his client on a recent project. When he asked the client to rate its project compared to previous experiences, the client said that DPR was not only the best GC experience he had ever had, but the best customer service experience, period. Not something you'd expect to hear about a construction company.

Customer feedback sessions are only one of a number of techniques DPR deploys. Another technique, called craft sessions, enables DPR to gather knowledge from employees and subcontractors on an ongoing basis. "Craft" is the specific building trade engaged to help build projects. To ensure that DPR employees and subcontractors are constantly improving, the company facilitates regular structured conversations to share best practices. In one session, for instance, a tradesman shared how he had discovered a new and faster way to estimate and install drywall, shaving 10 percent off the scheduled time while reducing waste. Another clued the group in to a newly discovered green product that had performed even better than less environmentally friendly products. At DPR, managers facilitate these calls in a structured way that verges on scientific, expecting participants to contribute and learn. Because of the formal nature of this collaborative learning, we might best think of these calls not just as standard meetings but as true "learning labs."

DPR also gathers knowledge internally through its Global Learning Group, charged with formal learning and development. As Cari Williams, DPR's head of people practices, told us, "Who we build is as important as what we build."[5] Rather than simply buying content and hiring trainers from outside the company, DPR challenges its people to develop their *own* content by taking stock of what they already know.

DPR didn't overlook the job site as a place for capturing knowledge. It launched Opportunity-For-Improvement (OFI) programs and charged every job site with seeking out either best practices or new ideas for improving everything from record keeping to tool use; employees recorded their insights on the OFI cards. Although the cards themselves hardly broke new ground, the intensity with which DPR deployed them did. The company eagerly took action in response to OFI suggestions, showing near-religious discipline in sharing the best of them across the company. Then in 2009, recognizing the difficulties that an organization of DPR's size has in scaling ideas, DPR created an Innovation Support Team whose sole responsibility was to take OFI-style cards and spread the insights they contained. The Management Committee appointed Jim Washburn, DPR employee number nine, to head up the Innovation Support Team, and allocated it significant financial and human resources, including implementing software to capture and track ideas from the OFI suggestions and other sources.

DPR has a series of successful knowledge management practices that have helped cement its position in the industry as a company with a strong point of view. It regularly solicits client input through facilitated sessions, and uses craft sessions to collect insights from its employees and contractors. It has formalized collaborative learning that is facilitated by strong leadership models, and it uses lab environments to support that learning. And finally, it engages at all levels, from the executive suite to the job site to ensure they know what they know.

Each of these practices was homegrown to suit DPR specifically, born out of desire to continuously improve and move ever forward. Embedded in them is a diverse set of viewpoints, coming from all parts of the business. The practices position DPR as a company clients want to engage—as the obvious choice for clients who want a thoughtful, well-informed contractor delivering on its multimillion-dollar investment. DPR has unshakable optimism and curiosity, and the courage to challenge assumptions, so it continually redefines its edge of disruption and learns from it. It takes courage to ask a customer for feedback, yet DPR does so all the time. When DPR employees see an opportunity to improve, they pursue it internally and externally. All of these efforts to learn about its edge of disruption gave DPR the strong point of view required to challenge industry assumptions about the bidding process and "how work gets won."

You may or may not be in a position to influence your organization's knowledge management strategy or implementation. But you can look around and think about how to capture what you and your team do best and to ask your customers (internal or external) how you can do better. Muster up the courage, the optimism, and the curiosity to ask the tough questions and fully understand the answers, then make a decision to take action. It takes hard work, but if you are committed, you can start to elevate your own perspective and that of those around you.

Homeplus, GHX, and DPR are examples of current companies that truly were able to define and learn about their own edges of disruption, where they could uniquely influence and differentiate themselves. Simply starting to elevate your perspective propels you forward in positive ways. You might be thinking, "That's great, but around here, there's no money, time, or appetite for learning." Interestingly enough, it doesn't always take executive support and investment to learn about your edge of disruption.

MOVE FROM IDEAS TO INSIGHTS

As we saw in the approaches taken by Homeplus, GHX, and DPR, learning about your edge of disruption and developing a strong point of view isn't about forming some esoteric view of the market's future. Most companies can do that with the help of any number of consultants, industry journals, and other sources, where they spend shedloads of money for very little in the way of actionable insights. You have to go a step further and understand the specifics.

An elevated perspective is more than marketing spin. It has real and measurable value in solving complex challenges, because it is grounded in hard data, deep understanding, and an appreciation for how it contributes to your clients' needs. Will customers actually buy a new offering? When you run the numbers, can you actually reduce their supply chain costs? Can you discover something that no one else knows about your industry? Do you do things better than even you might have thought? You have to invest time, energy, and other resources in your perspective; it has to be a priority. And don't just come up with a point of view. As you learn about your edge of disruption, produce original evidence to support it.

Ideas are not the same as insights. Ideas pop into your head in the middle of the night, or get doodled on whiteboards during meetings, and they are great to have. The work is in moving from ideas to insights. Insights are formed when an idea is tested in a real-world situation, and key distinctions are generated that test the underlying assumptions of the idea itself. Companies that contribute from the edge of disruption are committed to generating insights. By testing their ideas they flex them inside the market, using diverse viewpoints and taking intelligent risks. The companies we talked to that matter are able to develop an informed point of view about their edge of disruption and take it out into the world in effective ways. It is critical that this ability to define and learn about your edge of disruption be developed throughout the organization, not just in the marketing, R&D, or product departments. It must be ingrained in your company's DNA.

> It is critical that this ability to define and learn about your edge of disruption be developed throughout the organization, not just in the marketing, R&D, or product departments. It must be ingrained in your company's DNA.

Do a quick gut check. These approaches are available to anyone: as an individual, on a team, in a company. You can work to matter more in any capacity to the people you serve. As you work to define your edge of disruption and learn about it, you will need to figure out how to get out there in the world and test your ideas, convert them into insight, and have something meaningful to say. As we are about to discover, it's not just about what you learn at the edge of disruption. It's about what you do with what you learn.

As we close out this chapter, consider Homeplus one final time. One of the powerful elements of this grocer's subway experiment was that it was genuinely market facing, open to the general public, and the insights it generated were made readily available not just to the industry but to anyone with an internet connection. As a result, the experiment became a very well-documented case study (if you do a quick search for "Homeplus subway shopping" you'll get any number of hits about it), cementing Homeplus as a forward-looking grocer and building its reputation with customers. Years later, Homeplus continues to benefit from that six-week pilot run in one market.

If Homeplus had taken a "knowledge is power" approach and controlled every aspect of the test, we can easily imagine that it may have built out a subway station replica in a top-secret warehouse somewhere outside of Seoul and bused willing shoppers out there, under strict nondisclosures, in exchange for financial compensation. Then they would have filmed and analyzed the shopping behavior to the nth degree before deciding if they wanted to take the risk in the market.

Can you imagine the difference in the results? One approach yields a splashy six-week campaign with rich and insightful lessons that still get talked about today, which helped Homeplus to quickly deploy a shopping experience that led it to capture a lead position in a highly competitive market. The other hypothetical, we suggest, would have resulted in endless PowerPoint decks and business cases, expensive privacy protections, and likely no forward movement or learning. By publicly sharing the experience not just with its customers but also with the world, Homeplus positioned itself as an innovator—both as a grocery store and as a leader in technology, customer insight, and intelligent risk taking. Likewise, GHX positioned itself as a thought leader by including its market partners in its discovery processes.

Once you demonstrate to your clients that you don't just know yesterday's news but are discovering, defining, and sharing tomorrow's news, they will want to engage and partner with you as they push toward their own edge of disruption. In the process, this will break you free from the commoditized positioning that plagues most industry players. To leverage an *elevated perspective* into *elevated relationships*, you need to develop a platform from which you *share* what you have learned. You must find your voice and be heard for your perspective to propel and accelerate your journey to becoming the obvious choice. You must be known for what you know, as we like to say. In the next chapter we'll take a closer look at what that means.

Bring It to Life . . .

1. Identify three intelligent and controlled risks you could take to co-create with your customers, or to test your ideas in the reality of the marketplace and convert them to insight. (Your market might be your team, your internal customers, or your external customers.)

2. For each of these areas, reach out to two customers you believe would be excited to engage and would benefit from the process of exploring these emerging areas of opportunity.

3. Look around for untapped knowledge inside your organization that could help you better understand the areas of opportunity you have identified and contribute to the process of learning. Remember DPR's reach—it looks to customers, contractors, employees, and others for lessons learned and knowledge capture.

4. Combine the feedback you have gotten from testing in the real world with the collective of knowledge of your customers and existing team, and develop a set of insights about your edge of disruption and the opportunities for creating more value there.

CHAPTER 3

SHARE: Be Known for What You Know

HAMLET'S DILEMMA MAY HAVE BEEN "to be, or not to be"; yours, once you have a strong point of view, is "to share, or not to share." Only, we will suggest here that there is no dilemma. Share. Share freely. Share widely. Take the provocative, tested, and validated insights you have learned at your edge of disruption and share them with your customers, with their customers, and with your competitors, too.

"Wait, wait, wait," we hear you say. "Share what we have learned with our competitors? Won't that be like giving away trade secrets? Isn't knowledge power? Shouldn't we keep these insights under lock and key, in a safe deep in our vaults?" This assumption is *wrong*, based on what we learned about what differentiates companies that matter most from those that matter less.

Plenty of material already exists on content marketing and the tactics that allow you to package vanilla ideas and drive views and downloads, but this doesn't really differentiate you.

Companies that matter go beyond the superficial to become true thought leaders in their industry. When it comes to their approach to thought leadership, content marketing, applying their perspective to the sales process, and the way they share and proliferate what they know, companies that matter believe in four things that set them apart from their competition:

1. **Abundance**: To those who share much, more will be given.
2. **Quality**: Views and volume do not equal value.
3. **Provocation**: If an idea is easily accepted, and universally embraced, it's probably not thought leadership.
4. **Commitment**: Thought leadership is not a marketing tactic— it's a way of life.

SHARE ABUNDANTLY

In business we love concepts like "win," "beat the competition," and "get an advantage." It is natural in a competitive environment to think in these terms and to be protective as a result, as you try to eke out any advantage you can find. However, in the social and digital world, if you are not sharing, and someone else is, then who really has the advantage? Who has the ear and the attention of the senior buyers you most need to influence?

To put it differently, what is the point of defining your edge of disruption, building a strong evidence-based point of view, and then keeping it to yourself? Elevated perspective isn't just about what you know and what you see. It is about how your perspective is put to work by your customers, your sales teams, your industry, and even your competitors. It's about being known for what you know. Or as we came to know, to those who share much, more will be given.

Remember the key finding from our research: To be the obvious choice, you need to create more value. The place to create more value is from the edge of disruption, where you are delivering solutions to the complex and important problems facing your customers. Now ask yourself: When you are dealing with complex and important problems, what do you crave the most? Knowledge. Insight. Clarity. You are looking for someone with an elevated perspective to guide the way. If you become known for being in the know, people will look to you to provide that perspective, and it will differentiate you in ways your competition can't beat.

If you don't find a way to be heard, your elevated perspective will not add the value that it should. Instead of opening new doors and building your credibility, it will hibernate inside your organization until it reaches its expiration date, without elevating you at all. That creates two risks. First, you can become so enamored with your ideas, you don't realize they've expired; and second, you can fail to contribute in a way that ultimately associates you with the maximum possible value. Remember, by creating more value, you matter more—to your market, your customers, and your employees. Creating more value happens at the edge of disruption. And if you share, the perspective you gain there can be leveraged to elevate your relationships and your impact.

> Elevated perspective isn't just about what you know and what you see. It is about how your perspective is put to work by your customers, your sales teams, your industry, and even your competitors. It's about being known for what you know.

This was certainly true for The Integer Group (now owned by Omnicom), a creative agency based in Denver, Colorado. In the early 2000s, the manufacturers, marketers, and resellers of consumer products had a challenge: There was no generally available, consistently current data on shopper behavior. Today we know a lot about how customers surf the web, how they research products, and ultimately the path they take to buy online, but when Integer began looking into "the impact of shopping culture on brand strategy," the research to help understand that phenomenon was limited.[1]

What was available were typically generic and expensive proprietary reports that focused more on what people bought, rather than how they behaved when they bought. These reports were designed to be exclusive and hard to access, not readily available for decision makers in the categories they could serve. In a way this was ironic, considering that the reports were mostly historically based, not predictive, and therefore arguably less valuable. Integer staff believed that if you can understand how someone shops, you can use that insight to develop campaigns and strategies for the entire value chain. Campaigns could range from product development to in-store merchandising that could allow you to shift buying behavior. The Integer Group defined its edge of disruption as being able to deeply understand and make sense of changes in shopping behavior, in a way no other agency at the time had done. This edge was not only useful to Integer; it was also one of the problems that mattered most to its clients, and it was both market facing and internally motivating.

In 2007, a skunkworks operation led by some courageous, optimistic, and curious staff members started up a communications blog called *Shopper Culture* to collect and share insight about consumer shopping behaviors. The *Shopper Culture* blog started humbly, springing from a simple desire to engage in interesting dialogue. The Integer Group EVP of insight and strategy, Craig Elston, recalls that "the blog was started initially by, basically, three of us internally sending interesting stuff around to each other on emails and having these conversations at lunch. Finally we just said, Why are we having this conversation internally? Why don't we do it publicly and let other people join in?"[2] Later that afternoon, the three had a blog up and running for the sole purpose of exploring shopping behavior.

Sounds simple, and yet the belief system of most organizations would not have led them to launch a publicly facing platform, where they shared insights and opinions from this emerging edge of disruption. Their answer to Craig's question would more likely have been, "We are having this conversation internally because it is where our competitive advantage lies, and we would never want to share that with potential competitors." Out of fear of losing an advantage, or having their insight become too popular and therefore less scarce, companies consistently refrain from sharing what they know, and as a result lose the reputation and access advantages that would have come if they had. Advantages discovered by companies like Integer can generate far more reputational value than they do actual quality advantage in their day-to-day work.

For content, the group initially cut and pasted material they found, while sharing insights of their own in the course of daily client work. No one asked for permission or investment. Soon the business impact was so great that people weren't asking them to shut it down. Instead, they were asking them to replicate it in other parts of the business. Through the learning process, Integer was becoming the go-to place for data on shopper behavior, simply because a few guys had started to do research, ask questions, engage an audience, and build a repository that differentiated the agency from others in the industry. And it spent almost nothing to originate the idea and develop it into a corporate asset.

Things have evolved since those early days. Today, if you click on the *Shopper Culture* site, you'll find The Checkout and The Complex Shopper—branded content streams, consisting of signature reports throughout the year and ongoing commentary as the edge of disruption evolves. Both of these content streams today reflect deep, original research, including shop-alongs (accompanying shoppers in stores to understand the buying process and its influences more anthropologically), qualitative interviews, and even experiments with mock shopping environments (allowing Integer to investigate how changing the environment might alter shopping behavior). The agency's approach to learning has become more sophisticated and more intense as the value from sharing has accrued to the organization.

These reports have been downloaded more than 25,000 times, and Elston estimates that they have generated in excess of $3 million in PR for Integer, contributing directly to the bottom line in sales.[3] According to Maria Fox, who led new business development, Integer's thought leadership approach has had a "phenomenal" impact in helping to generate new revenue and clients for the agency.[4] When he was a planner at Integer, Brandon Fassino helped get *Shopper Culture* off the ground and noted in conversation with us that Integer "now [has] such a strong following of CPG [Consumer Packaged Goods] brands, retailers, and all of those are VP level, director level, those decision makers that influence our industry who are following, downloading, reading us."[5] In addition to supporting sales, an elevated perspective has a recursive effect—you are taking in so much broad data that you have the inputs to synthesize trends quickly and remain on the edge. It is a self-reinforcing activity.

Interestingly, clients have begun using the Integer research to elevate their own reputations in the minds of their buyers. Window and door companies like Pella used Integer's insights to help persuade buyers at Lowe's to carry more of their product. Individuals inside client companies have cited Integer's research in their internal meetings and presentations, building their own professional reputations with their colleagues and bosses. At candy maker Mars, an Integer client sent The Checkout around the company. When a colleague came back with a question, the client brought it back to Integer. "We could give them a lot more depth and a lot more richness around it," Elston told us, "and that client felt, well, Look how smart I am, look how smart my agency is." When you help your buyer win, you win, too.

> In addition to supporting sales, an elevated perspective has a recursive effect—you are taking in so much broad data that you have the inputs to synthesize trends quickly and remain on the edge. It is a self-reinforcing activity.

Armand Parra, who heads Integer's research efforts, agreed that such openness conferred a clear advantage: "If you're the originators of the thinking, and the whole world gets on the page that you've been on, that doesn't hurt you. That puts you in a fantastic position because you know [the content] best . . . by the time that curve comes around and they get back to being where you are, that was where you were two years ago. So now you've got two new years of stuff written and you are always ahead of the competition."[6]

We often think new leads and more revenue are the only real metrics of success. However, in an agency like Integer the stock in trade is human capital. And a critical contributor to success over the long term is the quality of talent the agencies are able to attract. The research has made Integer a magnet for the best and brightest talent in the industry. According to Craig Elston, "People want to come to work here, because they see so much of what we're doing. Recently I was interviewing for a VP-level position and VPs from competitive agencies were applying, and in their interviews asking, How on earth did you get that account? I mean, how do you get the resources to do that research? How did you, etc., etc.? They can't. They have nothing like it inside their own organization, and they're all looking at Integer and thinking I want a piece of that. I want to work there."[7]

This is not to be underestimated, considering agencies are essentially selling creativity. It is the quality of their creative assets—their people—that ultimately differentiates the work of one firm from the next. The thought leadership position established at Integer enabled it to punch way above its weight in the talent stakes.

Integer created something unique in its industry that continues to set it apart through an active and vibrant platform that is available to the world. Its abundance mentality and willingness to share generously have brought value back in spades. Craig's favorite moment, though, came when The Integer Group was invited to pitch for the account of one of the largest consumer brands in the world.

As he tells it, "We said, Why are you even talking to us? And they said, We see you at conferences everywhere, and we're reading your stuff all the time. We *had* to have you in the room. We couldn't *not* have you here."

This is a massive account, one any agency director would give their first-born child to win. Imagine how it felt for Craig Elston of Integer to hear that kind of feedback from this consumer products giant. It was, as Craig described, an "IBM moment," parodying the old line that no one gets fired for hiring IBM. Apparently, no one gets fired these days for hiring Integer, either.

Now for a powerful twist on the Integer case: It is important to realize that having an abundance mind-set is not the same as having unlimited resources. Integer elevated its perspective and became the obvious choice in what a Brit like Elston might call the "scent of an oily rag," or for an American, running on fumes. Elston and his team worked with an investment of less than $200,000 over the first three years. How? Elston inspired people to be generous with their time by providing a compelling scenario where everyone benefitted. In other words, he inspired the same abundance from Integer employees and industry players as Integer was embracing by sharing freely. He found people who genuinely cared about shoppers and were willing to share their expertise, and offered them a way to contribute and collaborate. He created space for dialogue between people who shared common expertise and passion, and leveraged that space to build meaningful insights. He didn't ask for much. As he said, it was "a very tiny percentage, a small amount of their time, some form of responsibility, whether it's some commitment to the blog, whether it's managing the vendor relationship for the research, whether it's writing issues of research, whether it's doing analysis on the data, so it's not any one person's responsibility. It's spread thinly, which allows us to get it done."

Elston also partnered with a sister company to exchange his sharing and co-branding of insights and reports for massively reduced fees for primary and specialized research. As a result of the cobbled-together network of experts and insights, Elston was able to make The Checkout, The Complex Shopper, and subsequent research reports available as a free download, when others in the industry were charging more than $10,000 for similar (but arguably not as good) reports. This helped avoid distracting the Integer salesforce from their strategic offerings by asking them to generate subscription revenue, and at the same time massively increased the potential audience who would be exposed to the Integer brand.

The access that resulted from reports being generally available led directly to elevated relationships, which as we know are critical to having an elevated impact and creating more value.

Integer's numbers look impressive: 25,000 report downloads, thousands of followers. But you'd be wrong to use these metrics alone to judge the success of your sharing efforts. Companies that matter have come to know that views and volume of consumption do not equal value. Value equals value. It's more important for the right people to access your perspective than for a lot of people to access it.

FOCUS ON VALUE, NOT VOLUME

Let's be very clear about one thing. Quality equals value when it comes to thought leadership. DPR is a construction company. Its biggest value is in being famous to its clients and in its market, to the industry influencers it wants to collaborate with, and to the schools and fields from which it recruits. It is not Doug Woods's goal to be famous as he walks down the street, or even when he logs into Twitter. Nor would it do DPR any good if he were. This is because DPR wants to be known for its elevated perspective by the people who matter most to its business, a fairly niche group of buyers and influencers.

> Companies that matter have come to know that views and volume of consumption do not equal value. Value equals value. It's more important for the right people to access your perspective than for a lot of people to access it.

The edge of disruption for DPR included rethinking the way work is contracted. Not exactly riveting stuff for your everyday consumer. As they worked to learn as much as possible about how to contract differently, DPR found that it made less sense to have large public-facing campaigns about that work. For DPR, more targeted B2B strategies and platforms were needed.

DPR has leveraged its obsession with improving its learning process as a platform, involving clients in continual feedback sessions and sharing its best practices broadly in their market. DPR is well known not just as a construction company, but also as a company that is rigorous in its collection of successful practices and its continual learning efforts. DPR does things differently in a visible way, for clients, employees, and contractors, because it brings everyone into its processes of collecting and cataloging lessons. DPR has tied learning and sharing closely together, so they reinforce each other. And it has involved its clients in the process, making everything visible in a way that generates buzz and an appreciation for DPR's elevated perspective in the industry. The company is known for what it knows, to the people who matter most.

For other companies, the people who matter most are in a broader set than for DPR, and as a result their approach to packaging, publishing, and platform development has to be appropriately broader as well. One company in our study, ExactTarget (ET), shared its perspective as impressively as any company we saw. It was able to change the dynamics of a fast-growing and evolving industry in the process. Founded in 2000, ET created software that brands used to manage their email marketing efforts. The software included the ability to build campaigns designed to engage customers and generate sales, and ways of automating and tracking marketing campaigns to engage and incite buying behavior. The company grew at a breakneck pace, rising by 2006 to #56 on the *Inc.* 500 list of fastest-growing private companies, and by 2007 to #43 on *Entrepreneur* magazine's Hot 500 list of fastest-growing businesses. Awesome, yes, but ET couldn't relax; more than twenty startups had emerged to vie for the same clients, all providing essentially the same service. Clients yearned for one of them to burst out, become the obvious choice, and consolidate the industry. What buyer wants to research and vet so many options when making a purchasing decision?

To become the obvious choice, ET knew it needed to develop street cred as the company with the elevated perspective at the edge of disruption. The moment was certainly ripe for it to do so: During the first decade of this century, the marketing field experienced rampant disruption. Social media enabled consumers to engage in multidimensional dialogue about products, services, and brands. Marketers could no longer control messages, especially with reviews and customer opinions just a click away. A recent report from Deloitte shows that among Millennials, close to half are influenced by social media for their purchasing decisions, and that consumers who leverage social media platforms to research their purchases are four times more likely to buy than those who do not.[8] Even B2B buyers are often as much as 57 percent of the way through purchasing decisions before they engage a supplier sales representative.[9] Most damaging of all, companies found it increasingly difficult to interrupt customers with marketing messages, no matter how targeted these messages were.

For ET, social media posed a direct threat. After all, ET's main services were connected to email, the oldest of the digital direct media, where consumers had become adept at filtering or ignoring what they perceived as "spam." ET knew with certainty that its real value to its customers was insight on how to create customer engagement, and social media was the bright, shiny, and new way to accomplish that. ET committed itself to build some bias-breaking data on how effective email remained as a direct marketing medium. At the same time, it pushed confidently into the future to build an elevated perspective on the emerging threat of social media–based marketing. ET invested right at the edge of disruption, at the intersection of the world as it had been (email), and the world as it would be (social media).

Remember the importance of optimism? No company would make that kind of commitment if the leaders weren't fundamentally optimistic about the future of their industry and the company's place in it. ET would not have dived into the relatively unknown world of social media if it weren't confident in its ability to profit from it. ET had developed (in a relatively short period) an unshakable belief that it was the best solution for its customers. ET was convinced that by developing an elevated perspective at the edge of disruption—social media—it would be able to leverage its thought leadership into broader access. This in turn would support ET's goal of building additional functionality into its core software program, allowing marketers to manage and optimize their activities in social media as well.

The question to be answered was which audiences needed to be influenced, and what were the best platforms to do so, to guide ET's approach to sharing. The answer was clear: marketers. And to influence marketers, three clear platforms emerged. The first was general business audiences. Every company is in the marketing business in some way, shape, or form, and most had some need for direct marketing capability and insight. The second was the industry-specific or geographic-specific marketing professionals, where direct and digital marketing was relatively more important than for others. And the third were the specific prospects looking to differentiate between ET and other competitive software vendors. For ET, bigger reach was not better—targeted reach was.

With this belief in mind, in 2009 the company launched a comprehensive research project to understand digital consumers, make data-driven predictions about their future behavior, and arrive at recommendations for marketers. Led by Jeffrey K. Rohrs and Morgan Stewart, respectively ET's VP of marketing and principal of research at the time, the research series was dubbed *Subscribers, Fans, & Followers* (SFF) and, according to Rohrs, sought "to seize the thought leadership high ground through objective insights about today's direct interactive marketing relationships—Subscribers (email), Fans (Facebook), Followers (Twitter)." If the research succeeded, Rohrs anticipated that it would "help the ExactTarget brand to move beyond email and into a broader association with the whole of social media today."[10] Today, SFF might sound like an obvious thing to do, but at the time no one had done such a cross-channel investigation, and certainly not at the scale ExactTarget planned. Tim Kopp, former chief marketing officer of ExactTarget, said, "If you aren't pushing the envelope, you are already behind."[11] Or as we'd say, if you aren't standing on the right edge, you're losing ground.

In addition to the investment in research, ET committed to packaging and publishing its insights in ways that would be relevant, useful, and powerful. From the outset, ET was determined not to produce another vanilla white paper that was too long and too dense to read. SFF would comprise seven individual reports that were short enough for people to read quickly but deep enough to establish ET's expertise. These reports had their own logo, design format, and highly visual style, and they were accompanied by fast-moving YouTube clips. As Kopp explained, it was "about creating ten- to twelve-page highly visual, highly engaging pieces of marketing that would . . . walk you through the key facts, the key takeaways, and then point to . . . key infographics that make it very hard-hitting."[12]

ET had clearly thought a lot about what would hook the three specific audiences it was trying to build its reputation with, and started with a report that had wide-reaching relevance to marketers across multiple industries and product categories. It was called *Digital Mornings*, and it reported on stunning research that tracked what consumers did first thing in the morning. As ET found, consumers didn't make coffee, or exercise, or kiss their significant other. Instead, they checked their phone for email, text messages, and recent Facebook posts. As you can imagine, the morning shows lapped this up, affording ET executives many opportunities to talk on air about their findings. Better still, ET was invited to share its findings at marketing conferences across the world, beginning the process of evolving the marketing industry and profession in meaningful ways by offering insight into the forces of social media and digital that continue to disrupt today. Downloads and sales leads followed.

ET's next report, released February 2011, followed in a similar vein, using a clever hook to dive into the reasons why consumers "break up" with brands. ET timed the release to coincide with Valentine's Day, and the report uses a romantic relationship paradigm to investigate consumers' relationships with brands. Since relationships help shape how consumers interact with brands, ET's insights about relationship dynamics were extremely valuable to its buyers, even as ET caught the media's eye. "It's what I love about this research," remarked one of ET's corporate communications leaders. "There's an emotional connection as well as a rational connection."[13]

The SFF research series yielded twenty-five reports, many of which narrowly focused on specific industry segments or geographic locales (one title, for instance, *Digital Down Under*, investigated Australian digital consumers, while another, *Retail Touchpoints Exposed*, focused on retail). These reports did not have anywhere near the views or volume of consumption that the headliner reports did, but that does not mean they were less valuable. If you ask professionals inside ET they would go as far as to say they were more valuable. *"Retail Touchpoints Exposed* is . . . very relevant for retailers," an ET salesperson noted. "I mean, that's something that my team can take work for or develop a campaign or develop a conversation specifically targeting retailers, whereas most of the [other white papers out there] are . . . more product- or issue-driven, which is much broader. I do think the more targeted we can get with it, the more relevant it certainly can be. It gives us the opportunity to take that piece of research and focus a campaign, focus efforts on specific prospects and clients that we know fall into that category."[14]

Following on from the more targeted approach, the SFF team realized that the sales interaction itself was one of the most powerful platforms for proliferating insights from the edge of disruption. Using research, the team produced a series of one-page cheat sheets on each industry vertical, giving ET's perpetually "too busy" sales folks the ability to start more strategic conversations with prospects. It created PDFs and PowerPoint decks highlighting specific parts of the research that these sales folks could use to get access and build credibility at the right levels inside their buyers' organizations.

Companies that are the obvious choice in their markets are not just abundant in their approach to sharing; they are targeted as well. They know and believe that views and volume are not the only measures of value. They put what they learn to work for them by developing and curating content platforms that make their insight, data, and points of view available to their most important customers. Sometimes that is in the form of awesome content that gets a broad audience activated, and other times that is more surgical and precise, focused on buyers in particular verticals.

Now might be a good time for you to start to think about how you can position your point of view about your edge of disruption, and with whom. Then consider how you would build a platform that will position your elevated perspective in a way that reflexively drives value for you and your customers. Just be targeted in your approach and abundant in your sharing, and please understand that it could be, and likely should be, provocative.

BE PROVOCATIVE

"Verbena, aloe vera, melisse, lemon-balm, and finally the usual apple; the palate as always is shady and cool, though more overtly mineral than usual, but the finish crescendos into a salty tide that clings and doesn't quit."[15]

This is the type of incomprehensible description of a bottle of wine that leads its potential purchaser to choose beer instead. Wine is complex, that's understood. But it's also really simple— it is nice to drink and should be accessible to more people than descriptions like this suggest. The world of wine has an air of sophistication to it, and the people in it have historically enjoyed the exclusion of others as a means to reinforce that sophistication.

At least it did until Belarus-born New Jersey entrepreneur Gary Vaynerchuk took on the wine establishment, and all its conditioned bias and beliefs, and won. Ironically, it was a win not just for him, but for the establishment itself, which was missing the opportunities hidden in plain sight at the edge of disruption. You can imagine, then, how well the establishment responded when Gary Vaynerchuk started regularly describing wine characteristics using terms like "popcorn" instead of "oak," and comparing good wine to the New York Jets and bad wine to New England Patriots fans, on his newly launched online platform, Wine Library TV.

If you are a wine drinker, there's a chance you've heard of Wine Library TV. If you haven't, you should check it out. It has great articles like "The Perfect Wines to Pair with Jersey Shore

Boardwalk Food"[16]—where else are you going to find the answer to that question? Believe it or not, only from Shoppers Discount Liquors, a small family business in New Jersey, launched in 1978 by Gary's parents, who had immigrated from what is now Belarus. Gary was three years old when his family arrived; by 1994, when he was in college, the business was doing reasonably well.[17] While at school, he reportedly had an idea for a new kind of wine business—one that would take advantage of the blossoming world of the internet and the broadening appeal of wine to new consumer segments. According to Vaynerchuk, this radical idea was largely dismissed by New Jersey's 2,258 liquor stores at the time, which gave him all sorts of reasons why the internet of 1994 would never disrupt them or their deeply held belief that wine was for sophisticated drinkers and special occasions, not everyday people. Still, in 1997, Vaynerchuk, then a successful college junior, persuaded his father to give him a small ad budget for the family liquor business. With that money he launched WineLibrary.com, which focused on educating consumers and making wine more accessible.

For Vaynerchuk, the edge of disruption had two fronts. One was wine, and broadening its appeal. The other was the role of the internet in local business—specifically, the wine business. Let's start with the latter.

What Vaynerchuk understood better and earlier than most is that the web presented an unparalleled opportunity to create a direct relationship with consumers, a platform for gaining direct and sustainable access to the right audience. We use the word "platform" in the sense of a pulpit or stage that even a small company like Vaynerchuk's family business could leverage to share what it knows, creating an elevated perspective to which customers would flock. His edge of disruption started out in the vicinity of learning how to use an emerging technology to connect directly with consumers. He started the platform early and built it over time, continually redefining the edge in a world that was changing quickly. He began pulling customers and prospects onto email lists for weekly content and marketing messages. In 2006, as broadband began to take hold and continued disrupting the consumer market, Gary graduated into video, launching a YouTube channel called Wine Library TV, now known as the Daily Grape. He reports that up to 100,000 people view it each week, and that his celebrity guests are a big draw.

By 2009, Vaynerchuk was famous not just for wine, but even more so for his use of social media as a platform itself. He was a guest on Conan O'Brien's show[18] and he got a ten-book publishing deal with HarperStudio. Suddenly he was not just a wine expert—he was an expert on building a platform! With that, he successfully launched VaynerMedia with his younger brother, and by 2014 they had 400 employees, $30 million in revenue, and clients like PepsiCo, the New York Jets, and General Electric, all from the value of a powerful platform and an identifiable brand or identity.

Don't make the mistake of thinking this is all about marketing. A platform like this takes personal commitment to sharing and a passion for your products and services. When you share what you've learned, you have to be authentic in your enthusiasm and conviction, otherwise your audience will quickly tune you out. Vaynerchuk has a big personality that drives his platform, and he had the courage, optimism, and curiosity to define new edges of disruption along the way, to learn about them, and to passionately share his perspective with the world through various channels. And he has his share of detractors.

According to a *Fortune* magazine article, "a common line of criticism against Vaynerchuk is that he is a snake-oil salesman, one of a growing number of Internet celebrity marketers who make their money telling eager beaver entrepreneurs that they, too, can get rich and famous by self-marketing on social media." The article goes on to say, "A 2009 Gawker headline called him a 'wine-loving Twitter twerp,' and . . . its tech site Valleywag wrote, Think of him as a sort of Deepak Chopra of selling bullshit with Snapchat."[19]

Unsurprisingly perhaps, traditional media outlets have been quick to criticize the guy who increasingly represents and touts the value of platforms that threaten their very existence: "The

Wall Street Journal called him 'continually overexposed.' The *New York Times* called him a 'tireless self-promoter,'" notes *Fortune*.[20]

He retorts in that article in typical Vaynerchuk style: "When someone says to me, You've only achieved this because you're big on social media, I say, Want to see my calendar?"[21]

The bigger idea is not whether Gary Vaynerchuk's personality is attractive or not. It's that new ideas and new approaches, including those from the edge of disruption, are always met with criticism—they wouldn't be disruptive if they weren't. When the future threatens the status quo, people become defensive and start to think, talk, and act out of fear. It is easier to reject a new elevated perspective than it is to consider it and embrace it. This is why in the next section we will talk about how companies that matter choose who they sell to and partner with as much as buyers choose who they buy from. For this chapter, though, it's about having the courage to stand by your point of view, and to shine a light on the edge of disruption itself.

> New ideas and new approaches, including those from the edge of disruption, are always met with criticism—they wouldn't be disruptive if they weren't.

Vaynerchuk's impact on the wine industry was as divisive as his impact on social media for businesses. Vaynerchuk wanted to make wine popular. He wanted to make wine the obvious choice among alcoholic beverages, and he wanted his family liquor store to be the obvious choice for customers who wanted wine. He succeeded on both fronts by reframing the popular opinions on what's important—to wine drinkers and to social media producers.

Although not entirely Vaynerchuk's doing, US wine consumption per capita had grown for almost two decades straight leading into 2010. According to the US Wine Market Council, total cases consumed went from 205 million to 276 million between 2000 and 2010, far outstripping beer and spirits for incremental growth, based on Nielsen data.[22] More interesting, though, and more clearly the edge of disruption, was that the growth came from trends in two specific areas.

First, across all segments, more people were migrating from occasional wine consumption (called *marginal* consumption) to regular (called *core* consumption). The shift toward core wine drinking partly has been due to the category becoming more accessible to everyday drinkers, precisely because brands and wine resellers like Vaynerchuk were making wine easier to understand and less intimidating to buy. It was no longer reserved for special occasions or the upper crust of society; it was something everyone could drink, every day if they liked.

And second, Millennials were the fastest growing of all the segments, clearly favoring the lower price points where bulk-import wines, like Yellowtail, dominate. Long the number-one selling wine in the United States, Yellowtail comes in two varieties, red and white, making it very simple for young and less sophisticated consumers to buy in the category without fear of embarrassment.

We believe the reason Vaynerchuk needed to go so wide with his sharing strategy is because his edge of disruption required that he educate the consumer. Unlike DPR, ExactTarget, and even Integer with their targeted customer strategies, he needed to improve sales not just for his local Jersey liquor store, but also for the category of wine itself. In an interview in 2011, Gary explained that "everyone is in the content business and I'm in the context business. That is the battle that I'm fighting. That's what I care about, it's what I think about, it's how I roll. Everybody wants to throw the football, I want to catch it."[23] Gary was an early challenger to the "content is king" mantra, believing that everything has to be in context. In his case, this means focusing on engagement with his audience within the context of his personality, rather than simply talking at them the way more traditional wine connoisseurs liked to do.

Vaynerchuk's willingness to move to the edge of disruption as he took on greater responsibility at his father's wine shop, and to share wide and loud his views on wine in a way that made it more accessible, contribute both to the success of the category and very much to his family store. Under this ambitious son's leadership, the Vaynerchuk family business grew from $3 million to reportedly close to \$60 million in revenue, as of 2013.[24] It has also changed names, becoming Wine Library in the process.

Defining, learning, and sharing at the edge of disruption is a way of life for Gary Vaynerchuk. As he describes, "Here's how I work: It's 2013, and most marketers are operating like it's 2009. I'm always trying to market like it's 2015, but not like it's 2020. A lot of my contemporaries who understand where the world is going, go too far out, and aren't practical. I have always prided myself on being visionary, with a heavy practicality."[25]

Gary is defining the edge of disruption in the wine market, the intersection of the old and the new. Not too far out into the future, yet not too focused on the past and present. For Gary, it is a way of life. We found that to be consistently true for the other companies we studied and people we talked to as well. They are incessantly focused on that intersection.

MAKE THOUGHT LEADERSHIP A WAY OF LIFE

Companies that matter don't just treat their thought leadership as a marketing strategy; they also grow their content out of a much broader mind-set and way of operating. Thought leadership infuses everything these companies do, from product development to learning. Everyone on staff has an obligation to think about the future. As a result, the value of these companies' insights goes way beyond typical content marketing. Specifically, they differentiate their thought leadership in three key ways:

1. They find and focus on the edge of disruption that is most impactful for them and for their customers, and that's where they spend time developing their most valuable insights. Their content matters more because it is about things that are of higher relative importance to the people they need to influence most.
2. Their ideas are grounded in experience, data, and collaboration. They go far deeper than imaginative predictions or

generic observations. Instead, they go to a depth of insight that enables others to think in terms of business models and future offers, and their own perspective is elevated in the process. It is true thought leadership.

3. It is authentic. Companies that matter are driven to challenge the fundamentals of their industry, their clients, and themselves. They want to break free of the world as it currently exists, and move confidently toward the world as it is going to exist. As a result, they are bold and provocative, and they leave people questioning their most fundamental industry assumptions.

Tim Kopp, whom we introduced earlier as the chief marketing officer of ExactTarget prior to its acquisition by Salesforce, hit it right on the mark when he commented that "you can't do thought leadership halfway. Either you're going to do it and get the whole organization behind it, or you ought just not to bother."

For example, ExactTarget's SFF reports supported many other parts of ET's business operations beyond marketing and sales. The firm used them to onboard new hires, shortening the time it took for employees to become productive and up to date. Even more importantly, SFF research influenced the evolution of ET's integrated software and accelerated the development of its new social media capabilities. Consumer insights that SFF uncovered became firmly embedded into the overall design and functionality of the platform. ET's Morgan Stewart explained, "To achieve executive buy-in, we had to generate interest in how to integrate the research into other organizational elements . . . it influenced where the investment of money came from on a product development standpoint as they saw the opportunity to translate insight into software."[26] Let us reiterate: Thought leadership is not content marketing. It is a way of life.

ExactTarget not only sought to move toward the learning edge of change; it also packaged its insight to position its brand as a leader in social media. This changed how buyers saw

ET, elevating its perceived value and reputation and winning it enough market share in the process to narrow the field of competitors so it could rise to become the obvious choice. ET's business saw high double-digit revenue growth for several years, making the company attractive to potential buyers. In 2013, the king of cloud computing, Salesforce.com, acquired ET for $2.5 billion, some ten times ET's revenue. Salesforce could have purchased any software company in the space, but it chose the company that had already become the obvious choice, in part by virtue of its elevated perspective, and it used ET's platform as the backbone of its expanded cloud offering. As ET's leadership team will tell you, going all in when developing both its insights and its platform was critical to that kind of success.

These are all things anyone can do, but you have to commit time, energy, and passion to them. If you aren't courageous enough to put your ideas out there, optimistic about the future, and curious about the present, and you can't couple these drives with a willingness to learn all there is to know about your edge of disruption and share it, you will not see the benefits that companies like Vaynerchuk's businesses or Integer, DPR, and ExactTarget have accrued. In each of these examples, the willingness and ability to share was crucial in *elevating perspective*, which in turn led to new client relationships and an ability to connect in a different way. Or to revisit Elston's words from Integer, "We said, Why are you even talking to us? And they said, We see you at conferences everywhere, and we're reading your stuff all the time. We *had* to have you in the room. We couldn't *not* have you here." That was from a big fish, a blue chip account. And it was saying Integer was its obvious choice.

Bring It to Life . . .

1. Package the most provocative and important insights from your edge of disruption.

2. Make a short list of the highest value forums, content platforms, and individual influencers where you could share the insights you have developed at your edge of disruption.

3. Share your packaged insights with the short list freely. Share without fear of recourse, and without fear of competitive advantage. Write when asked. Comment when requested. Speak when given the opportunity. Your position as a thought leader will not come if you don't give voice to your insights.

4. Consider giving more people in your organization the opportunity to make thought leadership part of the way they do business. Empower them to have a voice. Collaborate with them.

SECTION TWO

ELEVATED RELATIONSHIPS

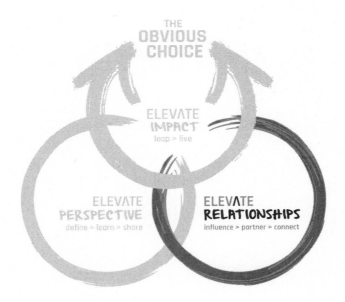

IN 2012, CANADA'S largest food and packaged goods companies held an industry conference, notable because the event was limited to CEOs and their strategic advisors. As the afternoon keynote and facilitator, we happened to be seated at the main table with the CEOs of PepsiCo Foods, Nestlé, Danone, and others, including Jeff Moore, CEO of a company called Lakeside. Lakeside was not quite the brand name that came with other people at that table, so it was a bit confusing. Why, at this CEO-only event, with sponsors allowed only in the hallway, was a Canadian logistics company CEO sitting at the same table as some of the largest food companies on earth? The CEO of Canada's largest grocery chain wasn't in the room, but Jeff Moore of this lesser-known company was. What was *that* all about?

It was all about Jeff Moore having made a decision to matter—to have his company matter in an industry that was deeply entrenched in legacy beliefs and assumptions about how work got done. Jeff began to challenge everything, with a commitment to remaking his business and positioning the company as a strategic partner to clients. In doing so, Lakeside became the obvious choice for logistics management partnership of some of the most influential companies in the market.

Validating Jeff's efforts to have Lakeside become a fully outsourced transportation and freight solutions provider, the company had made great headway in creating unique and perceptive insights that quickly became indispensable to its clients. It had created an *elevated perspective*, then put it to work for its sales efforts at the highest possible levels in its industry. The result? Jeff and Lakeside literally had a seat at the table, shoulder to shoulder with some of the biggest power players in the industry.

Jeff had managed to develop his company's *elevated perspective* and then leverage it into *elevated relationships* in his industry that gave him the influence, engagement, and connections for an even more powerful role with his key clients. It wasn't easy or fast. It took hard work and commitment over time to make the shift happen. But once it did, Lakeside was in a completely different place: delivering more value, standing above the competition, and truly being the obvious choice in its market.

Elevated relationships happen in three different but interrelated dimensions. First, you have access to the *key influencers* in your marketplace—the people who can say yes, and can make things happen inside their own organizations. They are typically your buyers. We call having access to these key influencers *playing high*.

Second, you *build partnerships* with the people who ultimately use or interact with your products and services, relationships that continually keep you fresh in understanding their needs and focused on the most complex problems they face. These partnerships are not necessarily with buyers (although they can be). Often they are with the people who enable you to create solutions that deliver outcomes that matter. We call this *engaging like you mean it*.

Third, you must make meaningful connections across what we call *the whole board*—all the various internal and external influences that create disruptions in your world. These connections go beyond the direct buy/sell relationships, or internally beyond your immediate circles, and into the broader ecosystem. No client or solution operates in isolation. Companies that matter understand this and thrive on the complexity it implies. They are master chess players on the board that is their market.

In Section One we introduced you to GHX, Piggly Wiggly, HomePlus, DPR, Integer, ExactTarget, and Wine Library TV, who all developed an *elevated perspective* that gave them access to a new space with their buyers. They found their edges of disruption and learned there. By sharing, they were able to offer consumers, buyers, and influencers something special. In each case, they were companies that mattered to their customers, their employees, and their markets. Each of them also took the next step and developed elevated relationships to increase the market value they provide. Like Lakeside, each of these companies is able to sit shoulder to shoulder with the right people in their markets to influence, partner, and connect in ways that drive incredible value for their customers.

This section is all about how companies like Lakeside have found success in elevating their relationships, and how you can, too. So how do you use your *elevated perspective* to create *elevated relationships*? Let's take a look, starting with Lakeside and Jeff Moore's vision of transforming his industry in a most startling way.

CHAPTER 4

INFLUENCE: Play High

W HEN YOU THINK OF COMPANIES that just *crush* the competition, the usual sexy consumer brands probably come to mind— Apple, Google, BMW. We've worked for each of these companies and can tell you that while they are impressive, and they "play high" with consumer buyers better than anyone, they are no more impressive than the smaller companies we studied, such as Lakeside. You may not have heard of Lakeside, but it has indeed become the obvious choice in its market.

Founded in 1986, Lakeside, which at the time was known as Lakeside Logistics, initially operated as a broker, connecting companies with goods to move and truckers who would move them. Founder Jeff Moore and retired partner Chris Magill built the business by forming relationships with the low-level traffic managers who were their customers, playing golf with them and seeing their kids at Saturday hockey games.

By the late 1990s, though, the business had gotten tougher and less enjoyable, not to mention less lucrative. Manufacturers no longer cared that their kids went to the same school or which sports team won. It became all about economic value, and a lot less about those long-standing relationships. As a result, Lakeside became engaged with customers on a strictly transactional basis, wooing them with the lowest possible prices. Sound familiar?

It got worse. Each Lakeside sales representative made twenty cold calls a day, asking customers if the company could bid on a single "lane" (a shipment route between individual cities). To "build relationships," like many in the industry at that time, Lakeside sent its salespeople to befriend low-level traffic managers by routinely sending them things like bags of candy, promotional items, and sports tickets. Even as a mid-sized competitor, Lakeside still had to bid on and execute tens of thousands of individual contracts every year, most worth less than $1,000. Customers called all the time to ask Moore to bid down thousands of truckers so that they could get the cheapest deal.

By 2007, Moore had had enough. Years and years of disloyalty, margin squeeze, and sweetheart deals had taken their toll, and he wanted either to get out of the business—or to transform it. He chose to stay, and he committed to making Lakeside a company that mattered, in a way the competition couldn't touch. And that's when Lakeside began its journey to becoming the obvious choice.

As a broker, Moore was connected with both logistics customers and suppliers; he was thus in an excellent position to influence at the highest levels through his understanding of his industry. He knew what companies needed to ship, and he knew practices truckers were adopting in order to meet customers' incessant price demands. He also saw inefficiencies in the system: Trucks leaving full on long-haul lanes but running empty excessive miles after making a drop or two on their way to other drops. Truckers being necessarily creative in imposing accessorial charges for all kinds of additional services due to the customer's inefficiencies (necessary to claw back margin lost by the price-driven competition). Moore had this unique understanding because of where he was standing—on the edge of disruption for himself, his business, and his industry with regard to how business "got done." He had the courage to challenge every assumption about how the logistics industry worked, and the optimism to believe that it could be different. Equally important, his perspective was deeply informed by reality—he knew his business inside and out.

Moore realized that the industry's cutthroat, price-driven competition wasn't actually reducing costs for shipping customers—often it was increasing the landed delivery cost per case of product. The low-level traffic managers Moore worked with were missing the bigger picture. Lakeside's sales team was appealing to customers with promises of saving them 5 percent on a single lane—a whopping $50. What if Lakeside could optimize the entire approach to shipping? That might save customers 10 percent off their *entire logistics budgets*. With budgets reaching $5 million or more, that was serious money. Which would you rather save, $500,000 per year or $50 on a single lane here and there?

Moore's plan, which coalesced between 2007 and 2010, was essentially to take over his customers' entire transportation function. Efficiency was the number-one goal. If a customer outsourced all its transportation to Lakeside, it wouldn't need in-house transportation staff anymore, nor would it need related administration. Lakeside would provide all services, saving the customer the expense and enabling it to focus on its core business. It would also compile and analyze logistics data for its customers more effectively than they could themselves, saving them money on systems and technologies. Lakeside would then use the insights it created from the data to help customers not only organize freight better, but also make better sales and marketing decisions, creating a scenario where doing business with Lakeside meant cost savings *and* increased revenue potential. It all boiled down to a revolutionary way of approaching the industry, one that would produce great cost savings and benefit both Lakeside and its customers.

Lakeside's new pitch was as follows: "Take your transportation department from a cost center to a profit center." It made great sense, but there was one problem: The traffic managers to which Lakeside traditionally sold refused to buy it. Lakeside had just run straight into one of the five key challenges you will encounter when you decide to play high.

INVEST YOUR ENERGY IN THE RIGHT PEOPLE

You can understand why traffic managers resisted. Not only was Lakeside challenging their sole focus on price; it was threatening to do away with their jobs! Saying yes to this new pitch meant that a logistics manager was agreeing to have his job outsourced to Lakeside. All those bags of candy, tickets to events, and lunches? Gone! And even worse, their jobs might disappear, too. As one of Lakeside's sales representatives recalled, "We'd show them all of the stuff. We'd tell them all of the features and tell them the benefits and whatever. They'd walk out of the room, and bury it. We did about twenty presentations. Great presentations. We didn't get anything."

Lakeside's *elevated perspective* on how freight could get done was met with resistance at their current buyer level. They needed to engage higher up the hierarchy to get any traction in the marketplace. However, at that time, Lakeside didn't have a relationship or, indeed, any interaction with the higher-level executives empowered to enact sweeping change to an entire function. Lakeside's leadership had ventured out to the edge of disruption in its industry and it was excited about what it saw—the company wasn't going to back away from it. It had developed an *elevated perspective* and was sharing it, but with the wrong people. Its buyers were trying to force Lakeside back from the edge, back down into commodity-based discussions.

This is a common problem that we saw over and over in our research. Elevating your perspective is critical, but alone it does not create enough value to make you the obvious choice. Innovative thinking and deep insights might raise your reputation, but to truly create the most valued outcomes, you have to leverage your elevated perspective to elevate your customer relationships. Lakeside was running right into the challenge of needing to figure out ways of engaging with customer organizations at levels *commensurate with the new value it wanted to deliver*.

We've seen some pretty creative approaches to getting higher access in organizations. If you have done your homework, developed an elevated perspective that is impactful, and coupled it with a platform that amplifies the message, you will find you don't have to get too crazy. In the case of Lakeside, it decided to perform an industry audit to understand what customers' challenges were and how to best address them. Taking what was learned and combining it with more than twenty years of industry experience, Lakeside began developing new offerings and models to address the challenges, and collecting evidence that these models really worked.

> Elevating your perspective is critical, but alone it does not create enough value to make you the obvious choice. To truly create the most valued outcomes, you have to leverage your elevated perspective to elevate your customer relationships.

The company then departed from its existing practice of advertising in logistics magazines, instead embarking on campaigns to target CEOs in specific customer industries. Lakeside identified the media and professional associations and organizations that engaged these CEOs, and then systematically began "earning their way into conversations," as Jeff described it, by showing up with something useful and interesting to say. Lakeside was generous in sharing what it had learned, and this came back to the company in spades. That's why Moore was at the food and beverage conference in 2012; and it's why, after only a few years, he was one of a very few strategic advisors invited to mingle with this illustrious band of executives. "From what I've seen," Moore told us, "the exposure that we get at an event like that is tenfold what we'd ever get putting that in a magazine, because . . . that's the audience that we're looking for. Those 200–300 people that are coming to that event . . . are the . . . people we're trying to get at." Again, it was not luck that Moore was there that day. His company had embarked on an intentional and targeted program of activities that enhanced its reputation in the mind of the people who mattered most, the only audience capable of saying yes to Lakeside's exciting new model. Companies everywhere interested in outfoxing commoditization should take note.

We often hear companies bemoaning their inability to reach the "right" people to influence at the highest possible level. Consider whether you are doing all you can to go to where your ideal buyers are, rather than either expecting to meet them in their offices or expecting them to find you. Take a hard look at where you are spending your time. Are there opportunities to claim different space and to create different conversations? We are willing to bet there are, and your elevated perspective creates the opportunity to do so.

You might think that the more comprehensive, advanced, and powerful thought leadership we are describing here is only for B2B companies. Think again. Consumer brands, both large and small, have also been using deep expertise to differentiate themselves from commodity providers, and are equally capable of focusing their efforts on a higher level. The difference is that to play high in the B2C world, they don't need to move up a hierarchy of people to do so. Instead, they need to move up a hierarchy of needs inside the consumer's mind. This usually means targeted segmentation, to ensure they are going after the right kinds of consumers, and then positioning against the higher-order needs those consumers have. These are the needs they see as more valuable to satisfy.

An example of a consumer products company that targets a higher-order need is Runners Roost, a chain of specialized athletic footwear stores with seven locations in the Denver area, where people like to run. Athletic gear is about as commoditized as it gets in the consumer world. You can buy running shoes almost anywhere: Target, Walmart, DSW, Amazon, Zappos, Sports Authority, Nordstrom—the list goes on. So a specialty store focused on running has to create an elevated perspective and bring that to bear in influencing the buyer effectively.

Runners Roost focuses on "selection and service," but when these folks talk about service, they don't just mean courtesy and good manners; they mean something else entirely. If you buy running shoes at the typical big-box sporting goods retailer, the salesperson (if you can find one) might give your foot a squeeze, spout a couple of buzzwords about the main brands, and try to upsell you on gimmicky, high-technology shoes you might not even need. At Runners Roost, be prepared to actually learn something about both yourself and running shoes during the sales experience.

A typical Runners Roost interaction begins with a conversation that covers the needs of the runner, their goals, and their desired outcomes. Trained staff members ask customers about their current exercise habits, the aches and pains they experience while exercising, and whether they're currently under a doctor's care for specific ailments. Then they watch customers as they stride across the store with their shoes off, and put customers on a special treadmill rigged with video recorders and computers. Afterward, software analyzes the footage for biomechanical patterns in the customer's gait. Staff members then sit with customers, watch the footage frame by frame, and explain what they are seeing as well as how it might affect the customer's shoe purchase. As customers try on shoes, staff members have them return to the treadmill to determine if the shoes really are supporting their gait and correcting for imperfections.

As you might expect, Runners Roost customers feel passionately about running and about protecting their bodies from injury. These customers want service, but more importantly, they want expertise. Getting the right shoe is a very important challenge indeed. For them, Runners Roost is the obvious choice as a retailer. Its name, its staff selection, and its sales experience are targeted directly at the sorts of consumers who value their athletic equipment more highly. It creates an experience that produces value above and beyond the underlying commodity product, and plays high as a result.

Imagine for a minute, though, what it takes to have a sales team that can execute on that type of service. It takes a commitment to stay current, an understanding of what's happening in the world of running, and likely being a runner yourself. Do you have the same culture in your organization? Are your own people using your products and services? Can your salespeople speak authentically about experiences with your goods? If not, why not?

Often it is because they believe selling is different from using a product. But legacy go-to-market processes like that impede a company's ability to elevate relationships. Companies operating that way are stuck in the past, continuing to negotiate on price instead of value and working too low in the organization to have a meaningful impact. Sales folks push back, saying they need more head count, they need cheaper products, they need to focus on monthly quotas, all the while missing the true opportunity to leverage an elevated perspective and engage in more meaningful conversations, and at higher levels. That's the way they've always worked—they know how to maximize their take-home pay in that system, and they might not love it, but they understand it. That takes us to the second challenge.

ALIGN YOUR GO-TO-MARKET APPROACH

Lakeside knew it had to create entrée into the more senior levels of its client organization. Doing so required new and different marketing, placement, and visibility from the most senior levels of the organization. At the same time, Moore quickly realized that he would need to overhaul the sales organization as well as marketing. In many companies, sales is the most coveted, most protected, and most rewarded group in the organization. After all, sales brings in the revenue. At the end of the day, everyone else is making products and supporting services that the world would never know about without the sales organization. At least that's the mantra we often hear.

Transforming sales and often marketing in any organization is not for the timid, that's for sure. But, it is completely necessary if you want to *elevate relationships* with your buyers and to put your elevated perspective to work for you. Time and again we've seen companies invest in building an elevated perspective only to have the sales organization reject it because "that's not how we sell," or because it can feel like a slower burn. Solving more complex problems is often a slower sales cycle than commodity-based categories. Companies that are working on the edges of disruption, that want to change how they matter to their customers, will push through that resistance, hold their nerve, and in the process often bring sales and marketing closer together.

Consider the situation at Lakeside. It was fighting for $1,000 lanes, and its salespeople knew exactly how to do that; it was what they had been doing for many, many years. It was hard work, but that's why it was called work, right? It's one thing to claim you will save a company 10 percent of its $5 million transportation budget, but quite another to *show* that company, as part of the sales process, that you can actually do it and

> Solving more complex problems is often a slower sales cycle than commodity-based categories. Companies that are working on the edges of disruption, that want to change how they matter to their customers, will push through that resistance, hold their nerve, and in the process often bring sales and marketing closer together.

have them believe you. If Lakeside was going to succeed, it needed a more sophisticated sales team, armed with data and intelligent arguments about the customer's current and future transportation spending. A traffic manager might want to talk about the weekend hockey game or be swayed by a lunch at a local sports bar, but the CEO wouldn't.

Like other companies we talked to, Lakeside devoted itself to revamping its sales team as well as the *process* by which it went to market. Rather than talking about itself during the sales process, as Lakeside traditionally had, the company began offering to do free benchmarking analyses for prospects. As part of each analysis, Lakeside would uncover the companies' true costs of freight and transportation. Further, Lakeside would compare these companies to similar companies whose analysis Lakeside had done as a result of its new go-to-market strategy.

If you were the CFO of a food or consumer products manufacturer, how could you say no to this? It was a no-brainer! Such companies were religious about understanding their total unit cost, and they could tell you down to the cent how much brand, advertising, materials, and other costs went into the end unit cost of each product. But in many cases, transportation and logistics were a mess, ambiguous at best from a cost perspective. And here was Lakeside offering to apply data and practical analysis to this mess, not just answering the cost-related questions but reducing the cost itself. Oh, and did we mention that Lakeside was going to do it for free, as a part of the sales process? That meant having salespeople who knew how to position the value of the analysis over and above the low cost of a particular lane.

Lakeside knew that most of its customers thought it did a "pretty good job" in transportation. To convince an organization to take a big leap and outsource its transportation to them, Lakeside would have to make a strong case that the client didn't actually do a pretty good job. "We have to tell them what they're *not* getting," a Lakeside executive told us. "We have to show them a lack of value as well as business sustainability that they have today." Once Lakeside had a clear picture of a company's current spending patterns, it could model how that spending would decline if the entire transportation function were outsourced. Lakeside would show the prospect hard evidence for a guaranteed percentage reduction in cost, and this would essentially clinch the deal. A cost savings of a large magnitude was a value proposition that no CFO or CEO could ignore, especially not when the data were there right in front of them and they knew Lakeside's flawless implementation track record.

Through this new go-to-market strategy, Lakeside created an upward spiral of success. The more analyses the company did, the more compelling these analyses and benchmarking exercises became. That's because each analysis created even more data that Lakeside could use in comparatively assessing a new company's situation, resulting in even more convincing arguments for outsourcing. In addition, as Lakeside's data grew more valuable, the company had an even easier time gaining exposure and access to senior executives (effectively improving how they dealt with Hurdle #1—getting access), which in turn allowed Lakeside to collect even more data, driving the process ever forward.

We don't mean to make what Lakeside did sound easy. It wasn't. A typical benchmarking analysis cost Lakeside at least $15,000, which represented more than fifteen times the company's historical deal size. Think about that for a minute. Lakeside increased its cost of sale to a level fifteen times its typical deal size. This is precisely what we meant earlier about companies that hold their nerve.

Even more important, when it wasn't the right fit for the customer or for Lakeside, salespeople had to be able to say "no" to lower-value deals without being penalized. To execute its strategy, Lakeside had to get rid of virtually everyone on its existing sales team. The company's previous salespeople knew how to sell in the legacy model, but that would no longer cut it in the bigger world Lakeside now sought to inhabit and the value they wanted to provide. The company needed people who were smart and technically skilled enough to perform sophisticated numerical analyses. Of the seven people on Lakeside's traditional sales team, only one remained as of 2015; the other six were replaced by financial and supply chain analysts. In essence, Lakeside's go-to-market team was now a consulting group—far different from what Moore had imagined his sales team would be when he started the company. Indeed, as the leader, Moore had to accept that the sales skills he himself had used to build the company were obsolete, and that he, like the company, needed to grow and evolve with the times. Lakeside is a fascinating example, but the truth is, so many of the companies we studied rebuilt their sales functions in similar ways. You must be willing to make some tough choices about a deeply entrenched function to truly break out of old ways of working.

Go-to-market principles are applicable for consumer models and internal teams as well. The way consumers shop, especially in a store experience, is critical—it determines what they expect and how they buy. Runners in Denver make a special trip to Runners Roost for the experience of interacting with the sales staff. Shoppers go to specialty bookstores because they know the staff will be able to guide them as well as help them find the book they want. If this approach to the market is starting to sound "consultant-y," that's because often the service piece of what you do is what makes you stand out, where you create more value and move beyond the competition. Whether it is expertise at Runners Roost, a private shopper experience at a place like Nordstrom, or the SWAT teams that Lakeside has put in place, the sales and service interaction presents an opportunity to engage at higher levels, either hierarchically in a B2B world, or conceptually in a B2C sense.

For internal teams, consider the times you've had to pitch your internal "customer" for funding to implement a new technology or process, or when you've had to do a budget review to defend your staffing levels. If you think of these as go-to-market activities, you will start to see that engaging these internal customers is not so different from engaging external customers. You still have to influence as high as you can, and along a needs spectrum that helps your "buyers" choose you instead of other options (going external, not investing at all, etc.).

> What we see happen most often is companies getting stuck in the middle. They neither solve higher-order problems, nor are they the best price option. As a result they are not the obvious choice for anyone; over time their volume drops, along with their margin, and in many cases they become targets for disruption or takeover.

At this stage you may be wondering if it is easier to just compete on price. You can certainly find ways to move a lot of volume and compete on price, but it will be tough to consistently win that way. The rate of commodification and the race toward volume and lower prices will leave very little room for anyone but the largest players. What we see happen most often is companies getting stuck in the middle. They neither solve higher-order problems, nor are they the best price option. As a result they are not the obvious choice for anyone; over time their volume drops, along with their margin, and in many cases they become targets for disruption or takeover.

If you choose to have a singular value proposition as the lowest-cost provider, you can find certain ways to do it and succeed. We'd just suggest that in many industries there is a higher calling that most customers look for, and most of the best talent does, too. Finding ways to solve your customers' higher-order problems at the edge of disruption will help you remain front and center in their mind. Whether you are solving a complex business problem, helping a consumer satisfy a highly important personal need, or even assisting an internal team focused on serving internal customers, you have the opportunity to matter—to solve the higher-order problems, create more value, and become the obvious choice in the process. But to do so consistently, you will need courage. The courage to say no. To say no to those who insist on pushing you back toward low-value work, and who don't understand the power of true partnership.

LEARN TO SAY NO

Both Lakeside and DPR did two interesting things when they decided to elevate their relationships by playing high in their client organizations. In addition to finding ways to engage with the right levels and revamping their sales teams, they did something that might seem counterintuitive. They created a "scarcity effect" when they started saying no: no to customers who were not interested in truly partnering with them to create the highest possible value, and no to work that wasn't right for them to deliver the highest possible value. Everything became focused on that one shining outcome—value creation. Working with the wrong people, and/or on the wrong work, became a distraction from the ultimate destination of creating value of the highest order.

That might seem unrealistic or simplistic to you, but consider this: Imagine if you took all the energy you put toward pleasing customers who aren't profitable to you and likely never will be—clients who keep pushing you into commodity conversations and ruthless negotiations—and instead directed that energy toward clients who are your partners and who most need the work you do best? We believe you'd become so valuable to those clients, you'd get the margins you need to do less (but more enjoyable) work and still thrive as a business. It takes clarity and courage to say no to work, but it is absolutely imperative if your goal is to become the obvious choice.

Let's go back to Lakeside as an example. Remember that Lakeside started gathering massive amounts of internal data from customers during the new and data-intensive sales process. You might wonder whether a client would wish to divulge details about its cost structure during a sales process. Lakeside initially thought the need for transparency might constitute a major obstacle. However, the *right kinds of customers*—those truly interested in embracing best practices—weren't all that concerned about transparency. "We had customers tell us to just go through the accounting department and look at the invoices ourselves," SVP and COO Tom Coates explained.

Imagine that: A customer trusting you enough to let you rummage through its business. It's the complete antithesis of the typical RFP process, where the customer guards most information tightly to secure a negotiating advantage. Lakeside wasn't just playing high; it was becoming part of the team. The importance of selecting clients who will welcome you as a part of the team can't be overstated; it is critical if you are going to bring your elevated perspective effectively into play to create the highest possible value for your clients.

> It takes clarity and courage to say no to work, but it is absolutely imperative if your goal is to become the obvious choice.

During our time at Lakeside, we had the opportunity to see this new value proposition in action. A notable moment came during one of our interviews with the company's sales leader. On the same day as the interview, a huge sales opportunity came knocking on Lakeside's door. This manufacturer had been hearing a lot about Lakeside's SmartSource solution and wanted to review the possibility of moving its $1.5 million freight spend to the "ideal transportation partner." You would think that Lakeside might have jumped at the opportunity. Not at all. As the sales leader told me, "We said today let's not jointly go down there and waste your time and our time, but let's reconnect at a future time when maybe we have something that would better fit for what you need, and you keep it in mind so as you get bigger and more complex, know that there's a place you can go, but you don't need us right today."[1]

Imagine that. Here was a business that only a few years earlier was scratching it out for $50 transactions on a daily basis, while also suffering massive amounts of disloyalty from customers and underhanded practices on the part of competitors. Now this same company was receiving—and *rejecting*—$1.5 million opportunities. We found it immensely satisfying to see the wave of pride wash over this sales leader's face as he realized for the first time just how far playing high had allowed Lakeside to grow.

Perhaps you're reading about Lakeside and thinking, *Inspiring story, but wow, that's an expensive approach to the market.* You'd be right; it's expensive. But that's precisely why Lakeside disciplined itself to partner with only a select group of customers: those who spent $5 million or more in transportation costs each year, and who also were dealing with complex freight needs (e.g., cross-border customs, regulation, and compliance) or controlled environments. Those were the customers where the Lakeside approach mattered the most, because it created enough value to offset the cost and to deliver outcomes that benefitted both companies.

Transforming the way a company manages freight was extremely complex and operationally demanding for Lakeside, as it had to customize outsourcing for every client. Moreover, all of this work and all of the solutions architecture (which you'll remember cost more than $15,000) happened *before* a client had even signed on the dotted line. Lakeside needed to be able to show real savings and value for the customer; only then would the customer take the massive risk of handing over responsibility for transportation to another company. To invest this much money in the sales process, Lakeside had to have complete clarity on who was a good prospect, and had to be completely disciplined to say no to customers who did not fit the ideal profile: high partnership potential and the right work portfolio. A $1.5

million client that once might have seemed like a gold mine for Lakeside now appeared as a very poor prospect, even though this client came to Lakeside proactively. As Lakeside's sales leader explained, a company with only a $1.5 million transportation budget "is harder to make a win-win solution, but at $5 million it's possible. So I push my business development manager to find these [$5 million] companies. You've got to bring the right one in. And before you even make a call, you've got to make sure that you're working on the right guy."[2] Before even reaching out, Lakeside would spend *days* researching a single prospect. Only that kind of effort would ensure a high enough hit rate as well as a warm welcome in the prospect's executive suite.

As you might have surmised, playing high seems to trigger the old chicken-and-egg paradox. You need to book the revenue in order to cover the cost of creating these higher-value solutions, and yet you will never have the capacity to do so if you chase transactions every day. As Moore told me, during the 1990s his company was spending "50 percent of our time winning lanes, and 50 percent of our time putting out fires."

To become the obvious choice, you need to break the chicken-and-egg dilemma. You need to hold your nerve and make the initial investments required to move to the edge of disruption, develop a compelling and elevated perspective, create valuable solutions based on that, and sell your solutions to higher-order problems. You must show determination to sell *only* to those capable of saying yes to these solutions. Otherwise, you wind up distracted, burned out, and as commoditized as everybody else. Remember DPR in the last section? Its cofounder Doug Woods told us, "You can't get . . . desperate because you think that [the] market's tight and start to fill in with a bunch of low-priced deals; you live with those things for a very long time."[3] For all of the successful companies we talked to, a willingness to *say no* gave management the bandwidth to do work that *mattered*, with clients willing to partner with them instead of bullying them like a typical supplier.

Companies that matter to their customers universally demonstrated the *clarity* to know where they added the most value and with what kinds of clients, and the *courage* to decline short-term revenue-generating opportunities. This ability to say no might seem startling, but you see the most successful companies do it all the time. Steve Jobs is often quoted as saying sexy things like "Put a dent in the universe" and "We made the buttons on the screen look so good you'll want to lick them."[4] Inside Apple, however, Jobs was famous for one word: "No." "Innovation is saying 'no' to 1,000 things," he would say.[5] This is how Jobs turned a company that once had only sixty days of cash left into the most valuable company in the world. He spent significantly less on R&D than his competitors did, yet he put out a superior product. He did fewer things, but he did them better, and in the end he delivered more value to his most influential customers—he mattered more.

How discriminating can a company be? Ask our friends at DPR. Doug wasn't kidding when he said you can't get desperate. Inspired by work the company did with management guru Jim Collins, DPR developed the notion of a "red zone" into which prospects must fall in order for DPR to consider them as potential partners. Collins suggests three questions a company should ask:

1. Is this something we can do better than any other company?
2. Are we passionate about it?
3. Will it fuel our economic engine?[6]

DPR went further, expanding Collins's approach into an eleven-question diagnostic, each question answerable with a simple "yes" or "no." It included questions such as "Would customers be fun to work with?" "Did they seek to buy a service as opposed to a commodity?" "Did they seem trusting?" and "Did they reside in one of DPR's core markets?" If DPR's sales team answered "no" three times, DPR would have a deeper discussion among the leadership team or refuse to pursue the job altogether. Now, that's picky!

Try it for yourself. What are your criteria for an ideal customer? What would it take for you to say no to a customer? What would it do to your current customer mix if you applied those two filters? It takes discipline and courage to say no, but it is absolutely critical if you want to elevate your relationships and deliver higher value.[7]

As a DPR executive related, "I'm really proud of what we've learned to say no to and who we've learned to say no to. So, it's cool. It's a really big, powerful feature of ours." By saying no when it needed to, DPR put itself in a position to say yes when it really mattered. It was snatching back its business from the jaws of commodification, recapturing the control that suppliers in its market had lost many years ago.

SET CLEAR STANDARDS

The most successful companies we talked to don't just apply strict standards to say no when choosing customers and work. They apply equally tough standards once they've taken a job as well, both to their own conduct and to that of their customers. DPR is very clear: They don't chase jobs; they *partner*. A given job matters, but the relationship with the partner matters more. As Jay Leopold, a DPR regional manager, remarked, "If you're chasing the job, you missed, you totally misunderstood everything that matters. You should be chasing the customers, trying to build a genuine relationship with them and with all our being, creating value based on what's important to them."[8]

DPR has a fascinating approach to a typically rough contracting process. At the outset of projects with a new customer, the company conducts a special session with that customer in which key stakeholders define the project's core values. Imagine a bunch of construction guys heading on retreat, singing "Kumbaya" by the fire, and agreeing on how they will treat one another during the project and beyond. Remember, theirs is an industry in which it is not uncommon for projects to end in lawsuits. It's true: These are multimillion-dollar, sometimes even billion-dollar projects that stretch on for years, so it's only natural that disputes will arise. Still, at their team-building sessions, DPR and its partners collaborate on processes for resolving disputes without lawyers, and they talk through the use of scorecards, reporting, and other tools that all parties can use to build a trusting relationship. DPR and its partners even write mission statements for each project.

It takes real courage to demand something greater from your customers and to adhere to these standards long after they are first defined. But the results are worth it. They include not just lasting, loyal relationships, but also more meaningful work. Mike Ford, a member of the Management Committee at DPR, recounted how when DPR finished a medical center for Kaiser Permanente in Virginia, the craftsmen working on the job showed up on opening day, helping to greet new patients as they came through the door. He explained, "They're just emotionally connected to this facility that's going to be providing community health in a brand-spanking-new building."[9]

> It takes real courage to demand something greater from your customers and to adhere to these standards long after they are first defined. But the results are worth it.

A big reason these workers felt so connected was because they felt valued themselves. Kaiser Permanente treated them right all along, opening the way for them to see the project as not another job, but something meaningful, something special.

You can be sure DPR is not satisfied even with this level of partnership. Executives at the company will continue to push hard, looking for ways to bring themselves and customers together as peers. Actually, they already have pushed harder, embracing a recent construction-industry trend called Integrated Project Delivery, which we will learn more about in the next chapter.

Of course, the setting of standards wasn't a one-way street for DPR and other similar companies; it was about setting higher standards for its *own* conduct in ways that feed its ability to influence at the highest levels. The ability to influence takes on special significance when it comes to telling clients no and turning down work. On one occasion, a major retailer came to DPR and asked the company to build a data center. Executives at the retailer had seen a DPR executive presenting some of the company's insights at a conference and were convinced that DPR was the right partner for them. DPR pushed back strongly against the client because DPR leaders didn't think the investment was a good deal for the customer. DPR saw how rapidly technology was advancing in this space, and executives felt the retailer was better off focusing on its core business and leasing an existing data center from someone else. Think about that: Here was a client offering to spend upwards of $20 million with DPR, and DPR was pushing back, suggesting that the client *not* spend that money to build its own facility.

Happily, such positioning usually rebounded to DPR's advantage over the long term. One DPR regional leader told us that his company had just won two coveted jobs without either of the jobs going out for RFPs. In both cases, "we were working with [the customer] far in advance . . . taking out their trash, almost literally, doing whatever it took. We wanted to work with them, we believe in them, and we found a way to get a small project with them and to kick butt, so that by the time the real job came, they trusted us. We insisted on doing the right thing, even when it may not have made short-term sense, so by the time the big opportunities came about, they knew us and they trusted us experientially and relationally."[10]

As DPR demonstrates, influence isn't just about whom you talk to; it's about *how* you conduct yourself, and how you expect your customers to interact with you. If you are influencing at the right level and insist that your clients engage as well, everyone will benefit. Isn't it refreshing to know that setting high standards and staying true to them really does work out for the best? We can be idealists and behave accordingly, and we will still come out further ahead than if we ply customers with gifts or scrap for every penny. That's the secret companies that matter know, and that many more organizations could stand to learn. It leads directly to the final challenge that you will encounter as you work to elevate your relationships—the need to *be true to your future self.*

BE TRUE TO YOUR FUTURE SELF

Herminia Ibarra advocates for people to *stay true to their future selves*, the selves they genuinely plan and hope to become, not their current selves, even when that future self might not be completely articulated.[11] We see this as applicable to organizations as well. All of the challenges we've highlighted so far in "Influence" hinge on your ability to do just this one thing: to be true to your future self. This is where clarity and courage kick in, and where it takes a certain degree of grit to see your way through to becoming the obvious choice. You have to know who you want to be in business, and with whom you want to be in business, and stay completely focused on that goal, while remaining open to changes in your industry and continuing to synthesize and maintain perspective on the edges of disruption happening all around you. Know who you want to be at a very foundational level, and it will allow you to focus where you need to, while keeping a broad connection to the ecosystem that surrounds you.

It sounds easy and hard all at once, doesn't it? Sometimes something as simple as a name can have great importance in defining your future self. In appealing to senior executives who might "get it," Lakeside initially had great difficulty getting anyone to pay attention. As Lakeside's marketing research showed, that's because the company was still seen as a typical "logistics company," a decidedly unglamorous category whose members ranged from one guy with a truck to UPS with 100,000 vehicles on the road. Somehow, Lakeside needed to reposition itself in the minds of buyers.

Once its business strategy and operational capabilities were in place, Lakeside then faced the obstacle of transforming how Canada's manufacturing industry sees the transportation function—a true paradigm shift from viewing transportation as a necessary cost of doing business to seeing it as a strategic function that injects value and business knowledge and fosters innovation throughout every corner of the business.

To address this challenge, Lakeside needed a strategic communications partner to help change the transportation conversation in Canada and establish Lakeside as a strategic partner in the minds of C-suite executives. Enter Jan Kelley, a Canada-based integrated marketing-communications firm with specific expertise in brand development, strategic communications, and customer experience mapping. Jan Kelley, in collaboration with Jeff and his leadership team, quickly recognized the opportunity to combine the heritage of the company with a tagline that both spoke to the caliber of people at Lakeside and presented the target audience with a powerful call to action. Thus was born "Lakeside. Be Smart." They then worked with Lakeside to evolve the brand in the market and translate this new position to its business development model. What resulted was a sophisticated consultative selling approach centered on a discovery process, which identified early on the fit between client need and Lakeside capabilities.

It wasn't just a name change for Lakeside. "Be Smart" was defining a new way of being for Lakeside, distancing itself from the negative perceptions of "logistics" in the market. With this cognitive barrier out of the way, Lakeside could then begin to build a reputation as being "smart" and ahead of the game—a company that has an elevated perspective. It was defining its future self organizationally. "By positioning ourselves as smart," Moore told us, "and declaring our value proposition as your 'ideal transportation department,' we were able to get out from underneath all the noise, and instead of being an apples-to-apples comparison to every other logistics company, we became an orange." Being "smart" was more than a tagline for Lakeside; it came to define its way of doing business. It dictated the way Lakeside sold, the way it marketed, and the way it built relationships with customers. In fact, it defined an entire industry model that Lakeside embodied and for which it advocated: "smart-sourced transportation." The company even built "smart" into its website URL (www.lakesidebesmart.com).

An interesting aside for insight into how much relationships matter to companies that matter: When we first wrote the Lakeside case study in this chapter, we left out Jan Kelley, instead focusing on Lakeside alone. Jeff was having none of it. He wanted to be sure credit was given where credit was due, and Jan Kelley was their partner. Lakeside demanded from itself the same partnership behaviors it demanded of its customers. We'll spend more time on the idea of partnerships in the next chapter, because they are critical to companies that matter.

Lakeside was true to its future self, certainly, and its "smart" positioning also suggested another dimension of future-oriented authenticity: building a brand that will allow you to interact with those customers you hope to serve. It's critical to represent yourself in the market in a way that gives you permission to engage at the right levels. Lakeside was ready to play a new role in its customers' lives, that of the ideal transportation partner. It needed to help customers understand that partnering with Lakeside was the smart thing to do. That by being smart, they could transform the way they did freight, saving a small fortune in the process while freeing themselves to focus on their core business.

We've spent a lot of time so far on mid-sized to large organizations. Interestingly, when it comes to defining and staying true to a future vision for your organization, we believe that smaller companies have certain advantages, and they can certainly learn to have influence that far outweighs their size. Consider the Littlefield Agency, a thirty-person marketing and advertising agency we studied in Tulsa, Oklahoma. That's right, Tulsa. Thousands of miles from the media centers of New York and California, deep amid what coasties call "flyover states." Celebrating its thirty-fifth year in business in 2015, Littlefield has always been proud of its regional business footprint, and even though it won national awards for its work, it wasn't trying to go national with multiple office locations. The company was plenty ambitious, but this did not mean executives there aspired for the company to be massive. They were far more interested in being a company that mattered in their hometown of Tulsa.

Since the late 1990s, Littlefield had been punching above its weight and fending off its coastal rivals while landing and retaining high-value accounts like the BOK Financial Corporation (one of the fifty biggest banks in America) and Ditch Witch, a leading international manufacturer of underground construction equipment. Littlefield had done this by insisting on being treated like a partner, and by being willing to challenge its clients when it knew they were making mistakes or taking unnecessary risks. Littlefield founder David Littlefield explained the way he saw it: "We work best, and our clients see the most robust results, when we are allowed a seat at their strategy table. Our outside-in perspective, representing the point of view of their customers, brings tremendous value to the candid strategic brand discussions that need to take place."[12]

Back in 1995, David Littlefield and his colleagues at the firm heard about the success some British ad agencies were having with a new approach to developing message strategy that relied heavily on qualitative research—small, interactive focus groups and personal interviews, even store and home visits—to get at what consumers actually think and feel. The Brits called this methodology Account Planning, and used a highly disciplined research study approach that delves into the psychology of how people make buying decisions. The discipline of Account Planning takes the guesswork out of the creative messaging process, as it produces evidence of the most relevant message strategy for the brand's best customers and prospects. This gives the client much more confidence to move forward with its marketing investment and an opportunity for a better ROI.

That might sound obvious today, but back then it wasn't how you did things in the middle of North America. Advertising was still dominated by *Mad Men* executives who regarded kick-ass creativity as the key to success. They sold creative ideas. Littlefield, by contrast, wanted to sell results. Sure, they had always embraced traditional research, but Account Planning is an approach that provides deeper, richer consumer insights, so Littlefield put this research front and center of the agency's value proposition, instead of the creativity of superstar individuals. Maybe because they were such a small firm in a remote location, Littlefield wasn't afraid to jump on the new approach and adapt it to its context. After all, what did the company really have to lose?

David and his colleagues brought this thinking to one of their clients, BOK Financial. The bank was used to driving positioning strategy solely based upon its internal perspective. Littlefield started saying, "But how do we know that message will be relevant to our customers?" Again, it sounds obvious, but ask yourself: How often do you *assume* you know what your customers want? How often do you develop your marketing and sales messages in the echo chamber of your internal meeting rooms with your internal team? How often do you truly test what resonates in the marketplace, and then build your value proposition around that? If you partner with Littlefield, you will have no choice but to test the market!

Trading on little more than passion and conviction, coupled with a change in the bank's marketing leadership, Littlefield convinced the bank to try out Account Planning. It paid off. The organization's messages became more relevant and targeted. Their customers related to it and prospective customers self-selected into a relationship. Such success fueled Littlefield's rise; its business with the bank increased almost tenfold, as did the value it returned. Instead of relegating Littlefield to the marketing function long after the strategy was developed, the bank engaged Littlefield to work with its most senior executives, ensuring that brand remained a key point of differentiation in an industry plagued by product-based commoditization.

How often do you <u>assume</u> you know what your customers want? How often do you develop your marketing and sales messages in the echo chamber of your internal meeting rooms with your internal team? How often do you truly test what resonates in the marketplace, and then build your value proposition around that? If you partner with Littlefield, you will have no choice but to test the market!

On the back of such success with BOK Financial and other clients, Littlefield committed fully to the underlying premise of this new, customer-focused research as it looked to its future—one based on the notion that outcomes for clients matter most, not maximizing your business or your artistic and creative aspirations. But if you don't understand the environment you're working in, how can you create value for the client and its brand? First you need a disciplined way to explore the marketplace. The Littlefield team was so convinced of the power of this approach that they drew a big line in the sand, refusing to work with new clients who didn't want to spend the time and money on Account Planning and instead wanted the agency to guess what was the right thing to say.

While most of Littlefield's clients liked the idea of Account Planning, selling them on it was a different matter. The research wasn't cheap. For a small client, research would add $75,000 to a typical project, and the charge for bigger clients would go well into the six digits. On top of that, Littlefield asked for three months to conduct the Account Planning work and develop the appropriate strategic and tactical solutions and storytelling options, while other agencies that skimped on research needed only half that time. Nevertheless, Littlefield eventually decided to go all in: no Account Planning, no deal. The company became willing to say no to clients who wouldn't partner at that level, and to work that wouldn't result in the types of outcomes it wanted to deliver.

Playing high is scary; Oklahoma is a small market, so Littlefield didn't have endless streams of prospects knocking on its doors. But Littlefield was too far into the journey to head back. As David remembered, "We didn't want to guess anymore and get fired if we were wrong."[13] This commitment led to the mantra that guides everything Littlefield stands for, and the value it brings to its clients: *It doesn't matter how well you say the wrong thing.*

In our research, we discovered time and time again that old paradigms of relationship selling have been discarded. The golf course and relationship tenure deals and the traditional back-slapping quid pro quo that once happened are history. Today it is first about value, or, as many of the executives we interviewed put it, "What have you done for me lately?" The way David Littlefield saw it, companies had been guessing about what mattered to their customers for too long, and that had to stop.

Littlefield believed that its ability to build long-term relationships at the most senior levels rested on its ability to get it right. That meant more discipline up front. Simply put, Littlefield had to hold its ground.

Like DPR, Littlefield chose its partners carefully. David Littlefield reviewed each prospective client before working with them, asking questions about whether the business had a product or service that inspired, if it required strategic leadership, and if it wanted to create work that would stand out—that would make an impact. These criteria went far beyond the usual concerns of "Can you pay me on time, and how much are you worth to me?" By being selective, David avoided that nagging feeling many of us have experienced that all of the decision-making power rests with the buyer. Like much bigger organizations, such as DPR, David simply seized back control himself. He described it well: "You simply cannot start a long-term relationship built on trust and values if you don't believe that you are the equal of the person sitting across from you. Even if you do get the business, is it really worth being treated poorly and being seen as inferior by the people that buy your services?"[14]

After Littlefield engaged on a project, the company pushed and pushed and pushed some more when it believed a course of action was right for a client. For instance, during the early 2000s, Littlefield proposed adding more digital content to the marketing mix for another client, Ditch Witch. The client was reluctant, saying that its customers in the underground construction industry were out working in the field, not tethered to a desk with a computer. Littlefield could see the importance the internet was going to have on businesses, in both the B2B and consumer spaces. Mobile technology would improve and people would have access to the internet outside an office setting, and Littlefield wanted to have a voice in that future.

So the firm kept raising the issue every year, even preparing examples, doing its best to be assertive on that issue without totally annoying the client. Then a lightbulb went on in the client's mind as it saw both the role social and digital media were taking in its employees' own lives and the advancements made in mobile phone technology. If Littlefield hadn't been persistent with its client all along, the client probably would have wondered what else Littlefield had missed—why Littlefield wasn't forward thinking, anticipating this. There would have been an account review, and the client probably would have hired an agency that specialized in digital media. Instead, having already done the homework, Littlefield could prepare a digital launch relatively quickly with an improved, easier-to-navigate, responsive website and a more aggressive social and digital media strategy. Because Littlefield stayed true to its future self, its *client* came back to its trusted partner and said, "You were right!"

Now you understand how a regional agency in Tulsa not only rose to be the obvious choice in its local market, but also has gained and kept a national reputation as a leader in its field. Having influence isn't just the province of large organizations. Anybody can do it. It happens when you have the clarity, courage, and determination to define and stay true to a future self. That is something everybody not only can do, but should.

Influence isn't fundamentally about what a company *has*. It's about what a company *does*, and even more profoundly, what a company *is*—what it's made of, its character. In this section, we've seen that companies accelerate their journey to becoming the obvious choice by positioning themselves to conduct business with the right customers and doing the right work. They go head-on to meet the challenges of gaining access, saying no to work, screening customers, revamping their go-to-market teams and processes, and being true to their future selves. And in doing so, they create organizations that can be selective in how they work, with whom they work, and the value they deliver—all the while insisting on delivering the highest possible value-for-effort combination.

> Influence isn't fundamentally about what a company <u>has</u>. It's about what a company <u>does</u>, and even more profoundly, what a company <u>is</u>—what it's made of, its character.

The companies we've researched raised their selling game, deploying techniques that you, too, can apply in your own organization. They worked hard to elevate their brand images, intentionally building brands aligned to and worthy of their desired market positions. They invested in a go-to-market function capable of appealing to a higher class of buyers. They focused on the *right* buyer, not just anyone with a checkbook. And they acted like a peer or a partner, not merely a supplier. All of this took serious clarity and courage, traits that are often, sadly, in short supply these days, but that we know you have (or want to have), or you wouldn't be reading this book.

It's not easy to stare commodification in the face, nor is it easy to leap ahead at considerable expense when all of your competitors are standing still. Yet as risky as it might seem to do what Lakeside, DPR, or Littlefield did, the even greater risk is to do nothing. Stasis feels safe, but you're placing a bet that nothing is going to change in your industry. But markets do change, every day and at lightning speed. In tomorrow's world, they'll change faster still.

You need to muster the inner fortitude, the self-confidence, to make that first move, even when doing so might seem crazy from a conventional perspective. You need to *earn* the right to engage with senior leaders by offering more value. The way you earn it is by stepping up and claiming your place, sometimes at a short-term personal cost to you. When commodification looms, don't compromise your values for the sake of landing a quick sale. Reaffirm those values, even if only a relative few people on the customer side "get it." Those few people are all you need. Select your customers, don't let them select you. And select your work—don't agree to do anything at all just to make a dollar.

Most importantly, figure out your future self and be true to it. It will pay off. The only way to avoid sinking into the morass of commodification is to actually be different, in a way that hauls you out of the depths of procurement negotiations and into the selection as the obvious choice. Not everyone can do it. But you can, if you are willing to stand confidently on the edge of disruption and to help your clients stand with you. Are you? If so, there's still work to be done, so let's keep going, by taking a look at two other critical areas of relationships that you need to elevate: building engaged partnerships and making connections by seeing the whole board.

Bring It to Life . . .

1. Do a "back of the napkin" estimate of what percentage of your time you spend focused on the senior, more influential people in your customers' organizations (or your own) compared to lower-level, less strategic people. How could you use the insights from your edge of disruption to gain access to and establish credibility with more of the senior people? Take an objective look at your current go-to-market approach. Does it enable you to play high consistently? Does it highlight your elevated perspective and encourage your customers to engage you in more strategic conversations? If not, what needs to change so that it does?

2. Based on the identified changes, develop a small number of pilots you can test quickly in the market and begin a process of doing so with a select set of customers and prospects. Review, refine, repeat.

3. Get together with some of your high-potential go-to-market team members (or those who interact directly with your internal customers) and do three rough customer profiles:
    a. High value: The customers you love and want more of.
    b. High potential: The customers capable of becoming high value.
    c. Low value: The customers who take up more time and effort than they are ultimately worth.

Now brainstorm a list of ideas for each of them:

a. High value: How could you spend more time and exchange even more value with these customers?

b. High potential: How could you migrate these customers to the high-value profile? What could you do immediately to begin migrating specific customers?

c. Low value: How could you engage in a constructive conversation with these customers that catalyzes them to evolve and move into the high-potential column? For those customers that will never migrate, how could you constructively and respectfully exit your relationship with them?

4. Be ruthlessly honest with yourself. Where are you cutting corners in your relationships (internally and externally), and behaving in ways misaligned with your future self? Prioritize which relationships you need to rebuild, start taking steps to do so, and begin the change journey to eliminate misaligned behaviors.

5. What one behavior do some of your customers consistently engage in that you know destroys value and is misaligned with your future self? What process or standard could you enforce that would reduce and possibly even eliminate this damaging practice?

CHAPTER 5

PARTNER: Engage Like You Mean It

H AVE YOU EVER HAD A RELATIONSHIP where no matter what you said and did, it always led to an argument or disagreement? Where it seemed like everything you did, even with the best of intentions, was further evidence to the other party that you were not to be trusted, which in turn triggered them to be even harsher in their assessment of you, leading you to react in a negative way that further cemented their impression, thus feeding the downward spiral and degeneration of that relationship? Most of us have had something like that happen in a lifetime, and it doesn't feel great. We hope that you can reflect on the experience but that you are not still in it.

Have you had the opposite? A relationship where each action you took and investment you made was welcomed and appreciated. One where the gratitude and positive feedback spurring you on to do more for this person in turn created a reciprocity in their words and actions as well. Where each step both parties took would send the relationship spiraling further up, and where the relationship fed itself?

When we encounter people, teams, and companies that matter—all of whom are the obvious choice in their markets— they are the ones that seek out and intentionally create such relationships. We call these *engaged partnerships*, and having the ability to build them consistently, with clients and other key stakeholders, is critical if you want to add more value.

The best companies invest in their relationships in such an authentic way that the returns they create are more than sufficient to justify further investments. They don't see relationships as a cost to be managed, but instead view them as critical to their ability to create value. They know that to not only see the opportunities at the edge of disruption but also have the understanding required to execute solutions that make the most of such opportunities, they need to create a partnership with a consumer or client beyond the typical cordial and sometimes adversarial nature of professional relationships. In our research we consistently found that the best companies create these kinds of partnerships in three ways.

First, companies that matter establish programs or models for engaging in partnerships with the clients and prospects that *create intimacy and understanding.* They do not rely on any one transaction, or the health and vitality of a relationship from the past. They are constantly reinvesting, re-creating the understanding needed to ensure they can create more value, and they build programs to support that kind of engaged partnership. The level of understanding achieved by these dynamic programs results in companies that are always "in the know," that see opportunities before the competition. Sometimes the programs are formal, and sometimes companies simply send their people to "stand in the traffic" with their clients. Either way, they forge lasting

> Companies that matter do not rely on any one transaction, or the health and vitality of a relationship from the past. They are constantly reinvesting, re-creating the understanding needed to ensure they can create more value, and they build programs to support that kind of engaged partnership.

partnerships that feed an understanding of customer needs that is critical to elevating relationships.

Second, the best companies reinforce the value they bring to partnerships by taking the understanding they have developed and turning it into an even more compelling and vibrant experience for their customers. They *convert their ideas into insights and their insights into application*. This positive outcome for the client encourages further sharing and openness from them, which in turn generates even more applicable insights and outcomes.

Finally, they *vest in the success of their customer* and remove barriers, in some cases financially tying their own success directly to that of the individual client. Vesting is not always financial—many programs create symbiotic business for the seller and the buyer of services, so when one does well, so does the other. These vested partnerships create a level of trust that inspires an elevated relationship. By creating transparency and removing conflicts of interest, the best companies create the environment for necessary collaboration to solve the most complex challenges, the ones that really matter.

> Vesting is not always financial—many programs create symbiotic business for the seller and the buyer of services, so when one does well, so does the other.

Companies that do these three things inspire the desire and willingness of their clients to seek them out as strategic partners. Together they solve problems that result in more value creation, ultimately making them the obvious choice in their markets.

For you, these partnerships might be with internal customers—the people you or your team serve every day. Or they might be with external customers—the buyers of the products and services your company produces. They might even be with suppliers, or with other industry players or groups that are meaningful to your business. Regardless of who they are with, these partnerships are engaged in ways that drive value that your competition can't replicate. Let's look at some examples of companies that have managed to create just that kind of engaged partnership in each of the three areas.

CREATE INTIMACY AND UNDERSTANDING

Even a quick look at Deloitte Canada affirms that it matters. Deloitte Canada has become the obvious choice, particularly for mid-sized companies in Canada. It is 40 percent larger than its nearest rival, and generates more revenue per professional staff member than any of the other major Canadian accounting firms. And it's not just with the big, publicly listed audit clients, either. It has built much of its success selling to the mid-market as well.

If you delve further into Deloitte Canada's story, you find that it has elevated its relationships in a focused and deliberate way with this critical market. How? In part through a ground-breaking program called Best Managed.

Deloitte Canada inherited Best Managed from Arthur Andersen in 2002, as Andersen was exiting the market. Mid-sized private companies (those with revenues between $10 million and $250 million) have become especially important for accounting firms since those heady days, because unlike publicly listed clients, they can buy tax, risk, and transactional services as well as audit services from a single provider. It is a challenging market. Mid-sized companies are a fragmented group, and no single channel or marketing platform existed from which firms like Deloitte Canada could connect with them. Since these companies were privately held, information about them had also been very scarce. What drove these businesses? What were their main challenges? Where were their hidden growth opportunities? How could professional services firms support that growth? It was almost impossible to develop a deep enough understanding of this marketplace to know what edge of disruption would be most meaningful, and where companies like Deloitte Canada could create more value.

Enter Best Managed. Every year, hundreds of mid-market companies vie to gain admission to the program and become known as one of Canada's best-managed firms. It's a rigorous designation that yields brand recognition to the winning firms, and to Deloitte and its program partners as well. If the program sounds like a public relations ploy, another one of those awards

programs that professional services firms give out, rest assured—
Best Managed is much more than that.

Administered by Deloitte Canada in a partnership that
includes, among others, CIBC, National Post, Queen's School
of Business, and MacKay CEO Forums, Best Managed is a meaningful designation that mid-sized companies can earn, much
as larger companies might earn recognition as one of *Fortune*
magazine's "Best Companies to Work For." Applying rigorous
criteria, Best Managed aims to benchmark and grade mid-sized
companies on the quality of their management and strategy,
distinguishing the relatively few companies that will endure
from those that likely won't.

To give you some sense of just how valuable the Best Managed
designation is, consider what Malcolm Hunter, president and
CEO of Deeley Harley-Davidson Canada, one of the largest independent distributors of Harleys, told us: "Our associates take so
much pride in that little Best Managed logo on our business card
or on our stationery or whatever, that I have started to believe
it is up there in their minds, with as much pride as the bar and
shield that we have for Harley-Davidson. I keep on telling my
associates here that I believe a lot of our success we've been
able to receive over the years is really the discipline around the
program that Deloitte Canada has done."[1]

Think about this statement for a minute. The Harley-
Davidson logo has likely been tattooed on more human skin
than any other corporate logo in the history of the world. And
here one of the company's most senior executives in one of its
most significant markets is saying that his staff has as much
pride in the Best Managed designation as they do in that logo.

Part of the reason Best Managed is much more than just a
PR program is that it drives incredible value to the participants,
well beyond any typical relationship they might have with a
professional services firm. In addition, the fundamental purpose of the Best Managed program is how it reflects Deloitte
Canada's commitment to supporting the health of the Canadian
economy. One of the partners who championed the program
early on told us that there are "many private companies that

are doing tremendous things, the backbone of the economy. You hear so much talk about the importance of the entrepreneur, and yet almost nothing was being done to understand and help develop these nationally significant leaders. And this was the genesis of the program—contribute to Canada by developing more of them."

Although we were impressed by Deloitte Canada's public-spiritedness (a trait we'll see again in Section Three, "Elevated Impact"), what especially interested us about Best Managed was how it completely integrated value for the participants and value for Deloitte Canada by creating long-lasting relationships that really mattered to both companies. The design of the Best Managed program creates an avenue for Deloitte Canada to not only understand more deeply its clients and their challenges, but also refresh and renew that understanding year in and year out. It is a program that perpetually drives intimacy between Deloitte and this critical market segment.

When we talked with Malcolm Hunter, he was in his eighteenth year of the Best Managed program. He shared that "I used to dread my interviews with Best Managed coaches because they're so good at what they do. You can't hide." When asked if it was easier now, he said emphatically that it wasn't. "It's hard every time. It hasn't changed. It's still painful because they keep on raising the bar." He so valued the challenge and rigor that his participation in the Best Managed program brought that he lined up year in and year out for the intensive process.[2]

At the most basic level, Best Managed is probably the most comprehensive survey available today that delves into the lives and practices of Canada's mid-market companies. In Stage 1 of the designation, companies enter strategic information about their businesses. This includes their performance, their approaches to strategy and management, and many other critically important areas. Up to 10,000 businesses are invited to participate in this stage during any given year, feeding a comprehensive and data-driven view of the market.

In Stage 2, the data collection gets even more intense, with companies participating in a qualitative "deep dive." Deloitte

Canada selects between 200 and 300 Stage 1 companies to engage in a time-intensive twelve-month coaching and examination process provided by CIBC and Deloitte Canada. The coaching, which is both high quality and free of charge to the companies, provides executives with ways to realize new levels of self-awareness about their behavior and competence. As coaches put executives through the paces, Deloitte Canada receives a unique viewpoint into these businesses, providing the insight needed to connect to common themes in their visions, their strategy, and even relationship dynamics among family members in these firms.

Can you imagine how valuable it would be to you if you were able to get free coaching from one of the world's leading consultancies, and at the same time have access to synthesized perspectives on how other companies similar to yours were solving their most complex problems? At the same time, the program enhances Deloitte Canada's ability to develop relevant content and services to meet the needs and desires of this high-value target segment; it makes them better advisors, providing guidance that matters to their customers.

The program generates the basic data most market analysis requires: size, growth rate, head count, and so on. But it also generates real insights about common behaviors, ambitions, and challenges of these companies. Deloitte Canada can benchmark hundreds of firms against one another in a way no one else can. In short, Deloitte Canada has developed an asset it can use to create value for its customers and itself. The outcome? Deloitte Canada can drive more thoughtful advice and more productive guidance for clients in this particular market, helping them to be more successful and laddering up to the desire to see a healthy mid-market economy in Canada.

Even better, the program builds an asset that clients and prospects engage in year after year, so it is always fresh. We have sat with these companies at the annual gala event and seen the connection between them and their Deloitte coaches. It goes beyond any typical business relationship. The program creates opportunities for insights that are not merely actionable but fresh, vital, and of the moment. Even the survey that Deloitte Canada repeats with thousands of companies each year represents the virtual pulse of the mid-market in Canada, offering an evolving glimpse into executives' moods and decisions. This fresh and insightful data makes Deloitte Canada the go-to company for mid-market clients.

Deloitte Canada's insight is the most current because it is based on relationships that are refreshed every year through the selection process. It is also woven into the very fabric of the organization. Deloitte Canada's senior leaders and decision makers, when faced with strategic decisions about where to invest in development of products and services, have at their disposal the current heartbeat of the firm's core target market. They apply this insight consciously and unconsciously to everything they do to create maximum value for their customers. To leaders of mid-sized firms, that level of knowledge and expertise is compelling and virtually impossible to find anywhere else.

One of the most intriguing elements of the Best Managed program is that it is able to keep its participants coming back. They come back because the value is there. The firm can benchmark mid-market company behaviors against financial performance, through multiple economic cycles. And Deloitte Canada can compare a given firm's financial well-being to that of hundreds of similar firms at different stages in their maturity and growth. The leaders at Deloitte Canada know better than anyone else the phases these companies went through, as well as the inflection points that are critical moments for mid-market companies. The firm could predict hot topics that CEOs will face, challenges they are likely to encounter, opportunities that will arise—the list is endless. Deloitte Canada's Best Managed program creates better insight than any one expert or CEO could about what it takes to grow a successful business—and it does so better than any white paper, because it provides the opportunity for dialogue and input from people who've been in the trenches. What's even better is that the more participants come back, and the more others join, the more powerful the program becomes for the participants and for Deloitte Canada.

As Deloitte Canada will tell you, participants who gain recognition as Best Managed companies go on to teach the next generations of participants. The insights they glean generate better companies, which in turn generate new and better insights. Designated companies refer other companies to Best Managed, vouching for the program and its value. The bigger the program gets, the more prestigious the designation becomes. The longer the program runs, and the more companies cumulatively participate, the more value the same process yields for Deloitte Canada. And the stronger the mid-market becomes, the better the market is for Deloitte Canada. Best Managed has become a program that truly matters to all participants and providers, and the value it generates is priceless.

Generating dynamic, constantly evolving relationships serves Deloitte Canada's business development in another way. It helps build goodwill by giving Deloitte Canada constant contact with the marketplace. In one interview we did, a Deloitte Canada partner told us that the firm invested in Best Managed in part so that it could always remain "in the traffic." This partner told us: "Business development in professional services firms is a long-term affair. And in a relationship development approach like Best Managed it can be five to ten years. In addition to bettering entrepreneurship in Canada, the initial investments into Best Managed were so we could be *in the traffic*—be in the marketplace and get to know lots of different companies, and lots of different CEOs. These firms will change; they will buy and be bought. And they will grow. And we will be right there in the room, advising them when they do. With goodwill and trust built over years of investing in them and companies like them."[3]

> Being "in the traffic" means standing shoulder to shoulder with your clients, essentially meeting them on their ground—being in the room, in the hallway conversations, in the planning meetings, adding value long before there is an economic opportunity for you.

Being "in the traffic" means standing shoulder to shoulder with your clients, essentially meeting them on their ground—being in the room, in the hallway conversations, in the planning meetings, adding value long before there is an economic opportunity for you. Deloitte Canada does that by embedding its leaders in the Best Managed vetting process. There are other ways to develop engaged partnerships that help drive similar levels of insight, without the organization and structure of a program like Best Managed. For example, some companies embed their partnership development into their account model with clients.

An especially good example of this type of engaged partnership is a promotional products company we studied; we'll call it ProductPromo. When you think of promotional products, you probably think of T-shirts being shot out of cannons at insane speeds, or bobbleheads of your favorite sports heroes. It's not cutting-edge stuff, and as you might expect, the promotional products industry indeed has a very low barrier of entry. Every day new players enter the fray, from the kid sitting in his college dorm room with a cool new idea for a T-shirt, all the way up to mega-chains like Staples with its promotional office-products catalogs. The fragmentation that results leads to an unsophisticated approach to merchandising at most customer organizations, with procurement officers treating merchandise as a commodity and bidding prices ever lower.

Good luck trying to buy this way from ProductPromo. Like Lakeside or DPR, ProductPromo would strongly consider not even accepting your order. The company requires that its clients be long term and large enough to justify the time and energy ProductPromo spends applying its resources to deeply understanding the client's unique needs and desires. Customers must also understand the power of merchandising in brand building, and they must be willing to let their merchandise partner jump in and help them create a brand launch and concept from scratch.

Talk about being in the traffic. Unlike its competitors, ProductPromo embeds itself or "co-locates" in the internal creative team of its customers, usually in the marketing department, where brand building takes place. ProductPromo wants a desk . . . a security pass . . . the works. And the company wants to contribute to brand development from day one, assuring that merchandising is used strategically and effectively to support the campaign. What results is a far more powerful use of merchandise for the customer. ProductPromo, meanwhile, develops a deep understanding of the brand, the product launch, and the campaign that can't be commoditized. Not surprisingly, this intimate go-to-market strategy allows ProductPromo to emerge over time as the obvious choice for supplying the merchandise. Who else would the customer buy from but the very originators of the promotional idea, the people who have become valued members of the creative team?

ProductPromo's co-location strategy ensures that the company's sales team is roaming the halls and having unplanned conversations with the client's team. The sales team becomes "part of the furniture" at their client's site, as ProductPromo's COO put it to us. People see ProductPromo personnel around all the time. They eat with them. Share ideas with them. Invite them to meetings for their input. This familiarity creates an implicit trust that allows ProductPromo to serve as a strategic partner rather than as a commoditized supplier. As the COO remarked, "Being engaged on client site from the very beginning allows [ProductPromo] to be a partner in the solution. Above and beyond the product, we are adding a lot of value from a creative perspective. Value that many of our competitors should and don't provide."

The case of ProductPromo reveals just how powerful a more active, engaged, collaborative approach to insight generation can be. The company controls the global promotional products spend for some of the most recognizable brands on earth, and has built from scratch a business generating hundreds of millions of dollars in revenue, in a market defined by smaller and more fragmented players. According to Promotional Products Association International, there are 23,740 such companies, with an average annual revenue of $425,000.[4] In fact 22,767 of them have annual revenues of less than $2.5 million. With more than ten times that in annual revenue, ProductPromo has become the obvious choice, and its strategy of co-location to ensure engaged partnership is at the core of how it generates opportunities at a size and magnitude that outstrips its competition. It affirms that companies in any industry can benefit from cultivating deeper engagement with customers. Even in an industry that seems hopelessly commoditized, stagnant, crowded, and lacking in innovation, there are ways to engage more deeply and to differentiate your organization as a result.

Because ProductPromo is in the trenches with its customers, it's the first to hear of any rumors about impending product launches, and thus the first to know of any likely need for merchandise in the future. These conversations happen months, even years before an RFP would be created in a traditional procurement process, leaving time for ProductPromo to create highly customized and differentiated merchandising solutions for the client's brand.

ProductPromo creates the opportunity for engaged partnership by insisting on being a part of the strategy and the process of building the larger picture of which it is ultimately only one part. It refuses to be relegated, and it commits to being present and contributing in a way that makes it the obvious choice for some of the biggest brands in the world. And Deloitte Canada has a bespoke program that helps to create a healthy and thriving mid-market in Canada, while building engagement and partnership at a level that would otherwise be hard to find—partnership that truly matters to everyone who participates.

> The idea of partnership isn't just for salespeople—it is for anyone who provides a product or service, internally or externally. And let's face it—in business, that's everyone!

Both are examples of ways to get in the traffic with your customers and to elevate relationships through a much deeper understanding than any of their competitors can replicate. What are some ways you might engage more deeply with some of your customers, whether they are internal or external, big or small? Are there opportunities for you or your team to get to know more about the people you serve internally and the way your products are used?

The idea of partnership isn't just for salespeople—it is for anyone who provides a product or service, internally or externally. And let's face it—in business, that's everyone! We believe you (and anyone else) have the opportunity to build engaged partnerships, in whatever capacity you serve—external or internal, sales or any other function.

CONVERT INSIGHTS INTO APPLICATION

If you really want to matter, you have to be able to add value in application, not just in theory. Doing that means having the ability to convert ideas into insights and insights into action for your customers. Deloitte Canada does that with the Best Managed program, and ProductPromo does it by being present with its clients. Companies that transform into the obvious choice are also able to convert insights about what they see in their markets into action for their brands, and to drive elevated relationships as an outcome.

These companies take the insight that comes from their elevated perspectives to make better decisions, shining a light on challenges and opportunities and creating products and services customers didn't even know they wanted. There is no better example of this in our research group than BlueShore Financial. This company has redefined a customer service experience in an unusual and remarkable way by converting a lot of data about its market into insight about how to best deliver to its target audience.

Stroll into a branch of your bank or credit union, and you usually find a pretty standard corporate environment: bland colors, run-of-the-mill office furniture, a flat-screen monitor or two advertising the latest interest rates, potted ferns in the corners. If you're like us, you've wondered: Why can't they make these places more pleasant, interesting, and meaningful for the people who bother to come in? After all, you've taken time out of your busy day to stop by; couldn't the place at least be engaging?

Someone has. And it isn't Citibank. Or Bank of America. Or any of the other American financial goliaths. It isn't even an

American bank. It's BlueShore Financial, a local credit union based in North Vancouver, British Columbia.

BlueShore Financial doesn't have branches per se. The credit union used to, but in 2006 it began rolling out "Financial Spas," boutique-like spaces decorated in the style of "West Coast Zen." They feature a stylishly minimalist décor, beverage and hot towel service, and concierges—all of which help create a more intimate environment for delivering expert financial advice (or as BlueShore Financial terms it, "financial wellness") to a higher-net-worth clientele in BlueShore Financial's area.

BlueShore's Financial Spas are all the more striking when you consider the organization's history. If you asked affluent Vancouver residents at the turn of the century whether they associated BlueShore Financial with a sophisticated, upscale banking experience, they wouldn't have just said no. They would have said no *and* given you a blank stare. Nobody had ever heard of BlueShore Financial back then because the organization was known at the time as North Shore Credit Union. And rather than serving the West Coast Zen crowd, since its founding in 1941 the credit union had catered to blue-collar workers in the shipbuilding and deep-sea fishing trades.

Today, Vancouver's upscale banking consumers *do* know BlueShore Financial, and they like it, enough that many of them have become members and consolidated their holdings there. In little more than a decade, BlueShore Financial's assets under administration have grown from $800 million to $3.5 billion in 2014. In 2014 alone, BlueShore Financial saw an 18 percent rise in deposits and a 16 percent rise in assets over the previous year, more than double the numbers of its closest competitors.

We were curious about how a fairly ordinary credit union came to pioneer the Financial Spa idea, so we sat down with president and CEO Chris Catliff in 2014 and again in early 2015. The first thing we discovered was that BlueShore Financial's innovation was even more unlikely than we had first thought. Prior to Catliff's arrival in 2000, he told us, the then North Shore Credit Union wasn't just stagnant as an organization; it was floundering. The emergence of new technology, the costs of compliance, and the relentless competitive pressure coming from Canada's five largest banks had left the credit union struggling. It had looked to merge with others to remain viable, yet prospective mergers fell apart. North Shore was grappling with precarious financials and high employee turnover.

Catliff realized that the time had come to do something drastic. The organization had to make a leap—and not look back. And that's exactly what he did. Catliff and his team forged a plan to transform a garden-variety credit union into a wealth-management institution focused on clients with complex and sophisticated financial needs. Does this sound familiar? The financial services company was creating a new future self to differentiate itself in the marketplace and raise its influence with a new buyer of its services.

It achieved this by clearly identifying its target market and serving this audience in a way that went beyond everyday banking transactions to offer a more valuable and personalized financial-planning experience. This strategic shift seemed to make sense: North Shore's member base of blue-collar workers had dwindled by the turn of this century. The credit union's local market footprint was shifting, with these traditional members being replaced in the local geography by swelling ranks of white-collar residents with complex financial needs. Indeed, at the time, the footprint included two of the five wealthiest postal codes in all of Canada.

Catliff and his team faced a choice: Keep the credit union rigidly attached to its founding market segment and become irrelevant or obsolete, or adapt to the changing socioeconomic patterns and create an organization that met the needs of this new demographic. It chose the latter and repositioned itself to thrive, grow, and take advantage of new opportunities.

In 2005, Catliff captured his strategy in a visioning document for employees that imagined what the credit union would look like in five years: "Due to our superior technology and quality of advice, we have been ranked as the #1 place to do business by the mass affluent/emerging wealthy segment . . . The various business lines . . . are using their business acumen and knowledge to produce superior rewards while mitigating risk."[5] Notice that Catliff clearly articulated BlueShore Financial's desire to become the *obvious choice*—a bold statement from a credit union about to challenge industry norms.

This outlook is just the sort of ambition required to stand out from competitors. It fell in line with the spirit of the other successful companies we studied. Notice, too, that like DPR, Lakeside, and Littlefield, Catliff also articulated very clearly which customer segments the organization would target: the mass affluent (those with $100,000 to $500,000 in investable assets) and the emerging wealthy (those with $500,000 to $1 million). BlueShore Financial would not actively target other groups in its geographic footprint. The concept of segmentation is obviously not new; what set BlueShore apart is the way it took this laser focus on a specific target group to create an unparalleled understanding of their needs and then apply the insights to shaping the actual experience and product offering of the credit union.

BlueShore even took the segmentation work a step further than we normally see. It pushed to create a "segment of one" that it used to create highly personalized financial planning and recommendations that would enable BlueShore to play a meaningful role in helping clients improve their overall financial well-being. The concept of segmentation is not radical; many companies do it. What was powerful about BlueShore is the way it drew clear boundaries around its demographic, the depth it went to in that segmentation, and its willingness to make the investments required to create a set of services, a model for engagement, and an experience compelling to those hyper-focused targets.

Catliff's strategy was not without its critics. Many credit union leaders and industry watchers perceived the strategy as an opportunistic move incompatible with the collaborative and cooperative values of the credit union system. Credit union–style institutions in Canada had always had a democratic, grassroots feel to them, founded as they were by customers who felt that banks were ignoring their needs. In openly targeting affluent members and those on the path to becoming affluent, BlueShore

Financial seemed to be sacrificing its cooperative roots for the almighty dollar.

Catliff and his team had two responses. First, the credit union's ability to thrive and grow organically was at stake. And second, its new strategy was not without a public service dimension. Even though on a national level the mass-affluent segments Catliff targeted held the majority of all wealth, few financial institutions were effectively catering to their needs. They were active members of the community and had growing wealth and increased financial-planning needs, yet they were "under-served," as they did not yet qualify for private banking. Why not have a credit union dedicated to serving them?

While developing their strategy, Catliff and his team amassed important insights about mass-affluent and emerging-wealthy members. Catliff heard from BlueShore Financial's time-depleted target market, "Look, I'm busy; tell me something I don't already know, something that makes me money or improves my financial well-being. And, ask me quickly if I want it, yes or no, preferably by email, and then just do it, so I know you've got my back." BlueShore Financial had discovered that these members wanted four basic things from a financial partner: they wanted their advisor to proactively contact them about their financial planning, to work with their best interests in mind, to make banking as easy as possible, and to assist them with their overall financial well-being. The credit union's edge of disruption would be creating solutions that brought these four needs together in a creative and satisfying way for its target market.

In particular, the idea of financial "well-being" is what prompted Catliff's team to focus on the retail experience and the creation of Financial Spas. As Catliff realized, for affluent clients, money was a highly emotional topic, linking to important concepts such as freedom, family, and opportunity. Just as people went to spas to attend to their physical well-being, they could go to a Financial Spa to attend to their financial well-being. BlueShore Financial's branches would become oases, places to relax, restore, and feel pampered by financial experts who understood clients' needs and who truly cared.

As part of its offering to meet these clearly articulated emotional needs, BlueShore Financial took its insight and applied it to both the in-branch experience and the focus on wealth management. It completely reimagined the way it feels to enter a financial services environment. The credit union was able to take its elevated perspective and connect it to an elevated relationship with its target market. By doing so, it effectively challenged some deeply held beliefs about what a branch really is, how financial advisory relationships should work, and what products the organization should focus on. By applying these lessons and deepening their understanding of their members, BlueShore Financial's team transformed the financial services experience and, in the process, better met the needs of their target market. This allowed the credit union to create more perceived value to its clients, and in turn become the obvious financial institution of choice.

But there is more to the story. Like the Best Managed program, these Financial Spas created deeper engagement with customers. The physical environment of the spas was starkly different from that of a typical branch of either a bank or a credit union. Most branches have physical barriers to intimacy and are set up only to efficiently process transactions. These spas were designed with an open, airy feel, to be a place to come and relax. To spend time. To engage in conversation. And to solve complex financial challenges. They stimulated intimate conversations and were more conducive to a human connection. The human connection triggered greater levels of honesty and openness, which in turn enabled BlueShore Financial to better tailor financial products and services to member needs. The increased relevance of these new applications inspired members to go deeper again and share more. On and on it goes, generating more value as each new action is taken.

Companies that matter know that clients will share information as long as the clients believe it will be applied to create a more compelling and relevant experience for them. Members of BlueShore Financial will share their deepest and most intimate goals and challenges, if they know the credit union will use that information to proactively create solutions that mitigate those risks and enable those goals. It's through the application of what they have learned that BlueShore Financial was able to elevate its relationships. And, as we are about to discover, it was by seeing the client through a human lens, rather than as a number on a spreadsheet, that the organization was able to do so.

> Companies that matter know that clients will share information as long as the clients believe it will be applied to create a more compelling and relevant experience for them.

Turning insight into action means having both the perspective and the relationships needed to understand data in a different way. Companies spend billions collecting all sorts of demographic and transactional information about their customers: where they live, how much they earn, what they've purchased in the past, and so on. Unfortunately, much of this data just sits there collecting dust; it doesn't yield insight into how leaders might appeal to these groups or alter the company's offerings to meet future customer needs. It is static information and therefore fails to deliver value. We are not saying quantitative insights aren't valuable. They are, but they can only take you so far when it comes to deeply understanding your customers. You need to know who your customers really are. How they live. What they hope to accomplish. What they fear. You have to study your customers, marrying sophisticated data analysis with an equally sophisticated interpretive, ethnographic perspective that leaves you with a rich and nuanced understanding that can't be found in the numbers. You have to go further than your competitors are willing to go in order to understand the customer you want to reach. It is often through qualitative work that you develop the insight you need to generate the most valued outcomes that are relevant to the end user of your product or service.

The idea from BlueShore Financial of converting insights into action plays out in almost any environment. Other companies have been able to create similar outcomes through their relationships with customers, including the luxury car market. Let's take a look at Mercedes-Benz in Australia for a perfect example.

Like every other car company, Mercedes had been collecting customer data forever. Executives knew the ZIP codes (or post codes as we call them down under), income range, and professions of many of its successful drivers. And what did it do with that information? It built dealerships and service centers located close to where customers lived. Yet one of the company's most breakthrough sales tactics didn't emerge from that data at all. It emerged from an insight Mercedes gleaned simply from connecting with *how* those customers lived, not where they lived.

In the early 2000s, Mercedes's service teams in Australia were frustrated with something they had long since known: Many of the professionals who bought Mercedes vehicles were too busy to service their car as often as Mercedes preferred. We say "prefer" because in many cases Mercedes dealers make more money servicing their cars than they do selling them. Yet for many customers, it was too much of a hassle to call, make an appointment, and hope they received a courtesy car that, inevitably, would be two or three notches down in status from their own vehicle. Since many of these customers leased their vehicles from Mercedes, they were more inclined to forgo the frustrations of the service experience. After all, they could simply return their car in three years for a new one, and any problems that emerged from lack of service would be someone else's problem.

Puzzling over this situation, Mercedes executives had an idea: What if the company could make it easier for customers to service their cars? Executives set out to understand not just basic quantitative data about their customers, but qualitative nuances about how customers lived and worked and how the Mercedes service might better fit with the lifestyles of their wealthy customers. A key observation emerged from this research: Many of Mercedes's best customers traveled a lot for work. Travel, of course, makes it inconvenient to service a vehicle. But what Mercedes did with this experiential insight was groundbreaking.

In 2005 the company announced an agreement to build Airport Express valet centers on airport property in Sydney and

Melbourne, just three minutes from the terminals.[6] The service was launched in 2006 and 2007, and customers could drop off their cars for service and safe storage, while a staff member would immediately whisk the customers off in a private vehicle to the terminal of choice, sending them on their way. For the customer, this was much faster than looking for a parking spot. While the customer was gone, a service person would arrive at the mini-dealership and drive the vehicle a few miles away to a service center to be worked on (Mercedes located the actual service centers offsite, since airport real estate was too expensive). When the customer returned, the service staff would already have the car waiting at the terminal, properly serviced.

What do you think happened with this system in place? Customers started servicing their cars far more regularly. Why? Because it was easier. Oh, and something else happened as well. Mercedes started selling more cars. Lots of them. The airport mini-dealerships became some of the most productive in Mercedes's network, selling more cars per square foot than the executives had foreseen.

Let's say that you have a day trip scheduled on Monday, and another one the following Wednesday. When you return Monday evening you are likely in one of two moods. Either you crushed it, and feel like a master of the universe, or your trip was less successful, and you feel overworked and under-rewarded. Both are mind-sets that suggest you "deserve" a new car. After the courtesy driver meets you at the terminal and takes you back to the mini-dealership, you see your C-Class is parked next to an even lovelier E-Class. Since you're going to be back Wednesday, you ask if you might take the E-Class home for a day or so, and return it when you fly again two days later. Of course, the Mercedes dealer says yes, knowing full well what two days in the E-Class will do to you. During the following thirty-six hours, you fall in love with the extra space and power. Your back problems disappear as you enjoy the "hot rock" massage in those executive-like seats. And your neighbors all get jealous of your shiny new ride. By Wednesday, the decision is made: You're not going back to your C-Class. You trade in your old car, even though the only thing you had intended to do that week was service your vehicle.

In designing its new service operations, through the human-centric lens of deeply understanding its customers and how they lived, Mercedes not only made it easier to service a car; they also generated a sales experience for the customer that removed the usual barriers inhibiting customer engagement. Instead of growing tired of their C-Class and then giving up a weekend with their kids to hunt for a new one, customers simply got their old cars serviced and inadvertently fell in love with the new one their car was sitting next to. Again, none of this originated in an analysis of the same old quantitative data. Rather, it emerged from insights generated through a more human approach, which, when applied, yielded more value for both the customer and Mercedes.

Mercedes was doing something else in addition to applying insights generated from more than just quantitative data. It was also, in a small way, "vesting" its interests with its customers. By entrusting its customers with higher-value cars, and believing that they would have a great experience driving them, Mercedes aligned its interests with those of its clients. Vesting is another way to elevate your relationships, and it actually goes much further than this example shows. It fundamentally aligns the interests of the buyer and the seller of products and services, and removes barriers to partnerships in ways that might seem amazing, but that are completely achievable.

VEST YOUR INTERESTS AND REMOVE BARRIERS

While Deloitte Canada was elevating its relationships through Best Managed, one of its competitors, another global consultancy, was learning through research of its own just how critical it was to build engaged partnerships based on deep understanding, applied insight, and as research would uncover, aligned and vested interests.

As was shared with us by leaders of the Australian office, this consultancy set out to conduct a human-centric study of client engagement. Its leadership knew the company needed to understand the key moments in a client engagement—moments that were critical to creating relationships capable of delivering the highest possible value, moments that would matter to the clients and the consultants. The leaders started by tracking emotional states for both consultancy staff and client staff during each of these key moments. The results were startling.

They discovered that the moments of celebration for the firm were moments of sheer terror for the client. After a big client project or audit sales win, the consultants felt cause to celebrate, and they often did so, by taking the client and key staff out for a high-end dinner, fueled with good steak and plenty of Champagne. However, when looking at what this *same moment* meant for the clients, it became clear that Champagne and steak were not what they wanted at all. In fact, clients were terrified at these periods, and were almost desperately in need of reassurance that they had made the right decision, that their careers would not be impacted negatively by this partnership. What the client wanted to see was consultants hard at work, mitigating risk and creating value; instead they were seeing expensive and exuberant celebration before any of the work had actually been done. As you can imagine, this consultancy has changed its client engagement process to reflect this new understanding.

An additional discovery in this work showed that clients of professional services firms were increasingly regarding the ability of these firms to serve as trusted advisors as the price of entry rather than a point of differentiation. It is no longer enough to have really smart people; if you don't, why are you in consulting? What clients really want is something more. They look for high-value reciprocal relationships. In other words, they want a professional services firm's success to be their success; they want a deeper relationship, mutually vested. They want to discover and exploit new value-creation opportunities together. They want their partners to be, well, partners—to succeed and fail together, with their incentives aligned.

This is part of why Best Managed is so powerful for Deloitte Canada. It's a vested program. Not financially, but structurally.

The more companies participate, the better the program is, and the better Deloitte Canada is able to serve its market. Unlike the more PR-related programs similar firms run, this one engages members of the firm so deeply in the lives of their prospects that they have skin in the game. Remember, the fundamental purpose of Best Managed is to build a vibrant mid-market in Canada and stimulate both the economy and economic prosperity for Canadians in the process.

This idea of vested partnerships is emerging in many industries we have worked with and studied. In her book *Vested Outsourcing*, Kate Vitasek details several case studies of vested partnerships that are driving innovation through highly collaborative business relationships.[7] Procter & Gamble is one company that is embracing a vested partnership, in this case with Jones Lang LaSalle (JLL), a commercial real estate and facilities management firm. The companies entered into a highly strategic outsourcing relationship to transform how P&G managed its facilities. Not an easy task when you consider it had more than 120 locations spanning 60 countries. As you can imagine, facilities management and maintenance is a massive expense.

P&G was aware enough to know that simply beating up suppliers could in fact have the reverse effect. Instead it chose to create a highly collaborative win-win relationship with JLL built on transparency of costs and putting a percentage of JLL's management fee at risk. However, the partnership was not simply about pushing risk to JLL. Rather, the vested partnership relied on shared risk/shared reward by creating economic alignment of interests. JLL received significant incentives to both reduce overall costs and achieve other business objectives. The more successful P&G was, the more successful JLL was.

In her book, Vitasek notes how P&G's Global Business Services has gone on record sharing the following results:

- Reduced Global Business Services cost as a percentage of sales by 33 percent;
- Service levels up 17 points (from 80 percent to 97 percent);

- Speed to market two times faster;
- Delivering 75 percent more service scope than seven years ago;
- Managing three times the number of complex initiatives;
- Acquisitions and divestitures time cut in half; and
- More capacity to innovate.

Under the partnership, JLL has been named P&G's supplier of the year for three years, a near impossible task when you consider JLL has more than 80,000 suppliers. "This kind of achievement can only be achieved by challenging the status quo and bringing innovation—the power of the *and*," explains Lydia Jacobs-Horton, P&G's director of global facilities and real estate at the time. "We expect our suppliers to bring innovative ideas to help us with our toughest problems and that is exactly what JLL has done."[8]

Simply put, a vested relationship is a win-win for both parties. It is interesting to learn that suppliers are also leading the charge to think differently about how they work with their customers. Vitasek also profiles how Genco (a FedEx-owned company specializing in product returns, as well as other supply chain services) is embracing vested engagements with customers such as Dell. John Coleman, general manager for Genco on the Dell account, explains: "For years, I had asked Dell to come up with a system to use wholesale as an additional option. It was a good idea, but Dell could not generate internal interest in investing in a project; Genco had no reason to make investments besides just contributing the idea." Under the vested agreement, Genco was highly incentivized to drive innovation that would benefit Dell and Genco jointly.

The results for both companies were positive, with a 62 percent reduction in scrap costs, while Genco also drove a 32 percent "cost per box" repair cost reduction in just nine short months after implementing the vested agreement. The effectiveness of the alliance has proven itself through radical improvements for Dell and hefty incentive checks for Genco. Coleman adds, "Before we were fighting tooth and nail and not even see-ing industry averages for margins on the Dell account." Under the vested agreement, Genco tripled its margins over industry averages.[9]

In the most vested of relationships, incentives are aligned, conflicts of interest are eliminated (or at least openly acknowl-edged and mitigated), and trust is allowed to create an openness and desire to engage fully that generates more creative solutions to challenging problems. People feel like they are on the same team, and feel supported by their clients and partners. DPR, which we looked at earlier, is a company committed to partner-ship with clients. As a part of that commitment, it is embrac-ing the idea of being vested through an approach known as Integrated Project Delivery (IPD) that is taking hold, with DPR as one of its biggest advocates.

The American Institute of Architects defines IPD as a proj-ect delivery approach that integrates people, systems, busi-ness structures, and practices into a process that collaboratively harnesses the talents and insights of all participants to optimize proj-ect results, increase value to the owner, reduce waste, and maxi-mize efficiency through all phases of design, fabrication, and construc-tion.[10] It sounds like a mouthful. Put differently, IPD is a more collabora-tive approach to construction, using technology, like building informa-tion modeling (BIM), and early engagement of all stakeholders to ensure the most efficient and effec-tive approach to construction. The real power in IPD, though, is in the alignment of incentives between the critical parties of any construction project: the client, the designer, and the general contractor.

> In the most vested of relationships, incentives are aligned, conflicts of interest are eliminated (or at least openly acknowledged and mitigated), and trust is allowed to create an openness and desire to engage fully that generates more creative solutions to challenging problems.

DPR and other companies using IPD are challenging the industry norms in contracting. DPR knows that things can go wrong on a project, regardless of the GC's competence. It could be any number of things. Poor decision making on the client's side. The weather. Changing economic conditions. Why, in such large investments, should one company bear all that risk? It's no wonder the vast majority of such projects end up in a litigious situation as the blame game develops and people try to share risk and the burden of mutually created overruns and inefficiencies on the project.

Under the more sophisticated IPD models, however, *all* parties share the risk. Margins and deadlines are defined up front. If a project finishes on time and ahead of budget, everyone shares in the dollars saved. If it goes over budget, everyone deals with the downside. The only losers in this situation are the lawyers who used to try the big cases when building projects ended up in court.

Mark Thompson, who leads DPR's sales efforts in the data center market sector, relates that DPR's adoption of IPD grew naturally out of its ethic of collaboration. Even when it wasn't as prevalent in the industry as it is today, the company was bringing all stakeholders to the table to collaborate and integrate project delivery to a point where everybody was clear about the result the team was working toward and what it would take to get there. "We've always believed that a rising tide raises all boats, and we see the advantages of an integrated approach for our customers and all team members both in reduced overall project risk and an enhanced opportunity for overall profit," said Thompson. "In an integrated approach, the team collaborates to validate the program and set a target cost. Then we openly share information and innovations, moving away from the typical hierarchical relationship. While collaboration sounds pretty straightforward, organizing the team across multiple companies is a big challenge, but once it happens the results can be game changing."[11]

Under IPD, all three parties are vested in making the others successful because if they each win, they all win. It's not us versus them. It's we. And in some cases it even manifests through the establishment of specific legal entities owned and controlled by the interested parties for the sole purpose of construction. The power of these models is that they align incentives and remove conflicts of interest. If you know that your supplier only wins when you win, you are less likely to wonder what they aren't telling you, and whether they are in this purely for themselves. This trust will yield greater levels of transparency and vulnerability. You move intentionally toward a purposeful interdependency, or as we would say, a deeply engaged partnership.

As one might expect of a company striving to be the obvious choice, DPR is partnering with a leading university, Stanford, to capture and package its experiences with IPD, using this knowledge to deliver better project outcomes and help move the industry forward. Remember that a critical part of creating an elevated perspective is cataloging what you know, and so is being known for what you know. Through its elevated relationships fostered with IPD, DPR is able to learn more about the contracting process, and use that knowledge to continually improve, applying these insights to create higher-value outcomes.

Vesting isn't just for B2B relationships. As companies look to create tighter alignment with their consumers as well, we see concepts of vesting coming through. In fact, we'd suggest that just about any warranty is a traditional form of vesting, as it is mutually reinforcing. The consumer wants the company to stay viable and therefore able to fulfill the warranty if necessary, and the company wants the consumer to be successful with the product or service to avoid enacting the warranty—there is mutually vested interest in positive outcomes. In a service example, lawyers have done this for decades, taking claims on zero fees, but for a percentage share of the settlement. While these traditional models of business contain elements of vesting, the digital world is opening fresh new opportunities for companies to vest with consumers. Waze, as of 2015 the world's largest community-based traffic and navigation application, depends on a social contract between users and the platform for mutual success. The more users contribute data, the better the application is for everyone. In some ways, this vests consumers not only in the platform provider, but also in one another, as it drives a dependency on a critical mass of users sending in valid data. Other digital platforms are emerging, such as the Vivino app for wine ratings, that will continue to explore how to vest users in each other and in the success of the platform. Amazon is another company that is exploring what can be seen as a vested relationship with its consumers. Amazon Prime provides incentives for people to use the Amazon platform. As Prime grows in membership, more capabilities are added, making the platform ever more valuable to both the consumer and to Amazon.

Whether you are in a formal, extensive B2B arrangement or looking to find ways to bind your consumers to your success, and you to theirs, vesting is all about finding ways to do business where everyone benefits. The goal is to do away with litigious, acrimonious organizational positioning, and to unlock the value of the relationships while driving higher-value outcomes for all.

As we said at the outset, there are no shortcuts here. Achieving the goal of becoming the obvious choice depends on your ability to bring more value every day. It depends on your ability not just to add value through new services, or to give trusted advice, but to leverage the strategic assets your clients need to help ensure their future success. You can't do this by reducing customers down to a spreadsheet or filtering them into two or three static data points. You have to know, understand, invest in, and partner with your customers. Let the best companies we've studied inspire you to engage more deeply with your customers than you ever thought possible.

As a Deloitte Canada senior partner told us during our discussions in 2012, "We recognized a long time ago that our business is people and our business is relationships. And so, if we can use the program to better understand this critical market and build relationships, then this will be a game-changer for us. And it is. In addition to access and depth, we now also have one of the largest quantitative and qualitative databases of mid-market companies on earth, are able to benchmark management practices with performance, and then share that with clients and prospects. The data alone is worth millions, the insights generated are priceless."

Build programs and approaches that ensure you stay close to your clients and prospects. Invest in developing insight, not just extracting data from those relationships, and apply the insight to improve the client's condition and/or experience. And where possible, proactively engage in interdependency and move to the level of partnership where you quite literally vest your success in the success of your customer. These are the things we have seen successful companies do to elevate relationships.

In the "Influence" chapter we took a look at how companies elevate relationships through their influence with customers, and here we've taken a hard look at what it takes to have deep and engaged partnerships. There is one additional consideration to elevating relationships that will help you to have a comprehensive view. You must cultivate and build *connections* with people, groups, and ideas beyond the direct buy/sell relationship, which will allow you to influence and control for things that are happening at your edge of disruption. You have to be able to see the whole board and respond appropriately. These connections are the third and final step of creating elevated relationships, and they will keep you moving on your journey to becoming the obvious choice.

Bring It to Life . . .

1. Identify the market segment you need to understand more deeply in order to truly create more value at the edge of disruption.

2. Create two lists: what is known and what is not known about the market segment that relates to how you could provide value from your edge of disruption.

3. Brainstorm with your team how to quickly and cost-effectively create understanding of your market segment. Think creatively of programs, being in the traffic, and voice-of-the-customer approaches. How could you get deeper levels of intimacy with this segment through go-to-market approaches, relationship management, and program development? Prioritize one or two ideas, and develop a plan to put them into action.

4. Map the customer experience from start to finish, both tactical and emotional. Map your experience on the same journey. Identify areas where your and the customer's interests are not aligned. Consider contracting, delivery, levels of engagement, pricing models, and incentives. Be as detailed as you can.

5. Using the insights from your brainstorming and the journey maps that identify disconnects, develop two points on the customer's journey where you could engage differently to support their experience.

CHAPTER 6

CONNECT: See the Whole Board

OR TWENTY YEARS Garry Kasparov was unbeatable in a game of chess. He was a man of impressive health and stature; his competitors used to refer to his physical presence and ability to intimidate his opponents in the same way one might in a more brutal form of sport. Others have joked that his achievements in the world of chess are only superseded by his political achievements, including attempting to run against Vladimir Putin in the Russian presidential elections in 2008 and living to tell the story. He never made it to the ballot, of course, but at least he survived.

Either way, anyone who knows anything about the game knows that Kasparov is considered by many to be the greatest player ever. Like those who went before him, and those who will come after him, he had an uncanny ability to see the "whole board." Sometimes called "board vision" in the world of chess, seeing the whole board is about not just seeing each piece in isolation, or a move in isolation. It is about seeing the spaces between the pieces—the relationships, if you will—and the impact of individual moves on the entire board. Players with board vision see their impact in the moment, and the potential future impact of subsequent moves as they begin to build to the crescendo that is the tension of the game.

Like a company that matters, Kasparov plays chess at the edge of disruption. He is able to paint a picture of the whole board two, eight, even thirty-two moves ahead. The "Beast of Baku," as he came to be known, was capable of producing moves that entire teams of Grand Masters would take days to unravel. In our research, and in our work, the companies capable of solving the most complex and valued problems for their customers are able to do so in part because, like Kasparov, they can see the whole board.

Connecting is about creating relationships that go beyond the buy/sell relationship, outside your organizational and market boundaries. It is building a level of knowledge and insight capable of identifying the interconnectedness of the moving parts in your world. It is being able to not just understand but also exert influence on how those parts work together and relate to each other. It starts with you seeing the whole board and builds through connecting the dots between the variables that exist on the board. From there, you are connecting moves into a broader set of relationships, which enables you to exert influence over the system, not just the immediate relationships that surround you and your company.

> Connecting is about creating relationships that go beyond the buy/sell relationship, outside your organizational and market boundaries. It is building a level of knowledge and insight capable of identifying the interconnectedness of the moving parts in your world.

If the goal of elevated relationships is to enable you to have an elevated impact, connectedness is the glue that makes it work. You need to elevate relationships across seemingly disparate areas and into the broader marketplaces that go beyond your immediate clients. You have to find ways to extend toward your clients' clients, suppliers, technology providers, industry groups, investment groups, and other key stakeholders in your market. It's the only way to convert the opportunity to create more value for your customers into actually creating this value for them.

CONNECT THE DOTS

Many companies that make it past startup last about forty to fifty years and then crumble from the inside out, or are taken out in a massive technology or social revolution. Companies on the S&P 500 have seen their average life span decrease from more than fifty years to fifteen.[1] The rare companies that are able to survive over a century and remain relevant and growing are the ones with the ability to truly see the whole board—what's going on in the world—and constantly adjust by connecting the dots and making bold moves.

One company we've worked with, De Beers, has done just that. When we think about becoming the obvious choice, there are really two ways to do so, outside of being a government monopoly. One is the path we've laid out in this book. The second is forming a supply-side cartel to effectively control the whole category. De Beers has done both. Much has been said and written about De Beers over the years, some of which is the most riveting and interesting exploration into commerce you can imagine. Many people have explored both the sometimes-dubious origins of the diamond industry and the marketing genius it represents, which largely originated with De Beers. While the origin story may be associated with controversy, its founders, Barney Barnato and Cecil Rhodes, had a vision in those early days, and the innovation that followed under the stewardship of its once-competitor, Ernest Oppenheimer and his family, in the 127 years since, might be unparalleled anywhere on the globe.

These days, De Beers participates in a highly competitive market, and yet remains the obvious choice in its extremely volatile category. It does it by seeing the whole board, a habit it cultivated from its very beginnings. Early on, the founders realized that scarcity benefitted them, and they created supply-side strength. At the same time, they focused on generating demand worldwide. Fast-forward to the 1940s, when Frances Gerety first proposed the marketing line "A Diamond Is Forever," and a marketing case-study legend was born (*Advertising Age* even calls it the ad slogan of the twentieth century). At the same time, an industry was born—diamond engagement rings. The stones were inextricably tied to rituals of love, marriage, and commitment, generating enormous downstream demand for De Beers's main clients, the jewelers who interacted with end buyers. De Beers didn't sell directly to the hopelessly lovestruck, but they controlled the supply and generated the demand that made those very buyers willing to spend more money than they ever had before on a symbol. Prior to World War II, diamond engagement rings in the United States made up less than 10 percent of rings sold, but by the end of the twentieth century, more than 80 percent of rings sold were diamond engagement rings. Try declaring your love for your significant other with a pearl or ruby, and you will miss the mark, thanks to the impact De Beers has had on its industry.

And it wasn't just a Western phenomenon. In Japan, the whole board was even bigger. Giving a specific type of gem wasn't in question there. Up until the mid-1960s, many Japanese marriages were arranged and were symbolized by drinking rice wine from the same wooden cup—a far cry from buying an expensive ring (something that the traditional Japanese culture would never condone). De Beers shifted a centuries-old Japanese tradition and created a new one as well, where young couples began giving a diamond ring as a symbol of marriage, conspicuously showing a break from tradition and embracing modern, Western life. In Japan, the market penetration moved from less than 5 percent of Japanese women receiving a diamond ring to more than 60 percent by the 1980s.

With a whole-board view, De Beers has also managed the threat of an exponentially expanding Russian mining industry, which included masses of smaller diamonds available to the market. A glut of new supply would not have been good in the long term for De Beers or for the category. De Beers leveraged its market-leading infrastructure and deep relationships to persuade the Russians to make De Beers the sole supplier of Russian-mined diamonds, and in the process preserved its ability to maintain an appropriate supply–demand balance that ensured the underlying value of the gem was preserved.

Underpinning so much of what De Beers had done through demand generation over the years was a set of attributes beyond just size (measured in carats) to create a diamond's "evidence-points" or, perhaps better put, "talking points," to perpetuate a story of value in stones of all sizes. The now-ubiquitous "4Cs" were used to grade diamonds and create a reference point for value in a category that for most consumers is opaque. For the most part, only a trained eye can really tell the difference between most stones, and yet prices would vary for same-size gems. The 4Cs were the answer. Beyond carat size, according to De Beers, three other attributes mattered: clarity, cut, color. By introducing the 4Cs to the consumer market, De Beers changed the way diamonds were bought for decades to come, allowing them to escape being commoditized for that time.

Fast-forward to the first decade of the 2000s, and add the internet to the mix, and the cost of comparing prices of readily available substitutes is virtually zero. A simple internet search will reveal multiple diamond-price comparison websites where you plug in your desired 4C combination, and competitors will essentially bid for your business. There is no greater recipe for commoditization on the planet. Coupled with De Beers's decreasing supply-side strength and the emergence of synthetic diamonds, the company faced imminent disruption.

Shifting geopolitical realities, trade sanctions, and increased competition were shifting the perception of diamonds in consumers' minds. Also, thanks in part to the internet and increased flow of information, buyers were becoming more aware of mining practices, and were starting to associate the gems with what became known as "blood diamonds." Something had to change. In the words of De Beers Group's CEO, Philippe Mellier: "The end consumer's desire for diamonds is the only true source of value in the diamond industry, so their confidence in their purchases is vitally important to our future success."[2]

De Beers decided to build three strategic pillars. It would continue to support demand and perception for the category, ensuring its health. It would, however, drive demand toward De Beers's controlled supply instead of generally supporting the industry branding. And finally, it would focus on integrity and trust, responding to the concerns buyers had about the industry as a whole by creating a De Beers brand promise. The diamonds would have to go beyond the 4Cs, making the source important again.

In typical De Beers fashion, they were able to connect the dots between the consumer trends and the supply realities, and developed an elevated perspective. *Diamonds needed a brand beyond the category brand itself.* To date, as long as the 4Cs were comparable, a diamond was a diamond, and who you bought it from didn't change the underlying brand promise. De Beers needed to shift that perception in the market and distance themselves from conflict diamonds, synthetic diamonds, and generic "4C" diamonds. De Beers developed a two-pronged approach to address its new vision of the market and the industry.

First, it created a branded gem that could be identified with a "trust mark"—a proprietary inscription to guarantee authenticity, quality, and ethical sourcing. Second, it would encourage diamantaires, wholesalers who buy the De Beers stones and then sell them to consumers, to build their own brands of diamonds and sell them through the independent channels.

De Beers ran some early marketing campaign pilots in Hong Kong, with positive results that also helped the diamond company learn more about how customers responded to its new positioning. Consumers liked the conflict-free and ethical sourcing guarantee, but they wanted a bigger story about why their diamond was special. De Beers shared what it was learning with manufacturers and resellers, and even went so far as investing with some of its buyers by providing capital for similar branded concepts. This had varied success, perhaps the exception being the success of "Hearts on Fire," which De Beers invested in early.

Together with the pilot success and an emerging understanding of Millennial buying behaviors, De Beers connected the dots and realized that it needed more than trust marks on stones. It needed a full-fledged consumer-facing brand that offered the promise of rarity, exclusivity, quality, and integrity. So it launched Forevermark, a diamond brand marketed by De Beers, sold (mostly) by independent jewelers, and carrying the trust mark inscription. Through Forevermark, De Beers is using its size and marketing reach to build a branded category where the independent jewelers benefit at the same time De Beers benefits—and it is working to restore trust in the category while maintaining price exclusivity. It is creating a new consumer preference model for De Beers–supplied diamonds, rather than generic diamonds, and linking to a broader ethos and value for what consumers now know is not necessarily a rare jewel. The scarcity has shifted to the way in which the gem is sourced, manufactured, and presented to the customer, rather than the scarcity of the gem in terms of mining volumes. For the independent retailers, it presents a powerful way to differentiate themselves from the price-driven online players who want consumers to keep on believing that a diamond is a diamond is a diamond. De Beers knows better, and to prove it, it's going to use its broad connections and ability to influence the entire industry.

Early results are positive. Launched as recently as 2008 in Hong Kong and China, and 2011 in the United States, Forevermark is already showing signs that it will be the obvious choice for consumers. More than $700 million of Forevermark gems have been sold at the retail level, and in China—fast emerging as one of the most important jewelry markets in the world—the Forevermark brand has already achieved the same recognition in consumers' minds as Tiffany & Co. That is tremendous equity for a brand that is only a few years old. De Beers has continued to play the whole board, watching moves in geopolitics, fair trade expectations, consumer preferences, supply chain realities, technology, and other disruptors in its industry. It maintains a healthy competitive position (at about 35 percent of the market today), and aims to have an impact in a meaningful way across the whole board.

Companies like De Beers, ones that matter in their markets and are able to sustain their position as the obvious choice for more than a century, understand that transformation doesn't happen in isolation. Problems are rarely solved between just two parties; transactions may exist between them, but the solution has much broader implications, and relies on a broader set of players to be executed successfully.

There are few times when the ability to influence, partner, and connect, applied broadly, matters more than when you are at the front of a new and emerging industry. Your ability to build a company that matters actually needs to start with creating an industry that matters. And that means building a bigger pie for all. LoyaltyOne learned this firsthand.

CONNECT BROADLY

LoyaltyOne is the obvious choice in Canada's loyalty-awards program industry. Its Air Miles Reward Program has achieved one of the highest per capita penetration levels of any national loyalty-awards program on earth. It did so because LoyaltyOne not only saw the whole board, but also built the wide-ranging relationships required to capitalize on what it saw via this strategic view: massive opportunities in the white space between brands and retailers, between retailers and consumers, and between retailers and other retailers.

For context, let's first dive into the role retailers have in the loyalty ecosystem. Canadian Tire, a Canadian chain comparable to Walmart or Kmart in the United States, was the first large retailer in Canada to have a loyalty program. Launched in 1958, the program, called Canadian Tire "Money," essentially amounted to discounting. When consumers made purchases at Canadian Tire stores, they earned Canadian Tire dollars (physical currency), which could be redeemed later at the store. In effect, this program offered a transactional exchange to consumers: loyalty in exchange for discounts. Given how massive Canadian Tire was, such a program seemed to make sense. The company was big enough to justify the costs of maintaining the program, and with the volume and frequency of consumer purchases, there was sufficient incentive for the customer to choose Canadian Tire over an equivalent competitor.

LoyaltyOne took a page from Section One of this book as it was developing its flagship program, Air Miles, in 1992, and asked an interesting question: Was Canadian Tire really fostering loyalty, or was it just competing on price? Executives also had been wondering: What if you could build a program that was not simply a discounting scheme? What if you could take the best of a Canadian Tire–type program and combine it with what airlines were doing at the time, giving flight rewards for flying or for purchasing with a specific credit card? What if you could encourage people to shop in your store not because they got a cheaper price, but because you enabled them to live out their wildest dreams? Things like new laptops for their kids, a trip to Mexico for a family vacation, or donations to charities of their choice.

LoyaltyOne, in short, saw an opportunity to create a loyalty program that was *aspirational*. It suddenly became clear that there was an opportunity to connect the retailer programs with the consumer's decision to shop somewhere, to choose a specific brand, or to use a specific credit card with something more meaningful than mere discounts. In envisioning the Air Miles Reward Program, LoyaltyOne wanted to be a dream enabler, and in the process generate loyalty.

But Air Miles wouldn't *just* be about creating emotional connections among consumers. Imagine that you are a consumer brand that sells product at Canadian Tire. You help pay for Canadian Tire's loyalty program by offering special discounts and cash contributions, and you do this in order to obtain increased penetration at Canadian Tire stores as well as access to specific consumer data. Well, what if someone built a program encompassing a *coalition* of retailers and brands, across hundreds of product and service categories, everything from liquor to financial services to groceries?

All of a sudden, you would gain access to a database of information covering the full range of a consumer's spending habits.

You would be able to track how spending changes as seasons change, as the consumer ages, and so on. You would know when a consumer got married, when she had kids, and when she bought a new house, and you would be able to respond to the shifts in consumer behavior that correspond to these and other life stage experiences. You would gain a direct understanding of each consumer's personal aspirations based on how he or she uses the loyalty points. And this database would contain information on *millions* of consumers and their purchase history. Talk about an engine for the elevated perspective needed to continually redefine your edge of disruption! Imagine how a consumer brand, bank, or retailer might use this insight to customize campaigns and reward offers to appeal to consumers' evolving wants and needs.

While most players in the retail space were simply thinking about their own vested interests and the specific, direct relationships they had with their consumers, LoyaltyOne was connecting the dots between industry players, recognizing and finding opportunities as it explored this edge of disruption.

The power of Air Miles lay in the whole constellation of consumers, retailers, and brands, and its success came from LoyaltyOne's ability to build relationships with all of them. Thanks to that breadth, the program knew more about what people bought and aspired to than any single discounting platform ever could have, and its results for brands and retailers were so remarkable that Air Miles created a bigger pie for *everyone* to share.

To fully appreciate LoyaltyOne's accomplishment, keep in mind that during the 1990s, marketers were not yet convinced of the value of loyalty programs. Loyalty as a concept required further development if it was to emerge as a strategy stealing marketing dollars away from thirty-second ads and in-store merchandising. As Bryan Pearson, president and CEO of LoyaltyOne, told us, "We were starting at ground zero. We were releasing a concept before we could sell anything else. And so, a lot of what we were doing was . . . recognizing that we were working with clients to . . . get them to understand this new type of marketing. Loyalty is really the term that ended up, kind of, moving forward. But when we started, it was very much to educate the industry on what loyalty programs were. What were they supposed to do? How did they work? You had old-school marketers who taught about mass media and circulars and what you did in-store. They didn't think about this new tool as a way to acquire and retain customers. So, we had to bring them up the learning curve."[3]

As LoyaltyOne came onto the scene, another key player in the market was Rick Barlow's consulting firm, Frequency Marketing, Inc. Barlow had helped lay the groundwork for loyalty marketing and, among other things, had created Colloquy, a thought leadership platform that brought together the best thinking in the loyalty industry, packaged it, and shared it generously across the industry via proprietary research, a magazine, a website, and industry events. Colloquy was a platform for connecting with the marketers in key decision-making positions across the entire loyalty industry, building the case for loyalty-based strategies in the process. A look at the whole board in those days didn't just present the coalition of retailers and brands that Air Miles capitalized; it showed a serious weakness in the value chain—demand! If retailers and brands didn't see loyalty as a legitimate and high-value strategy, industry players like Frequency Marketing, and indeed LoyaltyOne, would be left fighting it out for a small amount of available market.

In 2003, Colloquy started holding an annual summit that, over time, has become the premier event in the loyalty industry, an opportunity for everyone to gather and share best practices and information on the latest industry trends. Guess who now owns Colloquy? Not just the event, but the magazine, the website—everything? You guessed it: LoyaltyOne.

The Colloquy Loyalty Summit is unique in that it is a phenomenally cooperative group of competitors, all gathered in the same room. It was here, in 2010, that we first met LoyaltyOne's CEO, Bryan Pearson. Usually, a brand will host a summit, invite clients and prospects, and then bombard the audience with brand-specific and highly biased messages, sprinkling in keynotes by astronauts, ex-presidents, entertainers, and the occasional content-driven speaker from companies like ours. The Colloquy Summit couldn't have been more different. First, there were no astronauts. It was all content, almost exclusively case-study content from loyalty professionals themselves. American Express, Marriott, Tesco, and Starbucks all attended, their most senior marketers sharing freely. LoyaltyOne was there, too, but so were other loyalty program providers, consulting firms, and data and analytics agencies.

Why would LoyaltyOne/Colloquy organize and fund an event and then invite competitors? The answer is that LoyaltyOne wanted to build a bigger pie, and it therefore needed to be able to build the relationships required to grow that pie, knowing if it was successful, those it courted would share in the upside as well. Despite their maturity in Canada, loyalty programs remained a growth business. Pearson believed the pie needed to grow, and that everyone had to participate to make that happen.

"It's very simple," Pearson told us, in explaining LoyaltyOne's commitment to Colloquy. "[We want to] build credibility and reputation, be known for thought leadership. That should get you into the decision set if [prospects are] looking to do either deeper studies or consulting or potential, as they are looking for vendors that they want to partner with, as they are thinking about solving their problems."[4] Does this rationale sound familiar? Just as LoyaltyOne's service offering functioned as the glue for the end-to-end needs of a loyalty program, so Colloquy was equally ambitious in being the glue for the industry itself, bringing together the key players to share the latest and greatest best practices to build customer loyalty.

LoyaltyOne actually took all it had developed and went a step further. During the first decade of the 2000s, the company evolved its business model to take on a broader role in the loyalty marketplace and to help build up the market itself. Executives recognized that loyalty as a marketing strategy was still evolving. More players were getting involved, and new markets were emerging every day. As the pie got bigger, more companies in more countries wanted to build loyalty programs like Air Miles.

Having access to the experience, insight, and knowledge embedded in Air Miles would be invaluable access for these companies, and from that realization, a new line of business was born at LoyaltyOne. That's because by the early 2000s, LoyaltyOne had evolved into a full-service consulting company, providing everything from design, testing, execution, and back-end redesign of the customer's engagement strategies and in-store experience. LoyaltyOne knew that giving companies advice on the design and optimization of their programs would both generate revenue and position them at the very front of the sales cycle as well.

Nobody else in LoyaltyOne's market was well connected enough to tie together all the moving parts required to maximize ROI on a loyalty program, as LoyaltyOne was. The company aggressively and intentionally monetized its ability to be the glue between stakeholders and extract value across the whole board. For many large companies, LoyaltyOne is *absolutely* the obvious choice as a partner in developing and maintaining their loyalty programs, because it has successfully taken its vision of the whole board, and the broad relationships it had developed in Air Miles and through Colloquy, to exert influence over the entire market and grow the industry itself.

LoyaltyOne saw the need to grow the entire category through elevated perspective and broad relationships, and it found the opportunities that emerged when connecting the dots between converging disruptions and between multiple industry players. In other words, they saw the whole board. LoyaltyOne and De Beers both had the board vision they needed, and they used it to build relationships that resulted in influence at a system level.

INFLUENCE THE SYSTEM

Companies aren't the only organizations that have to be able to step back, see the whole board, and figure out the seemingly separate consumer behaviors, technologies, cultural phenomena, and market realities that need to be connected in order to see success. Nongovernmental organizations (NGOs, typically nonprofits or charities) often work in environments where otherwise unrelated data points are interconnected in ways that influence their ability to succeed. They have to be able to see the whole board and influence the system to generate the best possible value.

You've likely heard about the challenges encountered in the early days of HIV/AIDS treatment in Africa, where the drugs required the patient's adherence to a strict dosage timetable. This makes sense in a Western context, where we all wear a watch or carry a phone. Not so in much of Africa. Add to this the cost of the drugs being prohibitive for the vast majority of people in the area, the shortage of trained medical staff, and the lack of infrastructure and management capabilities on the part of local hospitals to administer complex programs to hundreds of thousands of people in remote villages, to name just a few of the most significant problems with treating HIV/AIDS in Africa.

And yet in a 2014 United Nations report, Michel Sidibé (director of the Joint United Nations Programme on HIV/AIDS) said, "The AIDS epidemic can be ended in every region, every country, in every location, in every population and every community."[5] *Ended in every region, every country, and every location*? Now that is an optimistic mind-set, from one of the most informed perspectives available. While challenges still exist in tackling this incredibly complex problem, NGOs like Doctors Without Borders, Catholic Relief Services, and untold other charity organizations are working together to solve these interconnected challenges and address the systemic challenges of cultural norms, supply chain, organizational capabilities, and others that prevent proven medical solutions from having their full impact. These organizations collectively see the whole board, and connect broadly—with each other and with the communities and influencers they seek to impact—to exert influence over the system and move the needle, both on infection rates in Africa, and on the ability of infected citizens to live high-quality lives. We are in awe of the work they do, the outcomes they have created, and the work they aspire to accomplish.

In a similar collective approach, the relatively new idea of "collective impact" in driving social change recognizes the often incredibly complex cultural context within which NGOs work to provide services. As described by the *Stanford Social Innovation Review* blog, collective impact aligns the goals of multiple service providers to help maximize the impact of each of them.[6] It requires influencing an entire system of services, customers, governments, and donors to create aligned value for the communities being served. It takes looking at the whole board, understanding what all the different interest groups, recipients, volunteers, donors, and other interested parties are attempting to achieve, and asking them to consolidate their efforts to maximize their impact.

One example of collective impact highlighted in the *Stanford Social Innovation Review* is StriveTogether, a Cincinnati-based nonprofit working to bridge the achievement gap and improve education throughout the city. Through StriveTogether, more than 300 leaders of local education-focused organizations agreed to participate in jointly advancing their common cause. As reported in the *Stanford Social Innovation Review*, "These leaders realized that fixing one point on the educational continuum—such as better after-school programs—wouldn't make much difference unless all parts of the continuum improved at the same time. No single organization, however innovative or powerful, could accomplish this alone."[7] And it seems to be working—as reported, thirty-four of the fifty-three success measures used to track StriveTogether are trending positively, including areas like high school completion and reading and math scores.[8] By stepping back and looking at the whole system, and engaging people who were passionate about different parts of it, everything from improving school lunch programs to assessing teacher quality became part of the continuum that the collective was impacting.

> Collective impact requires an organization that serves as the centralized point of infrastructure, coordination, and facilitation, with dedicated staff and processes designed to set up and deliver on common goals.

Collective impact requires an organization that serves as the centralized point of infrastructure, coordination, and facilitation, with dedicated staff and processes designed to set up and deliver on common goals. In the same way these organizations see the whole board, connect broadly, and exert influence over the system, the same opportunity to have collective impact—on customers, industries, and communities—exists for companies that want to become the obvious choice by being organizations that coalesce the common goals and objectives of the industry, and stand up to lead the way.

———

There is a war of sorts going on in the developing world. A war between consumer product companies, seeking to become the trusted brands—think "obvious choice"—for millions of new customers in emerging markets. According to *Forbes* magazine and the *Economist*, Unilever, with more than half of its business coming from these regions, is thought to be on top.[9] In addition to product-based innovations like locally inspired flavors and scents, the real secret to Unilever's success in this extremely complex market space is its ability to see the whole board, connect the dots, and then exert influence over the interdependent groups and behaviors required to ultimately drive the purchase decision.

Unilever is a huge company, and like all of its peers, it has its share of baggage in terms of its impact on the world; it doesn't necessarily always get things right. But it has also delivered some amazing accomplishments through its programs and commitments, and has demonstrated a consistent ability to drive positive community impact that is aligned with its strategic objectives. Recently, when Unilever stepped up its goals to penetrate the rural markets in developing countries, it started with a focus on hygiene products. The product introduction of Lifebuoy (its flagship "red bar" of soap), faced one seemingly insurmountable obstacle. Many of the potential customers in these regions did not wash their hands, or their hair for that matter. In addition to economic constraints, they haven't been raised to believe it is even important to wash with soap. Western brands take such things for granted. We assume that everyone believes in the efficacy of such hygiene behaviors, which is ironic given that it wasn't so long ago that even Western doctors saw limited value in hand washing, moving freely between the morgue, the operating room, and the birthing suite and unwittingly bringing germs along with them.

To increase sales of soap in Western Europe, Unilever would simply need to highlight the product attributes of its soap that make it superior, and maybe offer some discounts to drive demand in retail. There would be no need to explain the value of the activity itself. In a place like India, however, it is a different story. Given that it was reported in 2009 that there were more than 380,000 deaths per year of children under five from diarrheal disease, often preventable by routine hand washing, it is safe to say that the use of soap was not a "taken for granted" activity. With a view of the whole board, Unilever realized it needed to change the behaviors of an entire generation to create a market for its products. A complex problem indeed. But as a company that matters, Unilever didn't shy away from the complexity. Instead it sought to have the impact it desired, and launched a brand vision to "change the hygiene behaviors of 1 billion consumers across Asia, Africa, and Latin America, by promoting the benefits of hand washing with soap at key occasions, thereby helping to reduce respiratory infections and diarrheal disease, the world's two biggest causes of child mortality."[10]

Unilever knew it couldn't do this alone, so it connected broadly, establishing a coalition of organizations including the Red Cross, UNICEF, and the Millennium Villages Project to address the problem. Even with this coalition, to truly influence the system, Unilever would need scale, and that was not going to come by going child by child. But it would if the company went mother by mother, village by village, and enlisted them not just to change the behaviors of their own children (by embedding the idea of hand washing as a maternal duty) but also to share with other mothers the efficacy of the same behavior, as mothers are known to do.

In addition to this grassroots initiative, which Unilever branded Help a Child Reach 5, it exerted influence through more public messaging, launching Global Handwashing Day and other initiatives. For example, it linked hand washing with the most coveted and in-demand bread in the Indian culture. Every year, at Hindu festivals across the world, millions of these unleavened breads—known as roti—are consumed. And as a part of this campaign, on them is a message: "Did you wash your hands with Lifebuoy?"

According to an independent study by Nielsen, Unilever was able to reduce the incidence of preventable diarrhea (which can often cause death) in Thesgora, India, from 36 percent to just 5 percent, through its campaign.[11] Thirty-three percent more mothers started washing their hands, and kids exposed to the program washed their hands on two more occasions each day as a result.[12]

In a country where, as of 2009, more than 1,000 children under 5 were dying every day, over half from causes preventable by regular hand washing, Unilever was able to measurably reduce these deaths, while becoming the obvious choice for millions of new customers in the process. It saved these lives in the most vulnerable of populations, thanks to its elevated perspective on health and hygiene and its elevated relationships through which it connected an elegantly simple solution to a critical problem. The company saw the whole board, connected the dots, connected broadly, and exerted influence over the system, and in doing so laid the foundation for delivering a meaningful solution that would elevate Unilever's impact and make it the obvious choice.

It's no coincidence that Lifebuoy was the driving force of this massive social change and market creation initiative, because the brand itself was founded on the very same principle. When William Lever developed the first Lifebuoy bar as a means to reduce cholera, more than a hundred and fifty years ago, he created a product that matters. That product, together with other health and hygiene products, eventually turned into the company we now know as Unilever—a company that matters, after more than a hundred years in business. Your work can matter, too.

Having an *elevated relationship* is not just about knowing more, or playing higher with your customer or stakeholder. It is about having a more sophisticated and comprehensive view of your entire market. The best companies we studied, the ones that really matter in their markets, understand that creating the most value requires that you know how to execute in real life. And execution is about politics. It's about influence. It's about behavior change. It's about relationships.

Specifically, it's about the dynamics of relationships. It's about knowing how the actions of Player A impact the results for Players B, C, and D. You must understand so much more than the narrow transaction; you must grasp an entire interconnected system of different players bearing on the product's purchase and use. You need to see the whole board, and connect the dots between these players. You need to build relationships with them so you can exert influence over the entire market in a way that is good for you, good for the industry, and good for the customers downstream.

> The best companies we studied, the ones that really matter in their markets, understand that creating the most value requires that you know how to execute in real life. And execution is about politics. It's about influence. It's about behavior change. It's about relationships.

The point of connecting is both to identify opportunities that exist across the board and in the spaces between pieces, and to have the influence required within an industry to actually create more value for your ultimate buyers when the opportunity arises.

In the case of De Beers it was about understanding its customers, and its customers' customer—the end consumers and their emerging desire for branded diamonds from ethical sources. For LoyaltyOne it was to build a product and business model that resulted in a coalition more powerful than any one retailer could achieve, and to augment the industry platform responsible for bringing together the key people who would be responsible for growing the pie for loyalty players across the entire system. All of these companies focused on what mattered most: solving complex problems, adding more value, and doing something that none of their competitors were able to do.

It is in this process that your elevated perspective and elevated relationships begin to converge and reinforce each other in a renewable way. Think about De Beers and the Forevermark brand, or LoyaltyOne being able to evolve into a whole new business. Neither of these would have been possible without their commitment to seeing the board broadly and connecting with people in all different areas and mind-sets. Narrow, disconnected thinking around a product or a function would have stopped these efforts cold, if they had been identified at all. And it was the same for Unilever. The win-win scenario drove shared value for the community and for Unilever—an idea we will revisit in detail in the last chapter, "Live." They could not have had the impact they needed to have if they were unable to see the interconnectedness of the market and exert influence over it.

Average companies think small and narrow. They compete aggressively, usually on price, for the limited market that exists. The best companies connect broadly and take personal responsibility for building a bigger pie. De Beers and LoyaltyOne spent resources (both time and money) investing in the health of their entire industry, not just their own businesses. At Unilever it was the community at large. They all connected with different types of buyers and influencers, businesses that were adjacent to theirs or their customers', and they sought to bring their competition into the process where appropriate. They connected with industry and community players in new and interesting ways that redefined their roles and how they interacted with their markets. Better still, through specific relationships they had forged, they saw the whole board and identified places where they could have meaningful influence, not just for themselves but for multiple participants in their markets. In their commitment to mattering more, they appreciated how interdependencies in the value chain functioned; applying that insight, they found ways to deliver greater impact. This impact in turn differentiated them from their competitors, making them the obvious choice.

Bring It to Life . . .

1. Identify three people or organizations beyond your direct customer/client or supplier relationships that are most critical to your organization's future and to your ability to create value at your edge of disruption.

2. Take immediate action to establish and strengthen your relationships with those people.

3. Identify membership organizations you could join to gain access to and influence across a broader section of your industry. How could you not only join but also begin to play a leadership role in these organizations? What insights and thought leadership could you contribute there? Choose one and take the first step by joining and attending a meeting.

4. Based on your view of the whole board and your identified edge of disruption, identify one area where your future success is dependent on your ability to influence the system.

5. Brainstorm ideas with a cross-functional team for how you could exert that influence.

6. Pick the highest leveraged opportunity and start on the journey toward making the requisite changes happen.

SECTION THREE

ELEVATED IMPACT

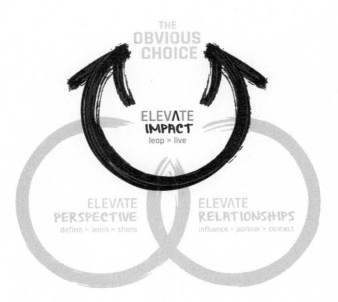

YOU MEAN TWITFACE, and stuff like that, what my grandkids play with?"

These were the words out of the mouth of one of the most experienced intelligence professionals in the world, at a conference designed to stretch his and his colleagues' minds on the impact of emerging technology on the intelligence industry. The year was 2010, the event was a private, executive-only affair for one of the largest defense contractors in America, and the speech was from a skinny-jeans- and sneaker-wearing PhD candidate from MIT on the impact of unstructured data and social media on intelligence.

Having been inspired by the TED-style conferences that were gaining momentum, the contractor's CEO decided to embark on a series of quarterly TED-esque events in an attempt to elevate the perspective of its most senior leaders. The sessions were meant to be provocative, and at the edge of disruption. There was a problem, though. These top brass were not as receptive to the ideas of this social media guru (who for the record looked like he might be eleven years old) as they could have been that day. This young-looking guy had an interesting hypothesis. Within a few years, he argued, social media would have far-reaching effects on national security and geopolitics, turning the entire intelligence community on its head.

It was this assertion that led to the "Twitface" question from a seasoned intelligence officer, who was responsible for sending spies into war zones to infiltrate local networks and gather information for various agencies that can aid military strategy and decision making.

"If you mean Twitter and Facebook," the speaker replied, "well, yes."

By the end of that year, the Arab Spring had broken out across the Middle East, beginning a process that would redraw the geopolitical map in that volatile region. The national security implications have been far-reaching, affecting not just the United States but countries around the world. And do you remember what initially supported the uprising, connecting people across formerly impenetrable social, geographic, and political boundaries? Social media.

It's not that those in the room that day were blind to the possibilities present at this edge of disruption, namely the wide-ranging capabilities of social media, which posed a threat to the contractor's current intelligence-gathering techniques. It's that the implication of what the social media guru was suggesting was so disruptive for their roles, their organizations, and the way they engaged with their customers that it may have felt easier to plod along, holding on to the legacy business models, and hope the changes would be slow and perhaps never eventuate at all.

This company had traditionally earned its keep by providing human "assets" to American intelligence organizations. The company would hire these individuals, pay them well, send them to war zones to gather data and intelligence, feed what they learned to intelligence organizations, and receive a fee that reflected their costs plus an additional percentage as profit. This contractor's business model was labor arbitrage; its product, spies.

The implications of what was being suggested from the platform that day were that this model would become mostly outdated, and that an entirely new way of doing intelligence would emerge. It would be an approach that would involve scraping the World Wide Web and social media for relevant content, analyzing that data for patterns using high-powered software, and then allowing trained analysts to further interpret the emerging insights, with a focus on the outcome of viable, reliable, and accurate intelligence. The likely business model would be software and licensing, but the product would no longer be the input—spies. It would be the higher-value outcome—intelligence.

The contractor had access to the elevated perspective it needed that day to understand the future of intelligence gathering. And as one of the largest outsourced providers of intelligence gathering for the US military, the contractor also had the relationships it needed to be the obvious-choice provider of this new approach to intelligence gathering. Its leaders just didn't have the appetite at that time to do the hard work required to get there. The Arab Spring changed that. It created a wake-up call for this company and all its competitors to respond to meet the evolving needs of their customer. The contractor had missed an opportunity to be ahead of the call and get a jump-start in becoming the obvious choice.

And this is what ultimately differentiates companies that matter. Ones that become the obvious choice proactively move to the edge of disruption, and when they see opportunities there to create higher-value outcomes, they do the hard work necessary to create them. They go all in; align their resources, people, and systems; and become the disruptor in their industry instead of waiting to be the disrupted.

> Becoming the obvious choice is about more than just investing in developing an elevated perspective and building elevated relationships. It requires the hard work needed to have an elevated impact as well.

Becoming the obvious choice is about more than just investing in developing an elevated perspective and building elevated relationships. It requires the hard work needed to have an elevated impact as well. Creating world-leading loyalty platforms that accomplish more than just package discounting, as LoyaltyOne did, is a serious undertaking. Taking on deeply embedded assumptions about how GCs interact with clients when millions of dollars are on the line is courageous, but DPR did it. And transforming the entire supply chain like De Beers did is hard work. Companies that matter do it anyway, leaning into the complexity and putting their hands up to take on the biggest client, industry, and community challenges. In doing so, these companies use their elevated perspectives and elevated relationships to ensure they have an *elevated impact* on the marketplace and, as we discovered, often on the world as well. Elevated impact happens when companies are delivering the most valued solutions in diverse areas to a variety of stakeholders—and when higher-value outcomes are being created. Remember that you cannot be the obvious choice if you don't create more value. And you cannot create more value if you don't have an elevated impact.

Something amazing will happen if you see this through. If you take all of your effort and you push through to do the hard work to elevate your impact, you will find it feeds your elevated perspective and your elevated relationships. That's right—it becomes easier and easier to maintain your place on the edge of disruption, because your elevated impact will make you more valuable to both your customers and your world. At the same time it will continually refresh your perspective about the new edges of disruption and the opportunities that live there. This in turn enables you to have an even more elevated impact. The cycle is self-perpetuating, and it gets easier as you go.

This section is all about how to take the final step and become the obvious choice. It is about companies that chose to be *relentlessly* true to their future selves by committing to doing both the *hard* work and the *right* work. So rally your courage, and read on to hear about companies that have done just that, and how you can, too.

CHAPTER 7

LEAP: Be the Disruptor

I F WE WERE TO ASK YOU, "What does Adobe do?" what would your answer be? We're willing to bet you would think about the software Adobe creates, such as Photoshop, Illustrator, Acrobat Reader, and perhaps its other document management and image-based content creation solutions.

That was exactly what we would have thought until one day in 2012 at the New South Digital Marketing Conference, one of the sessions was led by a young executive from Adobe. Adobe had long dominated the market for digital content creation, delivering award-winning clarity and grace in website designs. Like most attendees, we figured the executive would discuss how graphics software could make marketing materials more captivating—you know, he'd talk about pretty pictures and stuff like that.

It's a good bet that most of the audience was surprised—and we would be willing to bet most of our readers would have been surprised, too—when the presenter launched into a detailed discussion of how Adobe was reworking the online presence

179

of major retailers to meet the challenges of online competition. Rallying hard data, he showed how dynamic images, matched to a buyer's specific online behavior, could show measurable improvements in conversion (the percentage of website visitors who actually buy something) and basket size (how much stuff people bought when they purchased). The presenter was not just talking about the omni-channel world; he was showing people how to *win* in this world. He was unpacking how Adobe's clients, using Adobe products, were essentially managing their entire marketing function and e-commerce activities through Adobe's content creation suite and what is now known as the Adobe Marketing Cloud (AMC).

During the first decade of the 2000s, the Adobe most people knew was still selling packaged image-creation and document-management software to art directors and graphic designers. It had been a highly valued product, but over time the market was becoming increasingly commoditized. Manufacturers like HP and Sony were including competitive software with their devices, and Apple's software was exploding in market penetration. Adobe's products were losing traction and being pushed down in margin.

Fortunately, Adobe was able to define a new edge of disruption in its industry. It had spotted a higher-order value the market needed to have delivered. Executives in large companies were feeling increased pressure to present pages and online experiences, and to engage in social media in a way that actually boosted sales. Attractive content by itself was no longer doing the job. These executives needed to show the right content to the right consumer at the right time, in order to drive that consumer to make a purchase. Or as Adobe would now say, it would "need to make every pixel count."

Adobe saw an opportunity to combine analytics with its content creation offer, helping companies take their online experiences to a new level. If a retailer like REI could learn about individual consumers via their online behavior, it could then use this information to present itself more effectively online to those same consumers, thus driving more traffic to its site and stores, and increasing sales.

Instead of doubling down on its existing product offering and getting drawn into a price war, Adobe decided to do the hard work of solving a much more relevant problem. Forget about being a helpmate to art directors and designers; Adobe would now become a strategic partner to senior marketing executives, helping companies do three things: create and publish content across media and devices, manage documents online, and measure and monetize the content. And instead of selling boxed software, Adobe would offer these services on a recurring subscription basis as a constantly updated, cloud-based solution. Its elevated perspective and its ability to see the whole board helped Adobe identify the opportunity, and its elevated relationships exposed it to the specific customer needs. If it was to create a viable solution to this higher-order problem, and scale it profitably, Adobe needed to take the leap and become the disruptor of its existing model and that of its competitors, too.

That last bit is especially important when it comes to elevating impact. It is comparatively easy to have perspective and relationships. Converting that into impact, however, is a lofty target. It takes a degree of courage and commitment that, quite honestly, is hard to find in many companies. Doubters throw lots of stones, and in the case of Adobe, plenty of industry observers pontificated that Adobe might have been stretching a bit too far after such an ambitious goal.

> It is comparatively easy to have perspective and relationships. Converting that into impact, however, is a lofty target. It takes a degree of courage and commitment that, quite honestly, is hard to find in many companies.

The potential market for cloud-based services in 2009 was projected to surpass $56.3 billion, and at the time Gartner projected growth to $150.1 billion by 2013.[1] That was a reasonably attractive prize, but moving from being a traditional software provider to a provider of a cloud-based service would require massive change on Adobe's part. In 2009, when the company bought analytics pioneer Omniture, acquiring in the process a core component of what would become its cloud offering, Adobe's share price dropped 4 percent overnight. "Adobe Buys Omniture: What Were They Thinking?" read the title of a *Wall Street Journal* blog post.[2]

That's a moment when committing to becoming the obvious choice can start to feel pretty crazy, like a fool's errand. It is also the moment to trust your analysis as you forge ahead and take a leap supported by an elevated perspective, elevated relationships, and a clear opportunity to elevate your impact and create more value for your customers. You see, it is one thing to move to your edge of disruption and identify these complex problems; it is quite another to bring the solution to life in a way that has real impact and that cements a company's reputation with a new class of customer. Adobe accomplished both.

By March 2014, the cloud version of Adobe's traditional content creation programs had almost 4 million subscribers, 20 percent of whom had not been users of Adobe's traditional software.[3] Another part of Adobe's offering, Acrobat, had more than 2 million subscribers,[4] while the portion of the marketing cloud dedicated to measuring and monetizing web content grew 83 percent a year, making up more than a quarter of Adobe's revenue. In all, Adobe's revenues weren't much greater than they had been in 2012, but almost 60 percent of revenues were now recurring, up from only 5 percent, which is a story investors love to hear. No wonder that Adobe's share price has gone from $38 per share in 2013 to $78 in 2015,[5] and the 4 percent drop in price that happened when the Omniture purchase was announced has become ancient history.

Was it hard work for Adobe to reinvent itself as a cloud-based provider of strategic marketing services? Yes, undoubtedly. Was it an incredible leap? Absolutely. Here's our observation. Adobe set a goal and had clarity around its future self, and it relentlessly went after that, doing the hard work to get there. It could have continued to do a lot of hard work to compete in an increasingly low-margin business, and to scrap for every penny from the consumer on a commoditized product. Instead, it chose to do the hard work of moving to a new business model—a new operating model—selling to new clients in a new way, and realizing new revenue sources and streams.

Once you have made the leap in your mind and in your intention, it is critical that you follow it with the hard work. We found this to be a distinguishing feature of companies that matter. Instead of *working hard* on delivering limited value, companies that matter focus on doing the *hard work* to become their future selves, and they are willing to take that leap. Just working hard at what you've always done tends to yield diminishing returns, but doing the hard work of reinventing yourself and finding ways to move beyond the competition is what it means to elevate your impact—that's why it is the hardest step, the biggest commitment on your journey to becoming the obvious choice.

> Just working hard at what you've always done tends to yield diminishing returns, but doing the hard work of reinventing yourself and finding ways to move beyond the competition is what it means to elevate your impact— that's why it is the hardest step, the biggest commitment on your journey to becoming the obvious choice.

We actually found three distinct patterns of hard work in companies that took the leap, became the disruptor, and elevated their impact. First, they developed a mind-set, and *oriented their thinking around the outcomes they ultimately wanted to create in the market.* If they were to create more value, it would be by finding new and innovative ways to create outcomes clients valued, not by protecting the existing inputs of their current approach and business model. Second, they took their clearly defined edge of disruption, then *leaned into the complexity that was present, and moved confidently toward the disruption instead of working to avoid it.* They knew it was in the complexity that the opportunity to create a truly differentiated solution existed. And third, they *aligned the people, processes, and systems required to manifest their future self.* They knew ambition and intention were not enough. They needed to change the way people thought, acted, and did their work if they were to truly elevate their impact.

Think about those three patterns for a minute. All of them are underpinned by an elevated perspective and elevated relationships and tie back to many of the themes we heard in those sections—themes of courage, optimism, curiosity, embracing complexity, and doing hard work to change what you are doing today. Through the work of developing an elevated perspective, your edge of disruption is defined, and you start to formulate who your future self can be. Your elevated relationships give you the access and influence to bring your key stakeholders along as you undertake significant change. By using all of that together with the hard work we just described, you will have an elevated impact and be on your way to being the obvious choice. It all starts with orienting around outcomes, not legacy inputs and business models.

ORIENT AROUND OUTCOMES

Many leaders become blinded to opportunities by a less value-creating focus on building products or services instead of creating the right outcome for clients. As Clayton Christensen has argued, most customers do not make purchasing decisions because they favor a given product or service on the basis of its attributes.[6] Instead, they buy things in order to solve some basic problem; the product and its attributes are only the means or "inputs" that allow the problem to be solved. To the extent that companies focus too much on delivering a specific product or service and its attributes (e.g., "reliability" in a car, instead of, say, a transportation solution to get the customer from point A to point B), they can lose sight of what really matters to customers. This matters much more when an industry is being disrupted. As Christensen says on his foundation's website, "With an understanding of the 'job' for which customers find themselves 'hiring' a product or service, companies can more accurately develop and market products well-tailored to what customers are already trying to do."[7] Similarly, we would say companies can more accurately create outcomes that are more valuable because they are better aligned to solving the problems customers ultimately are seeking to solve.

Companies that have an elevated impact are able to do so precisely because it is the outcome that they focus on. Think back to the opportunity missed by the defense contractor you met in the introduction to this section. It was slow to

> Companies that have an elevated impact are able to do so precisely because it is the outcome that they focus on.

react because it was oriented around the inputs of its business (human assets who were building networks in war zones) and not on the actual outcomes its client (the US government) was buying—intelligence.

What business are you really in? What outcomes do your customers ultimately seek? Knowing the answers to these questions, and then aligning your focus and investments behind them, will help you to avoid holding on to existing business models for longer than is healthy, and allow you to leap, and become the disruptor in such a way that you have the future-focused solutions to the higher-value outcomes you are ultimately seeking to create for your customers.

And it is not just relevant for B2B and B2G (business to government) companies dealing with multimillion-dollar contracts. This applies to B2C companies as well—even those selling items as functional as a pair of sneakers. Just ask Nike. There are more valuable outcomes sought by consumers, and therefore more valuable roles you can play in their lives, in the seemingly commoditized world of athletic apparel. Decade after decade, Nike has pursued this edge of disruption and stayed ahead of commoditization, achieving both a price and choice premium over its competitors, precisely because it understood the outcome that both the highest-performing marquee athletes and the everyday athletes who aspired to be better were seeking. As Nike says, if you have a body, you're an athlete!

Let's begin at the beginning. Nike was founded with a mission: to enhance the performance of athletes, reduce their injuries, and support coaches and teachers in getting the most out of their athletes. From the early days in Bill Bowerman's kitchen, where he was destroying waffle makers to build a new running shoe, to its multibillion-dollar reality today, Nike has always invested in research and extensive testing, rigorously designing products to eke out even the smallest performance enhancements. As one former Nike executive, Ellen Schmidt-Devlin, explained to us, gold medals are won by hundredths of a second, and Nike was committed to creating products that would support athletes in pursuing that tiny fraction of a second.

That commitment to research and development remains foundational to Nike today. In 2013 alone it received more than 550 patents! The company's focus on developing products that are customized to athletes' needs in different arenas is unwavering. Enhancing performance through new technology, design, material, or even a new device is what excites Nike, as it focuses on the outcomes that are possible rather than the inputs it uses to create today's product line.

Consider Nike Free. In the early part of the twenty-first century, Nike started to build a body of research supporting a lighter, more minimalist running shoe, after a product representative learned that a Nike-supplied running coach was having his athletes run in bare feet.[8] While Nike was investing in research to support its 2004 launch of the Nike Free shoe, another company, Vibram, was working on its FiveFingers shoes, taking the minimalist trend even further. Nike stayed away, citing an absence of evidence in its research that the design would create the desired outcomes. Vibram ended up in a class-action lawsuit for its marketing claims, while the Nike Free shoe continues to be a profitable product on the market.[9]

On the heels of the minimalist movement, the world was introduced to "toner" shoes, primarily by Skechers Shape-Ups and Reebok's EasyTone line, both introduced in 2009. The toning shoe market was approximately $145 million in 2009, reaching a high of $1 billion in 2011.[10] Despite the sizeable growth market and some criticism from investors, Nike again stayed away, citing a lack of evidence regarding the positive effect of the shoes. By 2012, the Federal Trade Commission agreed—Skechers agreed to pay $40 million and Reebok agreed to pay $25 million in response to separate claims of deceptive advertising.[11] By staying true to the outcomes it sought to create and its commitment to supportive research, Nike managed to sidestep the trend and stay focused on driving athlete outcomes through validated products. With the same focus and discipline that makes companies like DPR so successful, if an idea emerges and research doesn't prove that it can deliver on outcomes, Nike has the ability to say no.

While competitors were busy with toner shoes, Nike was starting to do serious, in-depth research to create products that would drive positive athletic outcomes through behavior change. Nike has always had a commitment to building communities—around the athletes it sponsors, the sports it supports, and the products it sells—by connecting everyday athletes via common aspirations and role models. Technology was starting to play a significant role in the lives of its consumers, and in 2006, Nike announced the Nike + iPod Sports Kit, in a unique partnership with Apple to combine technology and athletic apparel. Thanks to significant upgrades driven by both partners year after year, the product was and continues to be a success. By 2013, Nike+ reportedly had more than 28 million users around the world. Users can create online "challenges," in which community members can compete and/or compare their results, creating self-reinforcing support of positive outcomes. The Nike tribes that once aggregated around world-class athletes now have become active, thriving digital communities online—still aspirational, but also connected to one another in new and binding ways.

Nike+ is a solution platform truly aligned with Nike and partner products. Companies like Polar (maker of heart rate monitors), Microsoft (Kinect), and of course Apple continue to innovate on the platform, and it has exploded as a place for solutions for the behavior change sought by millions of consumers. As of 2015, its active members had achieved more than 54.5 million daily goals, running billions of miles to burn over 100 billion calories. In succeeding with Nike+, Nike established itself as much more than a shoe and apparel company. It elevated its impact beyond the products it makes by connecting with the ultimate outcomes sought by consumers—higher dedication to and better results from their fitness efforts. Nike is now a company that builds great shoes and also delivers diagnostics, goal tracking, and global performance benchmarking.

Building on the success of the platform, Nike went to market with the FuelBand as an early entry to the technology "wearables" business. The FuelBand did well on the market, exceeding expectations in many ways. Yet Nike discontinued it after only two years. Why? They realized that even though FuelBand was one of the first trackers of its kind on the market, and it had healthy sales, Nike was better suited to partnering with the tech companies that had entered and rapidly saturated the field. Looking across the whole board, a single-function technology that used the platform wasn't the right place for Nike to spend its energy—it wasn't the right edge of disruption.

Instead, the company is looking toward smart materials. Imagine a shirt that changes its elements based on how hard you are training, the external temperature, and the sweat you are producing; a shirt that tracks and benchmarks the changes in your body temperature, heart rate, and other vital signs to guide you toward your optimal performance zone. That kind of product is at Nike's current edge of disruption, and knowing Nike, it will be in your closet soon enough.

No matter how technology changes, Nike will remain focused on the outcomes it seeks: enhanced athletic performance, reduced injuries, and support for those who coach and teach athletes. It will hold steady in focusing on the future, not being limited by current inputs and legacy business models, and it will pursue the very best ways to create those outcomes. It will lean into the complexity it finds there, and by solving for it, elevate its impact and remain the obvious choice for professional and amateur athletes the world over.

Thinking about how Nike remains committed to innovation backed by research and to focus on outcomes and value for the athlete as its absolutely highest-order calling, what are the higher-value outcomes you can align to in your market? How might you redefine the outcomes you create so that what you do matters more? To truly deliver on the promise,

> To truly deliver on the promise, you will have to move toward the disruption and embrace the complexity of what you find there.

you will have to move toward the disruption and embrace the complexity of what you find there.

LEAN INTO THE COMPLEXITY

Two years, 200 miles of cabling, and 100 high-definition interactive flat-screens are just some of the inputs required to bring Burberry's visionary new 44,000-square-foot store to life on Regent Street in London.[12] The manifestation of this 160-year-old brand's edge of disruption, this magnificent example of the future of retail is only part of the inspiring turnaround story of this iconic brand, which almost fell into irrelevance by failing to evolve with the times.

Upon becoming the company's CEO in 2006, Angela Ahrendts was asked by an industry analyst to name Burberry's most threatening competitor. Was it Louis Vuitton? Gucci? No, Ahrendts responded, "Burberry online." Ahrendts went on to observe that customers could now buy the same Burberry clothes or accessories online from e-tailers like Gilt Groupe and Net-a-Porter for up to 25 percent less than in a Burberry store; sometimes they could buy them on Burberry.com for less as well. Under Ahrendts's leadership, Burberry somehow had to figure out how to bring more paying customers into its brick-and-mortar stores. Ahrendts felt that Burberry stores could compete, but only if the company ensured that the in-store experience was worth at least 25 percent of the value of the product. Otherwise, the stores would lose out.

Think about that for a moment. Burberry sold products for which much cheaper functional substitutes were readily available. It did it by selling a story, an image. And here was the company's CEO saying that at least a quarter of the perceived value of that image for the customer had to be created through an in-store experience with the brand. How would Ahrendts and her team pull *that* one off? Digital and online disruption was squeezing retailers all over the world, and their typical response had been to dabble in online and digital commerce, but never really take it seriously . . . or just to ignore digital altogether and hope it would never truly threaten the underlying business.

Like Adobe, Burberry chose neither of these options, and instead confronted the disruption head-on, looking directly to it for inspiration. Even the most innovative retailers at the time were trying to win by replicating the offline experience in their online environments. Ahrendts and her then–creative director, Christopher Bailey (who was named CEO in 2014), thought that was backward. As they reasoned, brick-and-mortar stores were losing to online because online offered something consumers found both attractive and engaging: the opportunity to perform research, connect with friends, and make decisions. It was time to stop seeing online as a simple extension of business and branding as usual, and instead look to it for guidance on how to engage the next generation of Burberry customers. And it was time to stop treating social media as a "nice to have." Burberry's edge of disruption was to take the very best of online and integrate it into the in-store experience, completely shifting industry beliefs and assumptions in doing so. (We'll detail in a little bit what Burberry created for its in-store experience.)

In addition to digital, if Burberry were to remain relevant in the fickle world of high-end fashion, it knew it had to target Millennials. As Ahrendts explained in a 2013 *Harvard Business Review* article, Burberry "began to shift our marketing efforts from targeting everyone, everywhere, to focusing on the luxury customers of the future: millennials. We believed that these customers were being ignored by our competitors. This was our white space."[13] Millennials, too, have disrupted markets across every category, and for some brands they have proven elusive and too difficult to engage. Not for Burberry. The company moved directly toward this disruptive consumer segment, and with a focus on the outcomes this generation was seeking from the brands it wore, Burberry managed to become the most followed and "fanned" apparel brand in the world of social media. By the end of 2014, Burberry had more Twitter followers than Coca-Cola (or any other consumer products brand), and was being touted as a "role model" for others in its category for its ability to engage with this new generation in a hyper-personalized way—creating customer segments of one, if you will.[14]

Did its two-pronged strategy work? In January 2006, when Ahrendts joined, the share price was £441.50; by April 2015 it was £1,724. According to an independent report by Julian Easthope, published by industry watchers at Barclays in 2014, Burberry's success "reflects the investment made offline and online, in digital marketing and customer service. There was a strong acceleration in click & collect, and iPad sales now available in 131 mainline stores. Conversion increased both in stores and online."[15]

Burberry continues to grow in emerging markets and to successfully charge a premium for its products in a hyper-competitive market. We can safely say that in 2015, Burberry, having weathered the financial crisis, leaned into the complexity of digital disruption, and taken a leap, has assumed the mantle of exclusivity once again, claiming a price premium for its trench coat that is every bit as cool as it ever was.

It did it by not just moving toward the disruptions it faced, but embracing the complexity it found there. Burberry's vision to create a seamless digital experience, both online and in store, and to create customer segments of one using data and analytics, sounds great on paper. For a company like Burberry, or any other for that matter, these challenges are among the most complex problems that could possibly be solved. Layered in is the additional complexity of having to retrain sales staff and customers, retool the back-end systems, and bring the investment community into the vision—all complexities in their own right, meaning massive transformation was required.

It started with reimagining the store. According to Christopher Bailey, Burberry's then–chief creative officer, now CEO, the store aimed to bring its "physical and digital worlds together to create amazing experiences that encompass everything from fashion, to heritage, to music."

Reimagining the store helped to revitalize Burberry, and became part of a transformation that doubled revenues and operating income over the previous five years, as of 2012.[16] It did so by integrating an extreme focus on customer insight with advanced technology, a retrained sales staff, a commitment to new forms of engagement, and a massive investment of time and money to recapture a once iconic brand. As Burberry understood, its customers liked to feel supremely important—like the most important person in the world—and the only way to achieve that was to provide hyper-personalized service. In 2012, after 300,000 person-hours were invested in its development, the new store was opened and a new age of digital experience was created.[17]

You need to visit the store to get the full experience, but consider Burberry's use of RFID as one isolated element of the new technology it deployed to give the store the same feel as its website. It built RFID technology into the tags of many of its garments, enabling customers to pull clothing off the hanger, wave it in front of a nearby interactive mirror, and view footage of the artisan making the jacket. This helped customers find a "rational" justification for what, given the price, was ultimately an irrational purchase. Customers could also use the same mirror to see custom imagery of matching accessories and bags for the garment in their hands. Ahrendts summed it up by observing that "walking through the doors is just like walking into our web site."[18]

The store is the most visible part of Burberry's transformation to creating a customer segment of one, but it is by no means the only one—nor, its team would say, was it the largest. They resolved to build a deep understanding of each customer in a way that continually refreshes and provides new insight about that one individual. That required two things: the technology to capture data about each customer and transform it into insight at scale, and a culture of service that prompted in-store employees to use customer insight at any given moment.

Burberry's technology, called Customer 360, recorded customers' buying history, shopping preferences, and fashion phobias, and compiled the data into a digital profile that sales staff could access using handheld iPads. Customers contributed to this profile through their online behavior: Data from their social media activity streamed into Burberry's system, allowing Burberry to derive further insights about their personal preferences. Burberry might discover, for instance, that people who bought jacket A tended to like belt B, or that those who preferred style A from the previous year's collection tended to love style B from the present year's. Wielding their iPads, staff drew on that information during customer interactions. But as John Douglas, Burberry's chief technology officer at the time, explained, the possibilities went further than that, using the example of a "fashionable shopper" named "Natasha," "who takes a break from a conference in a distant city to browse through a Burberry store. The salesperson can greet her by name and use a tablet device to make recommendations using predictive analytics fueled by Natasha's buying history, Twitter posts, and fashion industry trend data. Natasha can examine raincoats that appear on the salesperson's screen and then view videos of those coats. If she sees a garment she likes, the salesperson can use the device to instantly determine if the coat is in a store near Natasha's hometown and arrange for it to be shipped to her or reserved for in-store pickup."[19]

Those same analytics engines also work in real time to influence other dimensions of the flagship store's experience. A twenty-two-foot-high screen beamed images of the latest collections, pumping sound through five hundred speakers. This screen changes what footage it shows based on the cumulative preferences of people in the store at the time (as well as on London's weather that day).

We could go on and on. The point is that this is extremely complex. Hard work, as we would say. Burberry didn't just move toward the disruption; it embraced and even reveled in the complexity it found there, and was able to create a brand and an in-store experience unparalleled at the time.

Considering Burberry's story, think for a moment about Adobe's key strategic move. The internet emerged as a powerfully disruptive force, and it was changing everything—the role of content, the role of the marketer, and the way software was developed and delivered. As we've seen, the natural tendency of most people and organizations when confronted with a disruptive force is to turn the other way and pretend it doesn't exist. Most of Adobe's competitors were holding on to their traditional model of developing and licensing out-of-the-box software; they weren't really confronting the disruption directly, just shying away from the complexity that cloud-based business models presented.

Adobe leaders decided instead to run right at it. They weren't intimidated. They were optimistic about the role they could play in the future of their industry and with their clients. And they were curious in seeking to understand the internet and engineer a way of exploiting new opportunities it might bring. The critical next step was to understand the outcomes Adobe could create to have its elevated impact, and to focus obsessively on those, instead of on the inputs, processes, and business models that enabled it to solve the increasingly lower-order challenges that had defined its past. It embraced the complexity that would follow as it sought to align its people, processes, and systems to deliver on this new opportunity.

> It embraced the complexity that would follow as it sought to align its people, processes, and systems to deliver on this new opportunity.

As Adobe's CIO, Gerri Martin-Flickinger, explained, "If you're a product company, you think about things like material masters, SKUs, and physical goods. When you're in the . . . cloud business, you think about entitlements, and subscription pricing, and the product itself being highly configurable with add-ons you can tweak each month. When you think about what that means to a company, it changes everything from how they build product to how they sell product. It requires different financial back office systems, and [a] very different way of doing business."[20]

It all left analysts questioning whether Adobe could truly pull all this off. As the leaders at Adobe discovered, you can't just leap by yourself and hope the organization follows. You need alignment—of processes, systems, and people. This includes your customers, your staff, and your investors, too. Adobe was able to accomplish it with aggressive management of its investor community and open communication, as well as by showing early wins and results. It went to the investment community early and often, explaining the expected drop in earnings and providing new metrics that it felt better reflected how to measure the health of the business.

CREATE ORGANIZATIONAL ALIGNMENT

Transformation expert Dr. Peter Fuda says, "Transformation is not just a matter of intention, it is also a matter of alignment."[21] This is our experience, too, and something companies that matter care about deeply. Major transformations will fail every time if alignment doesn't exist among a broad group of stakeholders who can also ensure that processes and systems are organized in a way to deliver. Leaning into complexity may be really tough, but doing it on your own is even tougher.

When Adobe shifted to offering software as a service rather than as an off-the-shelf product, many people needed to adapt—users, investors, employees, support teams, buyers, and others. In Adobe's case, it drove a pretty hard line on the vision, but a soft touch on the people. While not budging on the overall need to move to a software-as-a-service model, Adobe did understand that some staff would not want to be on this journey, and some would not be capable. It reskilled the ones it could, and offered generous severance and retraining programs to those it couldn't. That's right—Adobe had to make some restructuring decisions, but it made the tough call, and took the leap.

It was the same for customers. Imagine you had just purchased an expensive piece of creative software from Adobe, under the implicit assumption there would be a clear upgrade path available to you as features grew in time. Adobe was quick to offer deep discounts on the subscriptions to these specific customers, aiding in their transition and softening the blow, all the while painting the vision of the new and exciting capabilities the cloud model enabled on its platform.

Adobe also had to make its peace with allowing a certain segment of customers to leave as well. That has to be okay. To make a decision like this, you have to be able to look at yourself in the mirror and say, "Everyone is better off with the new model—the long-term value we can create for our customers far outweighs the short-term costs, and is beyond anything we were doing before." You will have to do the same. Think about your own situation for a moment. What stakeholders would you have to engage to fundamentally shift the outcomes you are producing? It might be for yourself, for your team, or for your whole company. If you are a public company like Adobe, it will certainly also include your investors.

Adobe's CFO related that the company had an extremely tough time getting Wall Street to give its new model time to unfold before delivering the right numbers.[22] Adobe's leadership held steady because it knew the new model was right, and it kept aggressively working with the investment community to help it understand its vision. "We had transparent communications for three years. We showed them the faster the P&L goes down, the better you are as an investor because more people were subscribers and over the long term we are better off as a business. We helped bridge them for quite a while, and then we got to a point where they were totally onboard and understood the new model. We kept giving them long-term guidance so they could see the light at the end of the tunnel."[23]

The need for alignment was no different for Burberry. Others in the industry may have dreamed of doing something this bold, but they didn't have the determination to make it happen. It wasn't impossible, but as Ahrendts and her team will tell you, it was very hard work for everyone involved. As Mike Thorpe, a former consultant on the program, shared with us, it was one of the hardest programs he's ever experienced, but also the most rewarding.[24] It was challenging enough to get the company's CRM system to talk to its Enterprise Resource Planning (ERP) system, but that was just the beginning of the systems and processes Burberry needed to align to its new vision. Burberry also had to train its sales staff to sell differently (at first, sales associates left their new iPads to the side, preferring to return to the analog style of service they knew so well). In addition, Burberry faced the distribution challenges posed by shorter delivery times to customers, to say nothing of the need to develop technology for running the company's complex analytics. As part of its strategy, Burberry also had to reposition the brand for a younger demographic, initially using Emma Watson of *Harry Potter* fame as the new face of the brand, and closing a number of established and entrenched resellers and stores around the world, thus ensuring that its brand was represented in a more controlled and exclusive way.

These moves are the real legends of the transformation, not the store itself. By aligning the people, the systems, the incentives, the supply chain, the capability of in-store employees, and the brand touchpoints, Burberry was able to reverse its fortunes. Some of the decisions were very tough to make, and others represented significant investments and equally significant departures from how things were traditionally done. This is the hard work of elevating your impact, and there are no shortcuts.

It was this same diligence and sustained commitment to the journey, and to aligning people, systems, and processes, that enabled BrokerLink (not its real name) not just to thrive in the face of disruption but to thrive because of it. BrokerLink found its market in the investment products industry threatened not by the internet, but by pending government legislation (notably Dodd-Frank), combined with a changing economic climate (thanks to the 2008 meltdown) and shifting client needs. BrokerLink was able to thrive against the odds by doing what so few of its competitors were bold enough to do: confront this disruptive environment head-on, and find important new ways to add value in new market conditions.

BrokerLink is a broker-dealer. Broker-dealers act as the research and back-office function for local financial advisors, selecting investment products and making them available on platforms to the advisors for sale to their end-user investors. They are the processes and systems that support advisors' businesses, and as such, if an advisor needs to align behind a new opportunity in the market, the broker-dealers will need to create processes and systems to enable it. Broker-dealers are directly vested in the success of their advisor clients—if advisors make less profit, so do broker-dealers.

In the wake of the financial crisis, it seemed everyone was making less and doing more. Advisors wanted their broker-dealers to step up and do more to help, particularly with Dodd-Frank's compliance pressures. At the same time, client demands for interaction and support were increasing.

Many broker-dealers reacted to these disruptions by complaining about the new legislation and lobbying against it. Considering how much trust the industry had lost following the 2008–2009 recession, it was a losing battle. Another choice was to look to the advisors to pick up more of the effort, but they were already overwhelmed not merely by compliance burdens, but also by investors who had come to want more real-time interaction to manage their concerns. Compounding the situation, advisors often ran fairly unsophisticated businesses. Many of them had haphazard processes, and their technology adoption was often quite low across the entire population.[25] Advisors also tended to be older (the average age of a US-based advisor was estimated to be over fifty at this time) and generally inclined to stick with what they knew and understood. Of course, not all advisors fit this description, but many did. When all is said and done, advisors had the most power in the value chain thanks to their direct link to the client, but they were often the weakest link when it came to innovation and adapting to change.

BrokerLink decided to take a leap: to find a way to turn the complexity of the new legislation, and changing investor demands, into an opportunity for its advisors to create more value for their investors. In doing so, investors become more valuable to the advisors who facilitated this win-win outcome. The optimistic question BrokerLink asked was not unlike the one Piggly Wiggly asked all those years ago: How can we turn the compliance burden of increased discovery and customer scrutiny that Dodd-Frank requires into a high-value advisor–investor interaction, which would drive greater revenue? BrokerLink didn't just want to get ahead of the legislation. It wanted to be a powerful catalyst for business growth and relationship building with its advisors. It took the leap by aligning its processes and systems to enable advisors to deliver on that high-value promise to their investor clients.

BrokerLink reengineered the entire client onboarding and discovery process for advisors on its platform. Specifically, the company did three things. First, it transformed the end investor's initial meeting with an advisor. The meeting went from an unstructured question-and-answer session to a systematic discovery and diagnostic process that produced a formal client report. Second, as part of this process, BrokerLink had its advisors speak about planning fees and compensation *much* earlier in the process, communicating the value advisors brought and anchoring the notion that advisors should receive compensation for it. And third, BrokerLink leveraged newly generated insight from the diagnostic process to identify a wider range of products and solutions that could meet investors' needs.

BrokerLink's new process was a huge success. Many advisors on BrokerLink's platform found that certain prospects became more interested in investment planning and advice than they had expected. These prospects were more willing to divulge information about their investable assets earlier in the process. Some advisors were so impressed by BrokerLink's process that they conducted diagnostics with existing clients as a way of renewing the relationships. Often they could easily reallocate clients' investments, making clients more money while generating new commissions. In some cases, advisors discovered that clients with whom they had worked for twenty years had substantial, never-disclosed assets to invest!

Talking about fees early in the process scared away some investors—which was a *good* thing. As we've seen, when

companies are the obvious choice, they focus on the right customers, not any customer. For advisors, that meant higher-value
clients who were prepared to invest properly in planning and
advice.

BrokerLink's use of the diagnostic tool to locate additional
products to sell to investors paid off as well. Life insurance sales
on the part of advisors on BrokerLink's platform reportedly rose
by 70 percent, while anecdotal evidence from advisors on other
broker-dealer platforms realized increases in only single digits
to the low teens from organic market growth during the same
period. Again, investors won, since this product would protect their families from catastrophic events that could destroy a
family's financial health. Advisors won, too, since they gained
higher commissions from life insurance sales.

BrokerLink won as well. Advisors came to value their relationship with the company more, seeing it as an even more vital
strategic partner. The amount of assets under management, the
number of wealthier customers, and the sales of high-profit
products like life insurance all increased, yielding much-needed
revenue and margins for BrokerLink at a time when the majority of broker-dealers were barely liquid.

BrokerLink had created a new solution that allowed its
advisors to build a new type of relationship with their clients,
understanding their lives and needs better and in ways that
perpetually renewed the relationship. This in turn elevated
BrokerLink's relationship with its direct customers, the advisors. Instead of merely paying lip service to being invested in
advisors' success, BrokerLink leaned into the disruption, and
became the obvious choice by creating more value and having
an elevated impact as a result. And it did it by aligning people,
processes, and systems to a new, more valuable way of serving
its customers.

Elevated impact starts with the shift from working hard
to doing the *hard work*. Adobe was working hard when developing, boxing, and shipping software for designers to create
beautiful graphics and video administrators to manage documents; the hard work was improving the ROI of marketing

dollars spent and helping brands navigate the emerging digital world. GHX works hard to deliver 99.9 percent uptime for its core exchange, and it does the hard work to bring the industry together in meaningful ways to co-create solutions to the toughest problems it collectively faces. DPR worked hard to win bids from clients the same way everyone else did, until it did the hard work of reinventing the process by which it engaged with partners to collaboratively build great buildings. These are companies that took perspective and relationships and then went the final step of finding ways to create an elevated impact; collectively that effort resulted in them becoming the obvious choice for their target markets. They truly became companies that matter.

Look at your own world and think about how you can do things differently. What elevated impact could you have on your part of the world? We're willing to bet there is a transformative opportunity in every group in every company, if you take the opportunity to think about how you might deliver more value, and how you might matter more in whatever form that takes for you. Elevating your impact means confronting your edge of disruption head-on, and leaning into the complexity you find there. It requires an orientation around the high-value outcomes your customers most seek from you, and a shift away from the inputs that have underpinned your offer and value proposition to date. And it means bringing others along with you— your employees, your customers, and others in your ecosystem. Think back to Lakeside, the logistics company that transformed itself into a comprehensive transportation partner. Most CEOs or CFOs would have been at least mildly intrigued by the idea. In the abstract, it sounds great: "We take over the customer's transportation function. The customer's cost goes down, while efficiency increases. Meanwhile, the customer's best and brightest people are freed up to focus on its core business." But the task of making this work at scale was enormously complex, which was precisely why Lakeside was interested.

As Jeff Moore, Lakeside's CEO, remarked, an opportunity to create more value "should have a level of complexity. The more complex, the more difficult for [the customer] to handle, the more value we can add." Under Lakeside's new business plan, "the quantity of [our] relationships has gone down, but quality has gone up. But with that quality has come complexity, right, because now there's so much more on the line. When somebody says I've got $15 million worth of freight spend a year, and it's 20,000 transactions, that's a huge amount of volume to put through a business, and when they say they want it all [outsourced to you], you get it, basically, all at the same time . . . They're putting so much more trust in you to deliver on the back side of what you're promising to them."[26]

> An opportunity to create more value "should have a level of complexity. The more complex, the more difficult for [the customer] to handle, the more value we can add."

It's precisely the intensity of work required to execute a new value proposition that cements the relationship between companies that have successfully become the obvious choice and their customers. These are companies that have embraced a whole new way of doing business, and so have their customers and investors.

You can stop at elevating your perspective and still have a lot of interesting things to say. You can stop at elevating your relationships and still have a lot of great interactions and latent potential. But if you do stop along the way, you will not transform your industry or your own company in the ways that will sustain it as the obvious choice.

Take the leap. Do the hard work. Be the disruptor. Use your elevated perspective and elevated relationships and make your move. Have an elevated impact! By doing so you won't just find the hard work that needs doing—you will find that the *right* work reveals itself, too. And this will inspire you to be the kind of leader worthy of your emerging position as the obvious choice. That's our last stop on the journey, the final task for elevating your impact: answering the call.

Bring It to Life . . .

1. By now you know your edge of disruption, and you have the relationships required to create value. Get into a room with the key decision makers, and answer this question: Are we going to move toward this edge of disruption or not?

2. Assuming you said yes, what symbolic move could you make that would send the message internally and to your key partners that you are serious about this, and that you want them on the journey? Make that move.

3. Work collaboratively to identify the single most important step to take if your edge of disruption is going to create the value it promises, and if you are going to find a sustainable business model in the solutions you generate there.

4. Develop a detailed approach to taking this step, and find ways to test ideas and potential solutions.

5. Form the internal team, establish the external partnerships, and allocate the necessary resources to run these pilots.

6. Execute, iterate, refine, and then repeat until you have a feasible, scalable solution.

7. Make a more significant bet on this solution, and be prepared to continue to refine and learn as you scale.

8. Make a list of the _one_ system, _one_ process, and _one_ person you most need to align if you are to make the leap and be the disruptor. Commit to making the changes needed for each, and take action immediately to begin making progress.

CHAPTER 8

LIVE: Answer the Call

IT'S INTERESTING, DON'T YOU THINK, how we like to refer to professional athletes as heroes for the way they play a game, entertain the crowd, and rise up in the face of adversity? Our provocation to you is this: If recreational activity like catching an air-filled, pigskin-covered prolate spheroid, or hitting a small white ball around a well-manicured garden, is worthy of such praise, then the journey to becoming the obvious choice is even more so.

Consider Nike again. When Nike says, "If you have a body, you are an athlete," it really means it. It doesn't, as one might think, just focus on athletes in big-name sports. It's worked with Paralympians, too, and recently came out with a shoe designed specifically for people with disabilities who want to wear sneakers. With its easy-entry rear zip design, the Nike Soldier 8 FLYEASE, designed in collaboration with a young man with cerebral palsy, will help millions of people who struggle with the daily task of putting on shoes.[1] This is work that matters, and is a core part of the culture that makes Nike so great in many ways.

We believe that the decision to do work that matters and become a company that matters, and then to go on the journey we have outlined to this point, is heroic. It's like all the great stories you have read since childhood. In each, there comes that moment when the hero answers the call and starts off toward his or her future self. We encourage you to take this just as seriously for your organization. Embrace the emotional and purposeful nature of what this book, and your customers, employees, and community, are asking of you. If you don't feel that way about it—inspired, if you will—you likely will not have the drive to see it through.

Joseph Campbell, writing about this moment, says, "Refusal of the summons converts the adventure into its negative. Walled in boredom, hard work, or 'culture,' the subject loses the power of significant affirmative action and becomes a victim to be saved. His flowering world becomes a wasteland of dry stones and his life feels meaningless."[2]

We'd compare that type of wasteland to the organizational existence of living in a hyper-competitive commoditized market, subsisting on volume and price equations that are negotiated further down every year. Surely standing confidently on your edge of disruption and making a choice to leap forward, to confront the challenges that lie ahead, and to make real change in your world, is the very same calling that our storied hero experiences—only this time you and your company are the heroes.

This is why it is important to do the *right* work—work that inspires, that makes a difference, that contributes to more than your bottom line. It's about seeing the humanity and social side of what you do. It is understanding that your customers, your suppliers, and your employees are all, at the end of the day, just people. People who crave purpose, people who want to leave a legacy, and people who want to see meaning in what they do beyond just economic gain. We refer to this as *answering the call*, and it is really about making a decision not just to have an impact, but to have a positive impact on your organization, your customers, and your entire community.

Milton Friedman believed that "the social responsibility of business is to increase its profits."[3] He wrote that in 1970, in an article with exactly that title. His influence over business models and organizational ethos in the 1970s through to today can't be understated, and that article has been frequently quoted by fierce defenders of ruthless business tactics. These tactics tend to work to create short-term gains, but when a longer view is taken and multiple factors are included, those gains become dubious at best. Friedman has to be taken in a specific context of short- or long-term success, and we believe most companies want to be around long term. Because we subscribe to a long view, we see companies as social actors, and believe corporate social responsibility (CSR) is a key dimension of long-term success, and a moral obligation for any corporation. We think this is in keeping with broader interpretations of capitalism, and ironically, perhaps, with Friedman as well, if you apply his logic to long-term rather than short-term returns.

We have had the opportunity to work with several of the world's largest and most successful companies, helping them with components of their CSR programs, and we know that these programs amplify their results in several dimensions. They keep their employees engaged and working hard on behalf of the company, they create a unique connection with their customers, and they drive long-term success by allowing companies to connect with potential new customers through the programs they support. To maximize profits and your positive impact over the long term, you might just need to aim in the short term.

We subscribe to Tom Zara's idea about the place of brands, and see it as a challenge for any company to aspire to meet. Tom is the global practice leader for corporate citizenship and strategy at Interbrand New York, and he once said, "A business, elevated by the power and purpose of its brand, can bring together various economic factors, resources, and skill sets, organize them and use them to not only maximize profit, but to bring the world back into balance."[4]

This aspirational goal of bringing the world back into balance is exactly what the best companies do. They take their elevated perspective, relationships, and impact and they create a new world order that truly matters to them, their customers, and the broader community within which they exist. They do work that matters, and they have an impact that makes them matter, too.

As we reflect on some of the cases we've studied, one overarching characteristic is in fact a commitment to the greater good, a sense of responsibility, and a second is an understanding that profits come from doing great things, not the other way around. For example, DPR wanted first to build great things, knowing that profits would come as a logical by-product of answering the call to change the trajectory of how its industry was functioning. As we heard from one of its executives, "Working at DPR Construction is about being part of something bigger than you. It is about contributing to the growth and success of a national organization deeply committed to serving customers and driving change in the industry. It is about building great things with integrity, enjoyment, uniqueness and ever forward."[5]

Deloitte Canada leaders, when describing the motives behind the Best Managed program, talk about enabling the economic prosperity of Canada by developing and supporting mid-market companies: "The vision for the program is to build a community of companies that can help each other, bringing insights and ideas to make all Canadian businesses successful."[6] This is all the more powerful when you realize it was conceived of prior to the internet, at a time when companies like this did not have access to insights like these.

> Companies that find ways to matter are extremely ambitious and deeply optimistic about their future. They take a long-term view of that future, and make investments in their customers, their people, their industry, and the community at large to ensure they remain sustainably profitable over the long term, even if it means saying no to revenue today.

And when leaders at CVS, a company we are about to look at, talk about CVS's 8,000 pharmacies, its 900 MinuteClinics, and its 200,000-plus staff, they don't talk about maximizing shareholder value, they talk about "helping people on a path to better health."

Let's reflect on the fact that DPR is profitable, Deloitte Best Managed does drive quality leads into the business, and CVS generates significant growth in shareholder value. This is not some Pollyanna chapter about companies putting community first and shareholders second. We also recognize that in each case, arguments can be made that these companies also struggle to "answer the call," at times with negative consequences for their environments. We cannot offer a single example of a perfect company, but we can offer many examples of companies working to make a positive difference within large and complex contexts. We believe that when profits or shareholder value become the sole purpose of a company, decisions become short term, focused on quarterly or even monthly earnings, and it becomes impossible for the company to stand confidently on the edge of disruption and make the bold decisions needed to confront that disruption fully. It gets in the way of answering the call to serve a higher purpose in a way that contributes to long-term profitability and success.

Companies that find ways to matter are extremely ambitious and deeply optimistic about their future. They take a long-term view of that future, and make investments in their customers, their people, their industry, and the community at large to ensure they remain sustainably profitable over the long term, even if it means saying no to revenue today. Likewise, the leaders of the companies we studied did not judge their impact based on any single reporting period. They looked at it from a systemic level, including the ecosystem, industry players, and the community at large, and thought about longer time periods both when reflecting on past performance and when considering future performance. Like Adobe, they have the courage to push back on Wall Street's demands for short-term growth when necessary to insist on longer-term commitments to deliver the most value to their market. This commitment to their industries, their people, and their communities was implicit in everything they did and every decision they made. It formed part of their DNA. And when asked why they go over and above for the customer or prospect, or share their insights and intellectual property freely with their competitors, or channel their expertise and capital to community development, they simply reply, "It's the right thing to do."

The most common phrase or notion in all the transcripts from all the companies we studied was "do the right thing," or some variation on that theme. Whether it is DPR spending so much time and energy partnering with Stanford and other universities to advance cutting-edge approaches to its industry; or LoyaltyOne deciding it would assume responsibility for building an entire market and educate all potential competitors in that space, to better its industry; or Deloitte investing in the health and development of the mid-market in Canada, these companies answered the call, and did the right work when the time came.

> The best companies attract the best talent because they do the right thing.

Here's another outcome that we heard about over and over again: The best companies attract the best talent because they do the right thing. Their commitment to playing a leadership role, contributing in return, and creating something bigger than any one company makes them the obvious choice for the best talent on the market. Why? Our work, and external research, has shown that the implicit social contract between employer and employee has shifted away from a traditional Baby Boomer model of being grateful for a job, willing to work hard for thirty-plus years and retire with a pension—the common model of the Industrial Age.[7] That implicit social contract involved trading security and longevity with a company for showing up and doing your work, regardless of the corporate value structure. As the 1990s rolled around, and outsourcing and "business process reengineering" gained traction, the implicit social contract changed as well.

Suddenly, employees were disposable "resources" or "assets" who could be easily laid off or traded in for more efficient models. As a result, employees started evaluating possible employers based on growth opportunities—where they could go to develop the most marketable skills, so when they inevitably got downsized they would be able to find work elsewhere. But we see a new disruption rumbling on the edges, and it is in this implicit social contract that it is shifting again. Today, many employees want to work for a company that gives them a sense of meaning and purpose, a company where they can make a contribution to both the economic success and the social impact of their company. In today's tight labor pool, this may be one of the most interesting reasons to take a hard look at the role your company plays in the broader community in which it exists. You will likely find that by offering new types of work, you will attract new types of workers.

TAKE A STAND

There may be no better example of a company that confronted disruption coming from social and cultural changes in recent years, and answered the call required to elevate its impact, than CVS Health. Its approach to tobacco sales in its stores cost the company money in the short term, but the longer-term benefit is paying off well. It is worth diving into how CVS approached this major disruption, and why we think it makes a good example of a company that matters in ways that are relevant today and in the future.

Drugstores and pharmacies are as competitive as any business on earth. Walgreens and CVS duke it out regularly as the biggest on the block, and then Rite Aid fills the spaces left behind.[8] Mixed in are Walmart, Target, Safeway, and other big-box stores looking for a piece of the action. Almost a third of current retail sales for the likes of CVS and Walgreens come from over-the-counter products such as groceries, beauty care, and other convenience-related items. As a result, big drugstore chains compete with gas stations, convenience stores, and even Amazon and other online retailers.

It's no wonder this industry has consolidated over the last decade or so, as the big guys seek economies of scale and a price advantage over their aggressive rivals. Discounting and com-moditization of both the products and the shopping experience are rampant. We can only imagine it is exhausting to continu-ally try to be a penny lower than everyone else. Strategically, Walgreens has made it pretty clear that it is going to focus on increasing store count and being on every street corner, compet-ing aggressively on price across not just pharmacy but grocery, too. CVS is leaping toward the complexity of not just healthcare reform, but healthcare delivery itself, and in the process it's seek-ing to elevate its impact on the health and wellness of Americans.

CVS's leadership team decided to answer the call to play a more significant role in dealing with the healthcare crisis in America. They were content to let Walgreens and Walmart slog it out on price and reach in the increasingly commoditized world of retail. CVS is confronting the crisis with a three-pronged strategy that includes in-store clinics, strategic sourcing part-nerships, and disease management for the highest spend areas of chronic health conditions.

Honestly, all of these pieces of strategy and execution are fairly imitable. Safeway, Walgreens, and others have spun up clinics, invested in research, and developed partnerships to lower costs. Those are good, solid strategies, but they don't necessarily make CVS stand apart from the crowd as the obvious choice. CVS's leadership team realized that where there is disruption there is opportunity, and eventually margin as well, but it takes a bold move to take advantage of that space. The converging forces of change in healthcare and population health presented the perfect opportunity to elevate CVS's impact and make it a trusted partner to both systems and consumers in all things health and wellness, if it could go a step further than anyone else.

And so the leadership team made an incredibly bold decision, one that immediately lit up the news wires and the Twitterverse with speculation about "What were they thinking?" (An aside: Remember the last company we talked about that got asked that question? Adobe ended up exceeding all expectations after that was posted in the *Wall Street Journal*.) The announcement was that as of September 2014, CVS stores across America would be free of all tobacco products.⁹ Pause for a moment and think back to the last time you were in a non–CVS Health drugstore. Perhaps you recall the wall-to-wall tobacco offerings behind the registers. Seems misaligned, wouldn't you say, to get your cigarettes at the same place you get your lung cancer medications? CVS thought so, and took the controversial move to ban them, forgoing at least $2 billion a year in tobacco sales as a result.

It was the first retail pharmacy to make such a significant commitment to the health of its consumers, which is amazing when you consider how completely incongruent it is to sell tobacco at a store focused on healthy living. CVS's leadership team decided it could not claim to be for the health and wellness of the American consumer while selling them things that science has long since accepted are very harmful to their health. It replaced the "real estate" with signage that read, "We quit tobacco. Ask a trained pharmacist or nurse practitioner to help you quit, too."

At the same time, CVS rolled out a series of products and services aimed to help people quit smoking. *USA Today* noted that "CVS was deluged with personal stories from customers who had quit smoking." Many called it "the hardest thing they had ever done," as CVS/pharmacy president Helena Foulkes said, but "the company is determined to make it easier for them." The CVS Health website was updated to say, "Some called it a bold decision. We called it the right decision," quoting their own CEO, Larry Merlo, in the process. As we have said, elevating your impact is not just about doing the *hard* work, it is also about doing the *right* work.

It's interesting to contrast this to Walgreens, which at the time came out and explicitly stated it would not drop tobacco. The position Walgreens took suggested that it did not get to the core of the cause of the issue, and that smokers would simply move to other retailers to buy their cigarettes. There is research to suggest that this is not necessarily true, and that when a trusted pharmacy brand like CVS Health makes a move like this, it can have an amplified impact and inspire smokers to make the same decision.

As Zara said, brands influence how people think, and in this case, we believe it is for the better. It acts as a timely contrast. Companies that matter are also passionate about making their customers and consumers better, their industry better, and their communities (which ultimately provide them with their social license to operate) better as well. And when faced with a $2 billion short-term decision like "Should we keep selling tobacco?" and the long-term opportunity to have an elevated impact on the lives of Americans, CVS chose the latter. It answered the call that was coming from the disruption it was seeing in the market, and got ahead of the game as a result. Some might say it was late to the game; after all, research has been available for years suggesting that quitting tobacco is better than smoking it. But CVS was still the first in its market to move, and it took advantage of the moment provided by shifting consumer attitudes and expectations as well as the science available.

So let's apply a little Friedman-esque perspective. Remember, we don't argue against Friedman's point that economic value is important, only the way it has been interpreted to make economic value (and short-term value at that) the *only* important goal of a company. By sacrificing short-term guaranteed revenue, in spite of a 0.4 percent drop at the time of writing in front-of-house sales as a result of the lost tobacco revenue, CVS Health profits were up 11 percent, and it could track $5.4 billion in new pharmacy sales.[10] Although this climb is not directly caused by their dropping tobacco, CVS Health CEO Merlo is quick to point out the symbolic value of the move when negotiating large, single-supplier contracts with key health plans who have a vested interest in cutting healthcare costs by reducing chronic conditions caused by things like smoking, and when negotiating with government as well.[11] And in the twelve months since the announcement was made, CVS shares were up 38 percent. At the same time, financial analysts suggested that even though the decision to stop selling tobacco would reduce CVS Health's earnings per share by $0.06 to $0.09, this decision will greatly increase its odds of renewing a prescription deal with the Federal Employees Health Benefits Program, which will add $0.16 to

$0.21 per share. Merlo observed that "the contradiction of selling tobacco was becoming a growing obstacle to playing a bigger role in healthcare delivery,"[12] so CVS took the courageous stance to remove that obstacle, and the result has been overwhelmingly good economic news. Getting organizationally aligned on a relevant issue created both social and economic benefits for CVS and its customers.

Let's take a look at two more examples of companies that have taken strong stands to change how they do business, the way their industry operates, and the skills and capability of the community at large. We'll introduce you to Domtar, an innovative fiber company that has single-handedly changed the face of the paper industry and in the process made paper a mostly renewable resource. Then, we'll share with you our experiences working with the Commonwealth Bank of Australia (CommBank) in its community partnership programs as it changes the financial capabilities of an entire generation of Aussie kids. Both of these companies faced a moment when they had to make a decision: they had to choose between short-term gain and staying true to the standards they had created for themselves. In choosing their standards, they invested money in ways that, at first glance, may not seem to maximize profit. Yet through a longer-term lens and an understanding of the social interdependencies that every business lives with, their choices have yielded and continue to yield economic value as well as social impact.

LEAD THE CHARGE

Domtar is a company in transformation. As North America's largest paper and pulp company, and the second largest in the world, you can imagine the challenges it currently faces with the structural decline of paper use since the onset of the digital revolution. Its edge of disruption is to embrace the complexity of more innovative and sophisticated paper and pulp products in the health and personal hygiene space, and to add more value to its underlying product.

Will it be successful? We think yes. In fact, it already is succeeding, with its share price up some ten times its lowest point in 2009. It's successful because it has transformed before, and because over and over again it has been able to elevate its impact, and answer the call in the process.

For Domtar it all really started in the early 1990s, when it made the conscious decision to answer the call—in the face of massive consumer and environmentalist pressure to change the way the industry sourced paper and pulp. Transparency found its way to the end users of paper products, and society began to turn its back on paper, in favor of the environment at large. This was a shift that the environmental nongovernmental organizations (ENGOs) leveraged to wage their war against big business, and Domtar was one of their biggest targets.

While waging war might seem like an extreme metaphor, it was not far from what happened. Greenpeace activists, for one, dropped a banner unannounced at the front gates of a Domtar mill in Cornwall, Ontario, and didn't leave until they were dragged away. It could be argued that a war was unnecessary, considering that the paper industry was only one environmentally impactful industry, and by no means the worst. Furthermore, Domtar was a better environmental steward than most at the time.

Perhaps even more important is to realize that environmental impact is a reasonable new phenomenon to understand. That's why the way Domtar responded, when it realized just how serious this was, is a credit to it as a company and to the paper industry as a whole, and is an example of the elevated impact a company can have when it chooses to do the right work.

Lewis Fix, VP of sustainable business and brand management at Domtar, explained, "That [Greenpeace] experience really opened Domtar's eyes to the fact that ENGOs were watching us and it also showed us the level of conviction they had. It startled us, because they didn't even ask us to talk first, it was a sense of shock and awe here." NGOs were using dramatic tactics to drive awareness, not just in the environmental space, but across human rights, social, and health issues as well. The confrontational style they preferred quickly created an "us versus them" mentality across the business world. NGOs and ENGOs established themselves as the "enemy," although their intentions were rooted in the right place. Not surprisingly, most companies readied themselves for battle, bringing in lawyers, lobbyists, and big budgets to fight back.

Domtar chose a different path. It felt the incident at Cornwall left it with two choices. It could meet ENGOs like the World Wildlife Fund (WWF) with the same adversarial intent and defend its environmental practices, which at the time were industry leading. Or it could acknowledge that there was opportunity for improvement, answer the call, and do the right work of evolving decades-old industry practices, directly confronting the disruption that was right in front of it. Domtar's leaders chose the latter. They stepped out of the echo chamber of their industry and decided

> They stepped out of the echo chamber of their industry and decided to do thing differently . . . As others in their industry may have said, they got into bed with the devil.

to do things differently, creating a coalition of businesses and ENGOs committed to creating more sustainable forestry practices in the paper value chain. As others in their industry may have said, they got into bed with the devil.

Rather than put up walls, close doors, and relegate ENGOs to the sidewalks and the airwaves, Domtar decided to elevate its relationships by connecting broadly with this new stakeholder group. It opened its doors to the very groups the industry had branded as "the enemy." Lewis Fix recalls that "at the end of the day, we figured that it'd be better for us to have a dialogue and work on having an open-door policy with them."[13] Domtar took a much more collaborative approach to solve the single most complex problem its industry was facing: how to produce sustainable, renewable paper products. For instance, Kathy Wholley, the director of advertising and communication at the time, explained that "Domtar was one of the first in the industry to commit to Forest Stewardship Council (FSC) certification when no one was willing to do that. It was a favorite certification schema of environmental groups, but it was definitely not a favorite of the industry."[14]

In addition to supporting the FSC, Domtar also collaborated actively with the WWF. The organization had been around for decades, conducting research, consulting, and lobbying in an effort to halt and reverse the destruction of the environment. It is the world's largest independent conservation organization, operating in more than 100 countries. When asked about the early days of working with Domtar, Hadley Archer, the WWF's then-VP, strategic partnerships and development, says that "at the time, we were not the ones who were out boycotting and pushing for absolutes, forestry or environment. We realized that forests are trees, trees are renewable, and if we could just work with pioneering organizations, we could learn to manage them properly to create thriving industry and ecosystems."[15] WWF had been reaching out to many businesses in the Canadian paper industry to get their participation in developing standards that the FSC had recently introduced in Europe. "It was often a tough conversation. We needed leading companies who were willing to change how they do business, up it to a higher standard from an environmental and social point of view, but also find ways to improve their bottom line with the ideal scenario," Hadley continues.

Domtar stepped up to be that company. WWF worked with Domtar and FSC "to help them achieve FSC certification for all of their managed lands in Canada," says Hadley. "We'd also help them push these standards and their importance throughout the supply chain." From a major player in an industry traditionally less modern in its approach toward understanding its impact on the environment, this was nothing short of extraordinary. By making this commitment, Domtar secured its place in the industry as a company having an elevated impact, making it the obvious choice for downstream value-chain participants like big-box retailers who were also being targeted by the ENGOs.

Staples, Office Depot, OfficeMax, Best Buy, and others needed help to effectively respond to the negative publicity and evolving consumer sentiment about the environmental effects of their product range, which was beginning to have a direct impact on their retail market. With its early involvement and willingness to collaborate to improve their practices, Domtar was well positioned to take advantage of and drive the sustainability message. No one else really knew how to do it, or had managed to cover as much ground as Domtar, so retailers flocked to it for its elevated perspective. Domtar brought these retailers into the discussion, showing that they could

> With its early involvement and willingness to collaborate to improve their practices, Domtar was well positioned to take advantage of and drive the sustainability message.

do more than just "stock their shelves with paper. [Domtar] could teach them . . . could show them how to set up a sustainability-related scorecard within their business . . . tell them what their hot buttons were with NGOs, and introduce them to those NGOs proactively instead of waiting for an incident," according to Dick Thomas, Domtar's SVP, sales and marketing.[16] Not only did Domtar have product in the market, but it also had unique advisory services to offer, thanks to all it had learned at its edge of disruption, and it leveraged this elevated perspective to gain access and influence with retail customers.

Domtar didn't stop with the WWF alliance. It also entered conversations with the Rainforest Alliance. "From the beginning, it was open conversations with Domtar," remarks Tensie Whelan, Rainforest Alliance president.[17] Domtar was actively searching for ways to improve how it was doing business to mitigate risks, but was also seeking new means for differentiation. The Rainforest Alliance had a respected brand name, a very strong chief of forestry, and ideas for how Domtar could continue down its FSC certification path, "green" its supply chain, and move the tarnished image of pulp and paper in the market. Through its collaborations with ENGOs, customers, and others in the industry, Domtar quickly realized it wasn't looking for small, incremental improvements. It wanted to see if it could create a paper product worthy of FSC certification. So in 2002, it launched EarthChoice, a product line that required *a lot* of hard work that was also the right work to do.

EarthChoice was a bold move that would require building an entire brand line around something that was credible, trustworthy, and robust enough to withstand demand fluctuations. This would mean new processes, new systems, new and revitalized machinery in the mills, new skills, and other major resource investments. It would take more than just shared goals, surface-level partnerships, and rethinking the status quo to get it done. As Rob Melton, Domtar's VP for specialty paper, explained, "We'd have to go beyond our customers to the actual end users of the product and try to really understand the value that they would like to have, and then work through the supply chain to make sure we're delivering that in these new products."[18] The development process required Domtar to fully confront the complexity it was managing across its entire system.

To do this, Domtar wrapped the whole organization around doing the hard work of reinventing its operating model, and doing the right work by committing to leading positive change in its industry. The result? The EarthChoice product was an amazing success. For years, Domtar was the only paper manufacturer that had copy paper in the North American market that was FSC certified and had the WWF's panda logo. It won the company new contracts with customers who felt heavy pressure to become more sustainable, it enabled Domtar to renew contracts with existing clients, and it elevated its positioning in the industry with buyers and the competition, as well as with employees. And as a pleasant by-product, Domtar enjoyed a better and leading-edge operating procedure.

A decade later, Domtar's EarthChoice paper is still one of the largest, most comprehensive lines of FSC-certified paper in North America, accounting for more than 20 percent of Domtar's total paper sales.[19] Those same NGOs and ENGOs that dropped banners in front of Domtar factories all those years ago now use Domtar as a leading example for how companies can do well economically while also doing the right work for humanity. Friedman acolytes might have pushed Domtar to squeeze the last viable dollar out of their old model, but we like to think Friedman himself would applaud the long-term view of social responsibility driving ultimate economic value. Since he died in 2006, we can only speculate (and debate) on that point!

We know it's worked for Domtar; has it worked for the environment, too? Consider the following data. According to a report released by the Society of American Foresters, replanting and reforestation efforts have helped keep forestland stable. There are nearly 750 million acres of forests in the United States, about the same as 100 years ago. Annual net growth of US forests is 36 percent higher than the volume of annual tree removals. The standing inventory of "growing stock" in US forests has increased steadily since the mid-1950s.[20]

Also consider that in 2012, more than 65 percent of the paper consumed in the United States was recovered for recycling. In a review of external reports, Domtar notes that since 1990, when the paper industry established its first recovery goal to advance recycling in the United States, paper recovery has grown by more than 85 percent. Comparatively, the recovery rate for metal is 35 percent; glass is 27 percent, and plastic is only 8 percent.[21]

Paper is on its way to becoming one of the few truly sustainable/renewable raw materials we use in everyday life. Combine that with the fact that the fossil fuels required to both produce and power electronics continue to be far more environmentally problematic than paper (and recycling batteries and other components is a problem that still hasn't been solved). If the industry continues to advance sustainable forestry management, assuming it can continue to promote and support the recycling of paper, we believe the industry has a bright future.

We are willing to bet you didn't know that. This perception, and the inevitable continued decline of paper in favor of digital, is a *big* issue for this industry. Perception is reality, as the saying goes, and paper is still struggling more than it should be. Who can possibly take this on? Domtar, of course. Under the leadership of president and CEO John D. Williams, Domtar has addressed this challenge head-on with a branding and demand-generation platform known as Paper Because, which serves the industry and consumers in a unique way.

In its simplest form, Paper Because is an education platform that includes articles, videos, and educational assets aimed to educate people about how paper is made, its impact on the environment, the role it plays in our life, and specific strategies for using it wisely. It includes an above-the-line advertising campaign, which has seen ads run in *Fast Company*, the *New York Times*, and even *National Geographic*. It involved Domtar staff and leaders presenting in both industry and non-industry forums, as well as kids' classrooms, about paper and the environment. And it even includes continued collaborations with powerful ENGOs like the World Wildlife Fund.

Through the Paper Because platform, Domtar provides in-depth data and analysis regarding the true impact of paper production and recycling, making it readily available to consumers, buyers, competition, and industry watchers. It tells the story of renewable and sustainable practices and also amplifies the more emotional role paper plays in people's lives. For many people, the way they use paper is a very personal thing. iPads are great, for example, but they don't feel the same as a personal journal. Digital books lack the feel of the pages and the connection with their markings in the margin, which represent something deeply personal for readers. Paper is not only sustainable, it is a connected experience, and Paper Because is telling this story on behalf of the entire industry.

Through Paper Because, Domtar doubled down on its industry, putting its own investment into relaunching not just its brand, but the entire brand that is paper. The company decided to remind people of the power of paper in their lives, and to tell the truth about its sustainability. Paper Because is a way to stimulate demand, slow the decline, and ensure the truth is being told about the business itself.

The elevated impact of all of this was not just a shift in the demand curve. It also influenced how people felt about using, producing, and buying paper. Paper Because was designed to instill a sense of pride that was lacking in the industry. Kathy Wholley, now Domtar's senior director of corporate communications, said to us in June 2015, "The reactions to Paper Because were 'Finally!' and 'Thank you!' The impact was felt beyond the intended audience of C-suite executives and environmental advocates. Our employees were excited to see the company standing up for them, and our competitors were relieved to have resources to rely on to help tell the story of the value of paper."

When we asked Lewis Fix at Domtar why the company continues to invest money in things like Paper Because and supply chain transparency, he simply replied, "High tides raise all boats."[22] It's a familiar sentiment from companies that matter: They believe that they can create the most value when they contribute to more than just their own success. Echoing this thought, Bryan Pearson at LoyaltyOne said, "At the end of the day, we're interested in having loyalty succeed, right? Loyalty and this idea of measured marketing and customer experience. If loyalty succeeds, then there's a lot more business that we can do over time. So, that's mission one." Companies like Domtar and LoyaltyOne are happy to put their hands up and drive an entire industry forward. It's the right thing to do, because truly a rising tide lifts all ships.

> Companies that matter ... believe they can create the most value when they contribute to more than just their own success.

We've shared CVS's focus on aligning organizational strategy with customer well-being, and how Domtar took on an entire industry's assumptions about how to do business in the spirit of doing not just any work, but the *right* work. They exemplify companies that matter—to their consumers, their industry, their employees, their communities, and their shareholders. We want to share one more case study with you before we finish, and that's the story of the Commonwealth Bank of Australia (CommBank). CommBank believes that it has a powerful role in its community, and even says so in its vision for the whole company: "To excel at securing and enhancing the financial wellbeing of people, businesses and communities."[23] It wants to live up to that vision and take on challenges worthy of its leadership role. Lots of companies these days are exploring the marketing potential of being community minded, but CommBank has taken a more authentic and "all in" position on the topic by making it a part of its vision, and by ensuring its social investments reflect that vision. That makes it a perfect example for how to matter and come out as the obvious choice.

BE WORTHY OF YOUR POSITION

It's astounding to think that a bank in Australia, a country with a population of only 22 million people, could be one of the most valuable banks on earth. In fact, CommBank is consistently in the top 100 most valuable companies on earth. It is the obvious choice for customers and for investors, precisely because it makes decisions worthy of its leadership position. CommBank strives to be a company that matters, and it acts accordingly.

CommBank has consistently led in offering features like its cutting-edge technology platforms, which enable omni-channel banking so consumers can bank anywhere, anytime, on any device. But cool technology is only part of its commitment to customers. Another key part of its platform is in community investments, and its flagship Start Smart program.[24]

Start Smart, an in-school education program powered by CommBank, has the audacious goal of transforming the financial well-being of an entire generation of Australians. To that end, in financial year 2015 Start Smart delivered more than 11,300 sessions reaching nearly 300,000 kids. And moving forward, CommBank has committed to doubling the investment in Start Smart so its reach covers half a million kids every year. When asked why CommBank would entirely fund one of the largest financial literacy programs on earth, Kylie Macfarlane, general manager of corporate responsibility, said, "We are committed to the financial well-being of Australian kids through Start Smart, while at the same time supporting teachers to create better education outcomes for their students, and rewarding excellence in teaching money management skills. We fundamentally believe better schools make a better country, and as Australia's largest bank we have an important role in creating that outcome."

Imagine booking half a million Aussie kids a year for a money management workshop. We can, because our firm, Karrikins Group, designed and continues to execute this program. The magnitude is staggering, and for one organization to take this on, to wholeheartedly invest, develop, and deliver on this type of commitment, is astonishing. For CommBank, it is obvious: It is the market leader, and this is how a market leader should behave.

When we talked with companies like CommBank and Domtar, this concept of a market leader behaving a certain way was a consistent theme. Companies that truly matter view their industry and community issues as their responsibility. If not us, who? And if not now, when? These companies are willing to take ownership of the unique role they can play, and they are willing to put their time, money, and energy into playing that role. They see themselves as social actors after all, but there is more to it for companies that matter. They do not just throw money at social problems, or give lip service to the issues. They confront the disruption caused by open social issues and develop programs worthy of their leadership positions. Consistently we found that companies like CommBank invest very intentionally in *measurably impactful, strategically aligned,* and *organizationally integrated* programs. Let's explore these three traits through CommBank and its Start Smart program, beginning with Start Smart's measureable impact.

> Companies that truly matter view their industry and community issues as their responsibility. If not us, who?

Businesses are not the only entities impacted by disruption. Citizens are, too. Cultures are shaped by technology, communication, transparency, and shifting attitudes about things like money and consumerism. Research by CommBank has shown that financial literacy is a massive challenge for our newest generations. Other research discusses how invisible (digital) money influences their psychology in different ways than cash. The whole experience of spending changes when you don't have to hand over hard-earned cash, and our credit-based world has created a whole new psychology of spending. At the same time, kids today are growing up constantly bombarded by images of people doing amazing things—for instance, on the latest social media platform (circa 2015, that would be Snapchat), they see a friend on a new Jet Ski, or someone taking a fabulous vacation. Money appears to be easy and everywhere, and the influence of product placement and branding is inescapable—it is in the shows they watch, the music they stream, and the social media they surf. Against that backdrop, learning reliable prudence in money management is a tall order for any kid.

Thankfully, CommBank is not the only group to recognize this, and in recent years we have seen financial management used to contextualize many parts of the school curriculum. A number of teachers are finding innovative ways to include financial management applications and instruction when teaching the basics. Likewise, CommBank has a deep commitment to education and teachers. It has answered the call to provide teachers access to best-practice learning resources to help teach financial management principles in classrooms. With all that said, teachers still have extremely challenging roles, and CommBank wants to do more than just provide resources and grants.

CommBank decided that there was a need, born from multiple disruptions in society, to create a program that further supported existing efforts of these innovative teachers. That was the foundation from which Start Smart began: an in-schools education program designed to arm kids with the skills and attitudes needed to make sound financial decisions in an increasingly consumer-oriented world. CommBank quickly discovered that the education sector was a demanding place to play, and that in order to partner with schools it would need to deliver a program that did more than fill the gaps. It would have to be measurable and credible as well. As the program developed, so did the bank's knowledge of what the most important things to influence were, and how to best influence those things.

Start Smart has evolved to focus on the following four critical areas for kids' educational outcomes:

- *Attitude*: Kids will be more interested in money and learning about financial management.
- *Self-efficacy*: Kids will believe they are more capable of managing their money.
- *Knowledge*: Kids will know objectively more; they will be more literate, so to speak.
- *Behavioral intention*: Kids will intend to engage in more financially sound behaviors.

It is fine for companies to subscribe to the notion that they need to pay their dues to the community, but that attitude generally results in either lip service or checkbook charity. CommBank took the outcomes very seriously, and insisted on evidence of positive impact, just like it would for any customer-facing program. It felt students deserved nothing less than what the bank offered its best customers—and that shareholders would demand the same.

Start Smart is only one part of how CommBank serves youth. For decades it has invested in a School Banking platform through its retail bank (Start Smart resides in CommBank's corporate responsibility team). Even though the two programs were not conceived of together and are run separately, with Start Smart being a purely education-focused program, there is an added behavioral benefit of school banking. Research shows that the sooner you can convert behavioral intention into actual behavior, the better it is for long-term behavior change. Not only that, but if you can create a structure and an opportunity for people to engage in a behavior consistently, you can form a habit for life. The School Banking program allows kids to do just that by enabling them to save regularly. Imagine half a million kids a year being taught about the importance and value of savings, with many of them also engaging in a weekly savings program. These community investments are now in the tens of millions of dollars a year, and once again we see the link between doing the right work and seeing long-term economic gain as a result.

All the companies we talked with about community impact tied it to business value. By aligning their community programs to their overall strategy, they realized a "twofer"—they contributed to their communities while growing their business. Let's see how CommBank does it through strategic alignment.

Major banks have long known that the first bank account you open is a "sticky" one indeed. Your financial needs will change throughout your life, but assuming that first financial services company you sign on with treats you well and solves your problems, you may indeed stay with it for life. Today, more than ever, this is critical to the long-term success of banks around the world. Why? One, deposits represent a cheaper cost of capital. Two, it's cheaper to sell more to an existing customer than to acquire a new one. So if banks can get customers when they are young, evolve their products as customers' needs evolve, and retain customers for life, they will be many times more profitable than customers who come in and out depending on life stage and rate-based incentives in any given month.

Consider the likely first transaction account a child will open or engage with today. In 2015 it is likely iTunes or the App Store. Kids buy increasingly more things across increasingly more categories using their smartphones and their store accounts. This feature isn't here yet, but as the application expands, we can easily see these customers depositing their paychecks or pocket money directly into this type of digital environment. In fact, PayPal already has a service like this. It's a thought that sends shivers down the spine of every bank executive on earth, because they know not only that it is technically possible, but that these technology brands represent a more relevant image and value proposition to these new consumers than any of the traditional banks do right now.

Setting a strategy to combat encroachment by newcomers like Apple means capturing the attention and resources of young savers as early as possible. It's obvious what role CommBank's School Banking platform can play here; Start Smart is an educationally focused program, however, and would never aim to directly acquire customers for the bank. But it is branded, and alongside its educational goal, Start Smart creates connection and affinity and relevance to the brand. Kids love the experience, teachers and parents love the impact it has, and Start Smart has a Net Promoter Score equal to that of some of the most respected consumer brands in the world. Start Smart enhances the brand, and School Banking closes the gap between behavioral intention and behavior, in the process bringing a new generation of customers into the bank. In addition, it produces a more financially capable generation that will make smarter credit decisions later in life, which is good not only for them but for the banks, their balance sheets, and their profits, too. It is the ultimate in shared value. And it is the sort of intelligent, strategic thinking companies can apply that matters both to their community and to their industry and customers.

CommBank invests in Start Smart because it embodies the company's vision, and supports its goals: investing in improved educational outcomes for young Australians, enhancing their financial well-being, and ensuring they have the skills required to participate in the workforce of the future. CommBank believes that "Better Schools make a better country." Start Smart and School Banking are important components of CommBank's role in the communities they serve, helping to build future capacity and capability.

> Companies that matter have high standards and look for the opportunity to link their social obligations with their strategy to create generative relationships that renew over time, cementing their place in the community.

Companies that matter have high standards and look for the opportunity to link their social obligations with their strategy to create generative relationships that renew over time, cementing their place in the community. CommBank has worked hard to ensure Start Smart's organizational integration works well for program recipients. As a result, Start Smart also provides an opportunity to connect CommBank staff to their local schools and community as well. Although it would be operationally impossible for local branch staff to attend every Start Smart session, they do attend some. CommBank's insistence on keeping Start Smart focused purely on educational outcomes builds tremendous brand equity and trust in their communities. CommBank staff can also volunteer to run the School Banking program at their local primary school, further engaging them in the communities they serve. And more broadly, CommBank staff, along with the local community, is able to nominate great teachers doing great work in teaching money-management skills to their students through the bank's annual Teaching Awards. This is critical to Start Smart's value because it aligns the organization to the success of the program.

CommBank takes its position as a leader in the industry very seriously—seriously enough to invest in a program like Start Smart. And it takes its investment seriously enough to make sure it is measurable, strategically aligned, and organizationally aligned. These three characteristics were common among the companies we talked with that felt called to take a role in their communities as well as their industries. Deloitte Canada talked comfortably about its role in supporting the economic engine that is the mid-market in Canada. In its Best Managed program, employees volunteer to be coaches and evaluators, supporting the program outside of their normal client commitments. Domtar is absolutely confident in its strategic alignment with its EarthChoice product line, and its employees support the effort it took to become FSC certified and ambassadors for Paper Because.

The list goes on, and the companies we engaged prove time and again that when you decide to matter, and you take the final steps of doing not just the hard work, but the right work, you will elevate your impact and in the process create more value. All of the companies we talked with expressed in some form their authentic commitment to doing well by doing good, and they had a sense of responsibility that permeated their strategy, their programs, and their commitments—all in alignment with one another.

Consider for yourself how you can answer the call. What is the right work for you to be doing? How can you elevate your impact by playing a different type of role for your community? As you consider these questions, remember to think about programs that create measurable outcomes—not just for your balance sheet, but for the participants. Then work on strategic and organizational alignment to build a self-sustaining program that will give back to the community and your business for many years to come. It is part of having an elevated impact, and you can't become the obvious choice until you do.

Bring It to Life . . .

1. Make time with your team to ask one critical question: Beyond making money, what do we want our contribution to be? Have a healthy dialogue about purpose and impact. Provoke them to think about what kind of organization they want to work for, and how to make your organization more like the companies they describe. Remember, "organization" can be at any level—a team, a division, a product group, or a business.

2. Where is there obvious dissonance between that vision and your current practices, product mix, and culture? Make the changes you are empowered to make, and begin exerting influence on those you aren't, to better align with your desired purpose.

3. What's broken in your industry? Where is the most value destroyed, and the most negative impact created? What role could you, your team, and your company play in resolving this problem? Start playing that role.

4. What areas of community development is your organization best positioned to influence, from which you would also get the most business value long term? Realign the investments your organization makes and the activities your team engages in to make a difference in this area.

The Matter Model

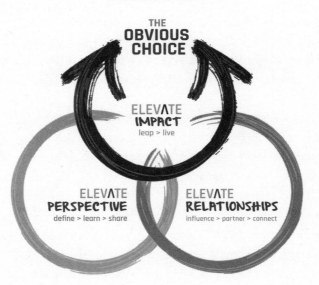

THE
OBVIOUS
CHOICE

ELEVATE
IMPACT
leap > live

ELEVATE
PERSPECTIVE
define > learn > share

ELEVATE
RELATIONSHIPS
influence > partner > connect

CONCLUSION

I
F YOU'VE MADE IT ALL THE WAY to the conclusion, we thank you. It has been quite a journey through some amazing stories of companies that are truly challenging themselves to matter in their markets. In that pursuit, they consistently find ways to add more value and drive higher-order outcomes, and as a result, they are the obvious choice in their targeted markets.

Along the way, they seem to have discovered a valuable secret: Once you start down that path and demonstrate to the world that you are the obvious choice, it can become second nature, something your employees, customers, and investors will expect. Instead of building the muscle to get there, you will have to guard against complacency, being vigilant to continually restart the process of elevating your perspective, your relationships, and your impact. If you act with intention, you will find that you will always be looking outward to a new edge of disruption, a different way to approach your business and stay out of the commodity game. The process, like the relationships you build along the way, becomes generative, with each element feeding the others in an upward spiral of differentiation.

Way back in Section One, we introduced the idea of finding your edge of disruption. Not what your competitors are doing, not what your investors want, not even what your clients are asking for, but *your* edge of disruption—the place where you feel you can create the most value in the system, where you have a passion to create systemic change. And we told you to go and spend time learning there, and then to share what you learn. Elevating your perspective is the first step because it forces you to get crystal clear on the value you hope to create, and everything else springs from there. Remember DPR pushing back on how work gets sold in one of the most cutthroat industries out there? Finding where you can make a difference and doubling down on your perspective lays the groundwork for elevating your relationships.

Once you'd established an elevated perspective, Section Two took you through the process of elevating your relationships. Elevated relationships mean you are influencing as high as possible in the organization or buyer's mind, building deep partnerships, and connecting the dots by seeing the whole board, cultivating broad relationships, and exerting influence on the market. Through these different types of relationships, you feed your perspective and create a platform from which you can have an elevated impact. It is also in this process that you begin to develop the muscle necessary to say no to work and clients who don't elevate you or help you to deliver the best possible value. Remember Lakeside coaching a potential client to wait to do business with them, because they weren't the best fit, or DPR being willing to walk away from clients who aren't interested in the type of partnership it desired? It takes courage and determination to realize a future self that is very different from where you are today.

Elevated impact, described in Section Three, is the critical final step toward being the obvious choice, and it is the one where many companies stumble. This is where the rubber meets the road, and you have to make tough choices about where to invest your time and money, how to set the future direction of the firm, and how you will answer questions about stewardship and longevity as you place big bets and do a lot of hard work. But if you stop before you get here, if you don't elevate your impact to create the maximum possible value, you will not become the obvious choice. We know it is hard; we challenge ourselves here, and sometimes we struggle. But it is so worth the effort when you see the impact you are capable of having on your clients and your communities.

And here's the really cool thing. Once you push through and elevate your impact, you will find you want to do it again and again. You will want to find your next edge of disruption, and you will have built the organizational fortitude to support taking the journey even further. It will become part of your culture to step out to that edge and leap over and over again as you learn, share, and increase your impact. Your ability to elevate your perspective, relationships, and impact will coalesce into a strength that will enable you to sustain your position as the obvious choice in your market. Being a company that matters will become your modus operandi, the most comfortable way for you to work, and you will join other companies that have enjoyed being the obvious choice year after year.

Our most sincere hope is that you take a combination of inspiration and aspiration away from the case studies and discussions we've provided, and that you are ready to take on your own journey to being the obvious choice. We know that it is hard, but we also know it is important. Our partners who contributed their stories to this book are all exemplars of the best types of companies—those that truly matter to their customers, employees, shareholders, and communities—and we believe you can be one, too. Choose to do the hard work on activities that move the needle in the right areas. Focus your team on the work that really matters to your internal and external customers. And commit to delivering more value and higher impact than anyone else in your industry.

We'd love to hear from you about your journey, what works and what doesn't, and how you have found ways to elevate in all three steps: perspective, relationships, and impact. Perhaps we can learn from and share your journey to becoming the obvious choice as well.

NOTES

Introduction

1. "A Conversation with Jeff Moore, Managing Director, and Susan Moore, Director of Sustainability, Lakeside Logistics," *Logistics Quarterly* 14, no. 6 (2008), http://logisticsquarterly.com/issues/14-6/interview1.html.
2. Nancy Hass, "Earning Her Stripes," *Wall Street Journal Magazine*, September 9, 2010.
3. DPR Construction, "Core Ideology: Vivid Descriptions," 2015, accessed July 25, 2015, http://www.dpr.com/company/ideology.
4. DPR Construction, "Awards and Recognition," 2015, accessed July 30, 2015, http://www.dpr.com/media/awards.

SECTION ONE: ELEVATED PERSPECTIVE

1. Karen Conway and Lana Makhanik, "Getting It Right at the Point of Care: Essential for Quality Care, Supply Chain Efficiency, and Revenue Optimization" (PowerPoint presented at the Spring 2013 IDN Summit and Reverse Expo, Phoenix, AZ, April 2013), http://idnsummit.com/2013Spring/Spring%202013%20Powerpoints/Tracking%20From%20Raw%20Materials%20to%20Point%20of%20Care-%20part%202-mahkanik%20conway.pdf.
2. Institute for Healthcare Improvement, "IHI Triple Aim Initiative," accessed August 26, 2015, http://www.ihi.org/engage/initiatives/tripleaim/Pages/default.aspx.

3. Bruce Johnson, interview by the authors at GHX Headquarters in Centennial, CO, August 18, 2015.

Chapter 1

1. Piggly Wiggly, "About Us," 2011, accessed April 22, 2015, http://www.pigglywiggly.com/about-us.
2. Willis Wee, "How Korea's Homeplus Brought a Smartphone Supermarket to the Subway," *TechInAsia*, June 25, 2011, https://www.techinasia.com/homeplus-virtual-store-south-korea; "Tesco Homeplus Virtual Subway Store in South Korea," YouTube video, 2:30, posted by "Recklessnutter," June 24, 2011, https://www.youtube.com/watch?feature=player_embedded&v=fGaVFRzTTP4.
3. Tesco, "Homeplus," accessed August 25, 2015, http://www.tescoplc.com/index.asp?pageid=314.
4. "Tesco Builds Virtual Shops for Korean Commuters," *Telegraph*, June 27, 2011, http://www.telegraph.co.uk/technology/mobile-phones/8601147/Tesco-builds-virtual-shops-for-Korean-commuters.html.
5. "CASE STUDY: Using a Digital Campaign to Drive Online Sales," GetMeMedia, March 7, 2013, http://www.getmemedia.com/ideas/case-study-using-a-digital-campiagn-to-drive-online-sales/cheil-worldwide.html.
6. Jim Tompkins, "The Data behind Breakthrough Webinar 'Competing with the Big Dogs: Standing Up to Google and Amazon,'" *Industrial Distribution*, January 29, 2014, http://www.inddist.com/blogs/2014/01/data-behind-breakthrough-webinar-competing-big-dogs-standing-google-and-amazon; Charles H., "Amazon's Foray into B2B Supplies: A Fight to the Finish?" *Scripted*, n.d., accessed August 25, 2015, https://scripted.com/cpt_experts/amazons-foray-into-b2b-supplies-a-fight-to-the-finish.
7. Richard Reese, phone interview by Peter Sheahan, July 2015.

Chapter 2

1. "Koreans Work Second-Longest Hours in OECD," *Business Korea*, August 26, 2014, http://www.businesskorea.co.kr/article/6035/working-hours-koreans-work-second-longest-hours-oecd.
2. Karen Conway and Margot Drees, interview by the authors at GHX headquarters in Centennial, CO, August 18, 2015.
3. "GHX Receives HDMA Distribution Management Award for 'First-of-Its-Kind' Traceability Pilot," press release, Healthcare Distribution

Management Association, March 5, 2013, http://hdma.net/news/2013-03-05-ghx-receives-hdma-distribution-management-award.
4. "The 10 Companies College Students Should Want to Work For," *Her Campus* (blog), January 11, 2012, last modified March 12, 2012, http://www.huffingtonpost.com/her-campus/best-internships_b_1184319.html.
5. Cari Williams, phone interview from Denver by Pete Gossin, August 7, 2012.

Chapter 3

1. Shopper Culture, "About Us," 2015, accessed July 30, 2015, http://www.shopperculture.com/shopper_culture/about-us.html.
2. Craig Elston, Katie Geraty, David Cole, and Patrick McGill, joint phone interview from Denver by Pete Gossin, August 1, 2012.
3. Ibid.
4. Maria Fox, phone interview from Denver by Pete Gossin, August 2, 2012.
5. Brandon Fassino and Michael Glunk, phone interview from Denver by Pete Gossin, August 1, 2012.
6. Armand Parra, phone interview from Denver by Pete Gossin, August 2, 2012.
7. Elston, Geraty, Cole, and McGill, interview.
8. Kasey Lobaugh, Jeff Simpson, and Lokesh Ohri, *Navigating the New Digital Divide: Capitalizing on Digital Influence in Retail*, 2015, Deloitte Development, LLC.
9. "The Digital Evolution in B2B Marketing," Corporate Executive Board Company, 2012, accessed September 22, 2015, http://www.executiveboard.com/exbd-resources/content/digital-evolution/index.html.
10. Jeff Rohrs, phone interview from Denver by Peter Sheahan and Pete Gossin, April 2, 2012.
11. Tim Kopp, phone interview from Denver by Pete Gossin, September 19, 2012.
12. Ibid.
13. Mitch Frazier, phone interview from Denver by Pete Gossin, July 31, 2012.
14. ET sales representative, phone interview from Denver with Pete Gossin, September 4, 2012.
15. Rose Eveleth, "Never Listen to a Wine Critic Babble about Tannins Again," *SmartNews* (blog), Smithsonian.com, January 29, 2013, http://

www.smithsonianmag.com/smart-news/never-listen-to-a-wine
-critic-babble-about-tannins-again-7955302/?no-ist.

16. WineLibrary Staff, "The Perfect Wines to Pair with Jersey Shore
    Boardwalk Food," WineLibrary.com, April 8, 2015, http://tinyurl.com
    /pmt2qgm.

17. Eric Asimov, "Pop Goes the Critic," *New York Times*, September 8,
    2009, http://www.nytimes.com/2009/09/09/dining/09pour.html
    ?pagewanted=all&_r=0.

18. David Segal, "Riding the Hashtag in Social Media Marketing," *New
    York Times*, November 2, 2013, http://www.nytimes.com/2013/11/03
    /technology/riding-the-hashtag-in-social-media-marketing.html.

19. Daniel Roberts, "Is Gary Vaynerchuk for Real?", *Fortune*,
    December 8, 2014, http://fortune.com/2014/12/08/is-gary-vaynerchuk
    -vaynermedia-for-real.

20. Ibid.

21. Ibid.

22. Rachel Nichols, "U.S. Wine Consumer Trends: Boomers' Tastes Evolve,
    Millennials Continue to Drive Market Growth," WineBusiness.com,
    January 24, 2011, http://www.winebusiness.com/news/?go=get
    Article&dataid=83196.

23. Mike Freeman, "How Gary Vaynerchuk Built His Empire," *Shopify*,
    September 15, 2011, http://www.shopify.com/blog/4072192-how-gary
    -vaynerchuk-built-his-empire.

24. Segal, "Riding the Hashtag."

25. Karen Geier, "Gary Vaynerchuk on What Investors Get Wrong,"
    Huffington Post Business Canada (blog), March 5, 2013, last modi-
    fied May 5, 2013, http://www.huffingtonpost.ca/karen-geier/gary
    -vaynerchuk_b_2807804.html.

26. Morgan Stewart (ExactTarget), interview by Pete Gossin, July 27,
    2012.

SECTION TWO: ELEVATED RELATIONSHIPS

Chapter 4

1. Dan Carruthers, Jeff Tapp, Brian Callan, and Mike Preston, joint
   telephone interview from Denver by Pete Gossin, January 8, 2013.

2. Ibid.

3. Doug Woods, interview by the authors, May 29, 2012.

4. Brent Schlender and Christine Y. Chen, "Steve Jobs' Apple Gets Way Cooler,"
   Fortune, January 24, 2000, http://archive.fortune.com/magazines
   /fortune/fortune_archive/2000/01/24/272281/index.htm.

5. Carmine Gallo, "Steve Jobs: Get Rid of the Crappy Stuff," *Forbes*, May 16, 2011, http://www.forbes.com/sites/carminegallo/2011/05/16 /steve-jobs-get-rid-of-the-crappy-stuff.

6. Jim Collins, *Good to Great: Why Some Companies Make the Leap . . . and Others Don't* (New York: HarperBusiness, 2001).

7. For a take on thinking differently about how you select your clients, see Larry Selden and Geoffrey Colvin, *Angel Customers and Demon Customers* (New York: Portfolio Hardcover, 2006).

8. Jay Leopold, interview by Pete Gossin in Englewood, CO, May 29, 2012.

9. Mike Ford, interview by Pete Gossin in Englewood, CO, May 29, 2012.

10. Leopold, interview.

11. Herminia Ibarra, *Act Like a Leader, Think Like a Leader* (Boston: Harvard Business School Press, 2015).

12. David Littlefield, telephone interview from Denver by Pete Gossin, May 14, 2012.

13. Ibid.

14. Ibid.

Chapter 5

1. Malcolm Hunter, telephone interview from Denver by Pete Gossin, December 4, 2012.

2. Ibid.

3. John Hughes, Peter Brown, and Kristen Dolson, joint telephone interview from Denver by Pete Gossin, September 6, 2012.

4. Promotional Products Association International, *U.S. Distributors' Promotional Products Sales 2013*, June 2014, http://www.ppai.org /inside-ppai/research/documents/2013salesreport.pdf.

5. Chris Catliff, telephone interview from Denver by Peter Sheahan and Stefanie Stolpa, April 14, 2014.

6. "Mercedes-Benz Airport Express to Set New Benchmark in Customer Service Excellence," *AutoWeb*, June 29, 2005, http://www.autoweb .com.au/cms/A_104707/title_MercedesBenz-Airport-Express-to-set -New-Benchmark-in-Customer-Service-Excellence/newsarticle.html; Mike Hanlon, "Devilishly Clever Customer Service from Mercedes-Benz," *Gizmag*, June 28, 2005, http://www.gizmag.com/go/4209.

7. Kate Vitasek, Mike Ledyard, and Karl Manrodt, *Vested Outsourcing: Five Rules That Will Transform Outsourcing*, 2nd ed. (New York: Palgrave Macmillan, 2013).

8. Kate Vitasek, Karl Manrodt, and Jeanne Kling, *Vested: How P&G, McDonald's and Microsoft Are Redefining Winning in Business Relationships* (New York: Palgrave Macmillan, 2012).

9. Vitasek, Ledyard, and Manrodt, *Vested Outsourcing.*
10. American Institute of Architects, "About the AIA: Programs & Initiatives," 2015, http://www.aia.org/about/initiatives/AIAS076981.
11. Mark Thompson, interview by Pete Gossin in Englewood, CO, May 29, 2012.

Chapter 6

1. Kim Gittleson, "Can a Company Live Forever?" *BBC News*, January 19, 2012, http://www.bbc.com/news/business-16611040.
2. De Beers, "Philippe Mellier's Speech Transcript from JCK Talks Series," May 30, 2015, http://www.diamonds.net/News/NewsItem .aspx?ArticleID=52420&ArticleTitle=Philippe+Melliers+Speech+ Transcript+From+JCK+Talks+Series+.
3. Bryan Pearson, telephone interview from Denver by Pete Gossin, September 11, 2012.
4. Ibid.
5. "UN: HIV Infections Decreasing, Epidemic Could Be Contained by 2030," *Al Jazeera America*, July 16, 2014, http://america.aljazeera.com /articles/2014/7/16/hiv-crisis-un0.html.
6. Shiloh Turner, Kathy Merchant, John Kania, and Ellen Martin, "Understanding the Value of Backbone Organizations in Collective Impact: Part 1," *Stanford Social Innovation Review*, July 17, 2012, http://www.ssireview.org/blog/entry/understanding_the_value_of _backbone_organizations_in_collective_impact_1.
7. John Kania and Mark Kramer, "Collective Impact," *Stanford Social Innovation Review*, Winter 2011, http://www.ssireview.org/articles /entry/collective_impact.
8. Ibid.
9. Indrajit Gupta, "P&G versus Unilever in India," *Forbes*, April 12, 2010, http://www.forbes.com/2010/04/12/forbes-india-pg-unilever-soap -opera.html; "Fighting for the Next Billion Shoppers," *Economist*, June 30, 2012, http://www.economist.com/node/21557815.
10. "About Lifebuoy," Unilever, n.d., accessed July 30, 2015, http://www .unilever.com/brands/our-brands/lifebuoy.html.
11. WASHplus, "Unilever Lifebuoy Handwashing Campaign Reduces Diarrhea," *Sanitation Updates*, March 27, 2014, https:// sanitationupdates.wordpress.com/2014/03/27/unilever-lifebuoy -handwashing-campaign-reduces-diarrhea.
12. Unilever, "Help a Child Reach 5: Saving Lives through Handwashing" (infographic), n.d., accessed July 30, 2015, https://sanitationupdates. files.wordpress.com/2014/03/lifebuoy-infographic1.pdf.

SECTION THREE: ELEVATED IMPACT

Chapter 7

1. Gartner, "Gartner Says Worldwide Cloud Services Revenue Will Grow 21.3 Percent in 2009," press release, March 26, 2009, http://www .gartner.com/newsroom/id/920712.
2. Michael Corkery, "Adobe Buys Omniture: What Were They Thinking?" *Deal Journal* (blog), *Wall Street Journal*, September 16, 2009, http://blogs.wsj.com/deals/2009/09/16/adobe-buys-omniture -what-were-they-thinking.
3. Tomasz Tunguz, "Adobe: The SaaS Company That Grew from Zero to 4 Million Subscribers in 2.5 Years," *Seeking Alpha*, March 23, 2015, http://seekingalpha.com/article/3021816-adobe-the-saas-company -that-grew-from-zero-to-4-million-subscribers-in-2_5-years.
4. Trefis Team, "Why Adobe Is Worth $70 per Share," *Great Speculations* (blog), *Forbes*, March 5, 2015, http://www.forbes.com/sites/great speculations/2015/03/05/why-adobe-is-worth-70-per-share.
5. Ibid.
6. Clayton Christensen Institute for Disruptive Innovation, "Jobs to Be Done," 2015, accessed July 30, 2015, http://www.christenseninstitute .org/key-concepts/jobs-to-be-done.
7. Ibid.
8. Amy Cortese, "Wiggling Their Toes at the Shoe Giants," *New York Times*, August 29, 2009, http://www.nytimes.com/2009/08/30 /business/30shoe.html?_r=0.
9. Matt McCue, "Vibram Agrees to Settle Class Action Lawsuit," *Runner's World*, May 6, 2014, http://www.runnersworld.com/newswire/vibram -settles-class-action-lawsuit.
10. Michelle Castillo, "Skechers Shape-Ups: Why the FTC Called Company's Studies Deceiving," *CBS News*, May 17, 2012, http:// www.cbsnews.com/news/skechers-shape-ups-why-the-ftc-called -companys-studies-deceiving.
11. Federal Trade Commission, "Skechers Will Pay $40 Million to Settle FTC Charges That It Deceived Consumers with Ads for 'Toning Shoes,'" May 16, 2012, https://www.ftc.gov/news-events /press-releases/2012/05/skechers-will-pay-40-million-settle-ftc -charges-it-deceived; Federal Trade Commission, "Reebok to Pay $25 Million in Customer Refunds to Settle FTC Charges of Deceptive Advertising of EasyTone and RunTone Shoes," September 28, 2011, https://www.ftc.gov/news-events/press-releases/2011/09 /reebok-pay-25-million-customer-refunds-settle-ftc-charges.

12. Tina Gaudoin, "Burberry Opens an Innovative London Flagship," *Architectural Digest*, December 2012, http://www.architectural digest.com/shop/2012-12/burberry-london-flagship-store-regent -street-article.

13. Angela Ahrendts, "Burberry's CEO on Turning an Aging British Icon into a Global Luxury Brand," *Harvard Business Review*, January–February 2013, https://hbr.org/2013/01/burberrys-ceo-on-turning -an-aging-british-icon-into-a-global-luxury-brand.

14. Denise Roland, "Burberry Has More Twitter Followers Than Coca-Cola," *Telegraph*, September 22, 2014, http://www.telegraph.co.uk /finance/newsbysector/retailandconsumer/11112035/Burberry-has -more-Twitter-followers-than-Coca-Cola.html.

15. Graham Ruddick, "Christopher Bailey Boosts Burberry Sales," *Telegraph*, July 10, 2014, http://www.telegraph.co.uk/finance/newsby sector/retailandconsumer/10960304/Christopher-Bailey-boosts -Burberry-sales.html.

16. Ahrendts, "Burberry's CEO."

17. Burberry, "Burberry World Live Arrives in London," press release, September 13, 2012, http://www.burberryplc.com/media_centre /press_releases/2012/burberry-world-live-arrives-in-london.

18. Ella Alexander, "Burberry Opens Regent Street Flagship," *Vogue*, September 13, 2012, http://www.vogue.co.uk/news/2012/09/13 /burberry-regent-street-flagship-opens.

19. Reza Soudagar, "How Fashion Retailer Burberry Keeps Customers Coming Back for More," *ForbesBrandVoice*, October 28, 2013, http://www .forbes.com/sites/sap/2013/10/28/how-fashion-retailer-burberry -keeps-customers-coming-back-for-more.

20. Peter High, "Adobe's CIO Helps the Company Move from Software Product Company to a Cloud Company," *Forbes*, March 23, 2015, http://www .forbes.com/sites/peterhigh/2015/03/23/adobes-cio-helps-the-company -move-from-software-product-company-to-a-cloud-company.

21. Peter Fuda, "An Obsession with Transformation," *An Obsession with Transformation* (blog), June 2, 2012, http://www.peterfuda .com/2012/06/02/an-obsession-with-transformation.

22. Noelle Knox, "Adobe Systems CFO: Managing Business Model Transformation," *CFO Journal* (blog), *Wall Street Journal*, January 16, 2015, http://blogs.wsj.com/cfo/2015/01/16/adobe-systems -cfo-managing-business-model-transformation.

23. Ibid.

24. Michael Thorpe, interview by the authors, June 29, 2015.

25. Steve Lockshin, "Is Your Financial Advisor Stuck in the Stone Age?", *CNBC*, June 18, 2015, http://www.cnbc.com/2015/06/17/is-your -financial-advisor-stuck-in-the-stone-age.html.

26. Jeff Moore, interview by the authors, January 2013.

Chapter 8

1. Belinda White, "The New Nike Trainers Inspired by One Cerebral Palsy Sufferer's Plea," *Telegraph*, July 16, 2015, http://www .telegraph.co.uk/fashion/brands/the-nike-trainers-inspired-by-one -cerebal-palsy-sufferer-s-plea-.
2. Joseph Campbell, *The Hero with a Thousand Faces (The Collected Works of Joseph Campbell)*, 3rd ed. (Novato, CA: New World Library, 2008), 49.
3. Milton Friedman, "The Social Responsibility of Business Is to Increase Its Profits," *New York Times Magazine*, September 13, 1970, 32–3, 122–4.
4. Tom Zara, "Corporate Citizenship 2.0: Leading Way to Skill-Sharing Economy," *Korea Times*, March 16, 2014, http://www.koreatimes .co.kr/www/news/biz/2015/04/331_153449.html.
5. DPR Construction, "The DPR Code," last modified July 30, 2013, accessed July 30, 3015, https://www.dpr.com/assets/docs/dpr-code -2013.pdf, 1.
6. John Hughes, interview by the authors, September 6, 2012.
7. William Whyte, *The Organization Man* (New York: Simon & Schuster, 1956).
8. "2014's Top Retail Pharmacy Chains, According to Drug Store News," *Drug Channel News*, May 6, 2015, http://www.drugchannels .net/2015/05/2014s-top-retail-pharmacy-chains.html.
9. Elizabeth Landau, "CVS Stores to Stop Selling Tobacco," *CNN*, February 5, 2014, http://www.cnn.com/2014/02/05/health/cvs-cigarettes.
10. Hoovers, "CVS Health Corporation Company Information," accessed August 26, 2015, http://www.hoovers.com/company-information/cs /company-profile.CVS_Health_Corporation.e8a792978e23c42d.html.
11. Jayne O'Donnell and Laura Ungar, "CVS Stops Selling Tobacco, Offers Quit-Smoking Programs, *USA Today*, September 3, 2014, http://www.usatoday.com/story/news/nation/2014/09/03/cvs -steps-selling-tobacco-changes-name/14967821.
12. Ibid.
13. Lewis Fix, interview by Pete Gossin, October 5, 2012.
14. Kathy Wholley, interview by Pete Gossin, October 12, 2012.
15. Hadley Archer, interview by Pete Gossin, November 26, 2012.
16. Dick Thomas, interview by Pete Gossin, October 1, 2012.
17. Tensie Whelan, interview by Pete Gossin, December 14, 2012.
18. Rob Melton, interview by Pete Gossin, October 12, 2012.
19. Enterprise Group, *2012 Annual Report*, http://www.egpaper.com /Company/Whats-New/Domtar-Annual-Report.

20. Mila Alvarez, *The State of America's Forests*, Society of American Foresters, 2007, https://safnet.org/publications/americanforests/StateOfAmericasForests.pdf, 25.
21. "Paper ≠ Bad," Paper Because, http://www.paperbecause.com/paper-is-sustainable/paper-is-not-bad.
22. Lewis Fix, interview.
23. Commonwealth Bank, "About Us: Financial Education," accessed August 25, 2015, https://www.commbank.com.au/about-us/who-we-are/in-the-community/financial-education.htm.
24. Commonwealth Bank, "About Us: Start Smart," accessed August 25, 2015, https://www.commbank.com.au/about-us/who-we-are/in-the-community/financial-education/start-smart.html?ei=gsa_generic_Start-Smart.

ACKNOWLEDGMENTS

IRST AND FOREMOST, thank you to the leaders who agreed to participate in the research, and for allowing us to share your inspiring stories and your company case studies. Without you, there would be no book.

Thank you to the original research team led by Peter Gossin, and including Shaylee Wheeler and Abby Loar.

Thank you to Stefanie Stolpa and Seth Schulman, who were instrumental in guiding the formation of this book, for shaping our arguments and style.

Thank you to all the critical readers, especially Josh Linkner and Peter Fuda.

Thank you to the BenBella team for their patience and partnership.

And last but not least, thank you to our colleagues at Karrikins Group, and our families, for sharing the load, tolerating our mood swings, and supporting the work.

INDEX

ABOUT THE AUTHORS

Peter Sheahan, Founder & Group CEO of Karrikins Group, is known internationally for his innovative business thinking and thought leadership. With staff in more than twenty-three cities across seven countries, Peter knows firsthand the challenges of growing a business in these rapidly changing times. Peter has advised leaders from companies as diverse as Microsoft, IBM, AT&T, and Wells Fargo. He is the author of several books prior to this one, including *Flip*, *Generation Y*, and *Making It Happen*. Peter has delivered more than 2,500 presentations to half a million people in twenty different countries, and he has been named one of the twenty-five Most Influential Speakers in the World by the National Speakers Association. He is the youngest person ever to be inducted into the speaking industry's hall of fame.

Julie Williamson, vice president for strategy and research at Karrikins Group, has decades of experience in management consulting and a PhD in organizational communication. Addicted to defining and exploring unanswered questions, Julie has an enduring belief in the power of asking different questions and breaking away from the assumptions that limit problem solving and opportunity seeking in business today. She spends much of her time with clients and students unpacking new ideas, converting them to insight, and creating positive behavior change that helps move that insight into action. Her work with leadership teams in companies large and small has helped inform her thinking on how people and organizations find and stay on their own edge of disruption and confidently execute from there. Julie believes that in doing so, people build teams, organizations, and products that matter to customers, communities, employees, and investors, and they can create solutions that are highly valued in their markets.